TORT LAW AND
THE CONSTRUCTION
OF CHANGE

TORT LAW AND THE CONSTRUCTION OF CHANGE

Studies in the Inevitability of History

Kenneth S. Abraham
and G. Edward White

University of Virginia Press • *Charlottesville and London*

University of Virginia Press
© 2022 by the Rector and Visitors of the University of Virginia
All rights reserved
Printed in the United States of America on acid-free paper

First published 2022

9 8 7 6 5 4 3 2 1

Library of Congress Cataloging-in-Publication Data

Names: Abraham, Kenneth S., author. | White, G. Edward, author.
Title: Tort law and the construction of change : studies in the inevitability of history /
　Kenneth S. Abraham and G. Edward White.
Description: Charlottesville ; London : University of Virginia Press, 2022. | Includes
　bibliographical references and index.
Identifiers: LCCN 2021027278 (print) | LCCN 2021027279 (ebook) |
　ISBN 9780813947143 (hardcover) | ISBN 9780813947150 (ebook)
Subjects: LCSH: Torts—United States—History.
Classification: LCC KF1250 .A717 2022 (print) | LCC KF1250 (ebook) |
　DDC 346.7303—dc23
LC record available at https://lccn.loc.gov/2021027278
LC ebook record available at https://lccn.loc.gov/2021027279

Cover art: The Two Rivers, Peter Blume. (Photographs in the Carol M. Highsmith
　Archive, Library of Congress, Prints and Photographs Division)

For Susan Stein and Susan White

CONTENTS

CONTENTS

PREFACE

THIS BOOK has evolved out of a series of jointly authored articles on torts that we published in law reviews between 2013 and 2021. We are grateful to John Goldberg for first suggesting that we consider using those articles as a starting point for developing a book intended for broader audiences than those to which the original articles were directed. In seeking to reach those audiences, we have identified a thesis that only in retrospect did we see linked the articles together—the notion that change in tort law, especially in the episodes in question, is "constructed." The result, we would say, is that the book is "derived" from the articles but that the book reshapes, reorders, and reorganizes the ideas they contain.

We thank the following law reviews, which hold the copyrights to these articles, for permission to derive much of our discussion and analysis in the chapters indicated: *Arizona Law Review* (chapter 1); *Maryland Law Review* (chapter 2); *Cornell Law Review* (chapter 3); *Texas Law Review* (chapter 4); and *American University Law Review* (chapter 5). The titles of the articles and full citations are provided in a note.[1]

A number of colleagues and friends have read and commented on portions of the book manuscript and the articles from which it is partially derived. Thanks to Tom Baker, Vincent Blasi, Andrew Delbanco, John Goldberg, Paul Halliday, Leslie Kendrick, John Langbein, Michael Lobban, Kyle Logue, James Oldham, Robert Rabin, Christopher Robinette, Frederick Schauer, and John Witt. Thanks also to participants in workshops at the Institute of Advanced Legal Study in London and the University of Virginia School of Law, where earlier versions of chapters in the book were presented in 2016 and 2020. Once again we are indebted to the superb research assistance of the reference librarians at the University of Virginia School of Law's library, headed by Kent Olson.

The dedication reflects our gratitude to our wives, Susan Stein and Susan White, for their forbearance during a long interval in which the authors of the book, being largely house-bound along with family members, indulged themselves in almost daily phone conversations. The authors are good friends and colleagues who have enjoyed doing scholarship together, but it would be unseemly to dedicate the book to one another, and the contributions of the two Susans to our well-being over the years have been incomparable.

K.S.A. AND G.E.W
Charlottesville
November 2020

TORT LAW AND
THE CONSTRUCTION
OF CHANGE

INTRODUCTION

THIS BOOK is about the way that the common law of torts describes, and thereby constructs, change. The common law—law made by courts rather than legislatures—has a distinctive way of proceeding through time. For centuries, the courts indulged in the fiction that the common law did not change. Judges merely "discovered" what the common law had always been. Although open adherence to that fiction long ago disappeared, the values that lay behind it still influence the process by which the common law changes. There is tremendous emphasis in the common law on continuity. Yet continuity and change are, in a sense, incompatible. The common law nonetheless reflects the efforts of the courts—sometimes commonplace and interstitial, sometimes heroic—to reconcile continuity and change.

As the title of this book indicates, we believe that much change in tort law has been and is "constructed." By this term we mean that what the courts say the law is, and how they say they have or have not changed the law, is an important ingredient of what the law is. In this sense, change is constructed, or built. We also mean that change occurs by constructing, or construing, the meaning of the past. Strictly speaking, in law the term "interpretation" applies to the discovery of meaning while the term "construction" means attributing a legal effect to a word or phrase. Construction of tort law thus comprises both interpretation of the past and making law about the meaning of the past. In this sense, ours is a project mainly in intellectual legal history, rather than social or cultural legal history or jurisprudence.

We recognize that in addition to the ways in which the common law is constructed by courts, the application of that law in practice, to actual litigants and other people in the world, is critically important. But in the development of the common law, what the courts say the law is, and how they say that are predicates for, and constitute significant features of, the ways legal rules and doctrines are applied in practice.

Although the term "construction" is not typically used to describe decision-making in the common law generally or tort law in particular, the message in our title is by no means a new recognition or insight. That recognition, however, has usually been at a level of generality so high as to be abstract, or so concrete as to be difficult to generalize. Celebrated jurists and scholars, Justices Oliver Wendell Holmes and Benjamin Cardozo among them, have written about the manner in which common law change occurs.[1] Those and other general accounts, however, do not, and by their nature could not, examine change in a particular common law field in an intensive and sustained way.

In tort law, the subject of this book, there have been countless studies of the ways that the law has changed. But those are mostly studies of a particular sort. They are about the external forces that have caused change, and how those forces have resulted in particular substantive changes in the law of torts. Many such studies in recent decades have adopted a focus on the reasons of principle and public policy underlying the development or developments in question. This has been the chief characteristic of scholarly work on the development of tort liability for bodily injury and property damage, which was quantitatively the most important change in tort law in the twentieth century. The focus of that work has mainly been on substantive changes in tort liability, such as the movement from negligence to strict liability, the demise of the assumption of risk defense, the relaxation of causation requirements, or the rise of no-fault liability for auto accidents.

In contrast, our interest here is not in the specific substantive changes that have occurred in tort law or, in the main, the forces external to the tort system that have been the impetus for change in tort doctrines, although at times we allude to the role of such external forces in discussion of particular doctrines. Our primary interest is in the intellectual and conceptual mechanisms for constructing change in tort law, and in the ways in which courts have attempted to maintain continuity between the law of the past and the new law they are making, as they make it. Our analysis takes place at an "intermediate" level of generality; it is neither a granular examination of individual cases nor a grand inquiry at the level of Holmes and Cardozo. We believe that insufficient attention has been given to the actual ways in which the courts, having decided to make a change in tort law, must confront established tort doctrines, and have sought to accomplish change while preserving at least the appearance of doctrinal continuity.

In particular, we are interested in developments in tort law that do not fit comfortably into the dominant but often oversimplified model of common law change: gradual, step-by-step change in which an exception to a rule expands to the point at which it eventually becomes the rule. Under that model, change is reconciled with continuity by rendering individual changes in the law almost imperceptible. Only after a series of judicial decisions, no single one of which accomplishes substantial change, is change of any great significance understood to have occurred. As Cardozo put it, "The work of modification is gradual. It goes on inch by inch. Its effect must be measured by decades, even centuries."[2]

We say that this model of common law change is "dominant" not only because it accurately describes how much common law change occurs but also because, as a consequence, it is the most salient emblem of the nature of the common law itself. A good deal of change in tort law has occurred roughly in the way this model describes, but not all change, and not all important change. We chronicle a series of episodes in the history of tort law in which change was not constructed in the seamless way the dominant model envisions, and in which the nature of the relationship between continuity and change therefore warrants extended analysis. In each episode, the weight of history was an inevitable—by which we mean inescapable—influence on the way change was constructed, but the nature of that influence varied, at times propelling change forward, and at other times constraining change.

Not only do the episodes that we examine not fit comfortably within the dominant model of common law change. These episodes lie outside the mainstream of modern tort law scholarship and history for two additional reasons. First, all five of the episodes involve lost history of one form or another. By uncovering these episodes, we aim to help remedy the incomplete understanding of the way tort law has developed that the traditional history of tort law embodies. Second, our focus departs from the principal focus of tort law scholarship over the last century, liability for accidental bodily injury and property damage. Two of the episodes that we examine involve tort law generally, rather than liability for physical harm exclusively. And three of the episodes do not involve liability for physical harm at all. Rather, the subject matter of those episodes is liability for what is often called intangible loss—emotional, dignitary, and economic harm. The history of these forms of liability, including history about them that has been lost, is worthy of greater attention.

Because tort law is very much a creature of its time, for long periods of its existence tort law was inhospitable to the potential claims of racial minorities and women. Some of this insensitivity was substantively embedded in tort law doctrine, but only some. For example, as we document in chapter 3, until late in the nineteenth century there was no tort liability for intentionally causing emotional distress or suffering, unless it resulted from physical injury. At that point, the courts began permitting recovery of damages for what was eventually recognized as "intentional infliction of emotional distress" (IIED). A claim for IIED could only succeed, however, if the infliction was "highly offensive" and occurred under conditions that were "extreme and outrageous." The result was that any racial insult, offensive touching, marital assault, distinctively emotional injury, or even macro-aggression (let alone micro-aggression) that would not have been understood by a (usually white male judge or jury) to be both "highly offensive" and "extreme and outrageous" had little chance of succeeding. To oversimplify only slightly, tort law in the Jim Crow South (and often in the North as well) was mostly Jim Crow tort law, and was generally unresponsive to emotional harm claims by female plaintiffs as well.[3]

Thus, harm resulting from what could and should have been recognized as tortious wrongdoing received little or no vindication. In some ways—perhaps many ways—that is still the case, especially in the continuing calculation of damage awards in ways that are systematically biased against racial minorities and women.[4] But thanks in part to the seminal work of legal scholars who have identified those deficiencies, and in part to changes in our broader culture, we hope tort law is becoming more hospitable to such claims.[5]

In addition, however, even the tort law that did protect African Americans and women *on paper* undoubtedly protected them less *in practice* than it did in theory. In the entire period between 1865 and 1920, there were only 132 appellate decisions in eight southern states involving African American plaintiffs seeking recovery for physical injuries.[6] Although other legal scholars and historians have been analyzing racial and gender bias in tort law for several decades, we think that the evidence of biases they have uncovered is just the tip of an iceberg.[7] The dearth of cases in which African Americans even made an effort to recover damages in tort actions suggests to us that race and gender operated as constraints on the access of African Americans and women to courts in the first place.

It is striking, for example, that in an era when injuries resulting from the operation of railroads and trolleys were increasing exponentially, and tort law was emerging as a means of redressing those injuries, plaintiffs in personal injury cases overwhelmingly remained white males. If there are so few reported cases involving tangible physical injury, then there naturally would have been even fewer cases involving the kinds of intangible emotional and dignitary harms that are the subject of several of our chapters, since in tort law at large any cases involving intangible injury have always been a small fraction of those involving physical injury.

The explanation, we believe, is that there were considerable barriers to African American plaintiffs filing suits in court *at all* during the nineteenth and much of the twentieth centuries. The small number of African American lawyers, the difficulties African American plaintiffs had in getting white lawyers to represent them, the barriers facing many African American plaintiffs in accumulating damages from physical or emotional injuries because of their limited access to medical services, and a perception within the African American community that most judges and juries in tort cases, being overwhelmingly white, might not be receptive to their claims likely combined to result in comparatively few tort cases in which African Americans were plaintiffs even being brought, so that a very small sample of such cases exists for most of the period covered in our book. Two of the few works about race and tort law, for example, do not cite a single case involving an African American plaintiff suing for intangible injury such as emotional distress or dignitary invasion before 1950.[8]

Although we note certain racial and gender biases in the law of torts, and other deficiencies in tort law, in the chapters that follow, our principal purpose in the book is not to chronicle any particular strengths or weaknesses in tort law as it stood during the periods on which we focus, or at present. Nor is our purpose to examine the external causes of change in detail. Rather, we are seeking to analyze the way that tort law has described and justified the changes it has undergone, and the inevitable influence of history on those descriptions and justifications, whether the changes have involved moving away from regressive doctrines reflecting racial and gender bias and toward more progressive doctrines, away from protection against certain kinds of significant personal harm in order to provide greater protection for freedom of speech, or toward the recognition of liabilities that do not fit comfortably into any conventional ideological category. Our contention is that tort law tends to describe and justify change, when change occurs, in distinctive and recognizable ways that transcend disagreement over or variation in substance. Our subject is the ins and outs of that particular tendency.

The Nature of Tort Law and Tort Liability

Tort law addresses the obligations of individuals and enterprises for injuries and losses that they cause to others when no breach of contract or promise is involved. Tort law is "private" as opposed to "public" law, in that the government is not a party (as it is, for example, in criminal law and administrative regulation), except when government causes or suffers harm itself. But private law, including tort law, still involves the government. In tort law a branch of government, the courts, sets the rules governing the obligations of private parties to each other, provides a forum and mechanism for determining when the civil obligations of private parties have been violated, and decides what remedies are available for those violations. The result is that, by specifying the conduct that will result in the imposition of liability if the conduct causes harm, tort law identifies the conduct that counts as wrongful, tort law influences the behavior of those whom it threatens with liability, and tort law assures the compensation of parties who suffer wrongfully caused injury or loss.

In specifying the civil obligations and liabilities it covers, tort law necessarily takes into account the social and cultural contexts in which it operates. Through the doctrinal frameworks that embody tort law's rules, it makes an effort to reflect this context, and to alter the content or scope of rules in response to changes in those contexts. Over the course of American history, the content and scope of tort liability have changed, sometimes dramatically. At one point, recovery in tort for injuries caused by negligently manufactured products was limited to individuals in contractual relations with the manufacturer; now the liability of manufacturers or retailers for such products extends to any individuals who can show that their injuries were caused by the manufacturer's negligence in designing, making, or distributing a product. At one point, individuals who otherwise would have been entitled to recover damages in tort were totally barred from recovery if their negligence contributed in any way to their injuries. That is no longer the case.[9] At one point, mothers who witnessed their children killed or injured by negligent drivers had no right to recover from the driver for the emotional losses that they suffered from being present when that occurred. Now they can recover, even if they suffered no tangible physical harm themselves.

In those illustrations the scope of tort liability has expanded over time, resulting in more people being compensated for their injuries and more parties that might engage in risky conduct being encouraged to take steps to reduce risks associated with their activities. But there have been other instances in which changes in the content or scope of tort liability have served to reduce the amount of tort liability associated with particular forms of conduct. Defamation law, which we discuss in chapters 3 and 4, furnishes an example. For most of the history of tort law, oral or written false statements that lowered the reputations of others subjected those making the statements to liability in slander or in libel. Liability was imposed even when the statements were not negligently made, such as when a typographical error in a newspaper article resulted in a person's being mistakenly identified. The law also presumed that a defamed individual had suffered damages. But liability for defamation on the basis of those old rules has contracted substantially since 1964.

There are numerous other instances in which the content and scope of tort liability has contracted or expanded. Our interest in this book is not so much in charting the course of expanding and contracting tort liability in particular areas, although we do some of that. In fact, we need not take a position about whether the expansion or reduction of tort liability was desirable, or whether it would have been better for legislatures rather than courts to take the lead in changing tort law. We are interested in the ways that tort law proceeded to do its work in the past, and how tort law will proceed in the future, if it continues to be dominated by common law decision-making. That process has usually maintained the underlying continuity of tort law while simultaneously responding to the forces and conditions promoting change. The process of accommodating change to established doctrine has taken a distinctive form, which has been a product of both the nature of judicial decision-making and of legal reasoning within the American common law system.

Aspects of the Inevitability of History in Tort Law

We suggest throughout this book that the judicially fashioned expansion or contraction of tort liability has been affected by what we are calling the "inevitability of history." Changes in judicially fashioned tort rules and doctrines do not take place in a manner akin to legislation, where the institution given authority to govern various aspects of American life, a legislature, can enact laws changing the rules by fiat, without supplying reasoned justifications for the changes other than its delegated authority to make them and the fact that a majority of its members voted to support the changes. Rather, courts deciding cases that follow, depart from, or modify precedent by changing what was done in the past must explain and justify what they do. And they comply with this requirement by interpreting history, in the form of precedent.

Precedent and Continuity

Judicially fashioned changes in the rules or doctrines governing common law fields are not treated as legitimate if they are perceived as being made by fiat. Longstanding convention and the separation of powers that is part of the American governmental structure require more from courts. Courts are expected to provide justifications for changes in the law, and those justifications need to be grounded, to some extent, in established legal rules and doctrines, because judicial authority, and the legitimacy of judicial decisions, have traditionally been associated in American jurisprudence with the capacity of judges to discern and apply authoritative legal sources that are deemed to be separate from, and transcendent of, the particular views of judges on matters of social policy. When judicial decisions are perceived to be merely grounded on social policy, as distinguished from authoritative legal sources, the specter of judicial fiat is raised, with the accompanying concern that many judges are not elected officials and thus not politically accountable for their decisions.

This means that judges have a strong interest in justifying their decisions by appeal to authoritative legal sources, by way of confirming that the decisions are not simply a product of their own policy inclinations. Although lay people are often most familiar with judicial decisions that have overruled precedent, in fact express overruling is very rare. A court that often overruled past precedent would not long retain its perceived public or political legitimacy. The power to overrule precedent is a precious resource that most courts spend only with great care.

The rules and doctrines of tort law tend to be announced in judicial opinions accompanying the decisions of cases. Those opinions typically not only resolve a particular legal dispute between the parties but also advance reasons why the legal rules governing the dispute favor one party or the other and lead to a given outcome. Those rules are often articulated in the form of a legal "doctrine," which simply means a proposition of law designed to govern more than one case. The process by which judges fashion rules that both decide particular cases and may apply to additional cases gives judicial decisions a dual character. They not only resolve legal disputes but also offer guidance for future potential disputes by promulgating doctrines whose authority is intended to extend beyond a particular dispute.

Judicial precedents thus promote the values of stability and predictability in common law fields. If lawyers can discern that a common law doctrine has long been established in a jurisdiction, they may expect that, absent unusual circumstances, it is not likely to be abandoned, and the lawyers will conduct themselves, and advise their clients, accordingly. The accumulation of judicial precedents fashioning doctrinal propositions thus serves to foster stability, not only within common law fields but for parties who regularly rely on knowing the "state of the law" on legal subjects. Closely allied to stability in this regard is predictability: lawyers and their clients want to be able to predict what legal doctrines will govern their conduct and whether those doctrines can be expected to remain in place. An accumulation of judicial precedents helps in that prediction process. Moreover, stability and predictability in common law fields arguably help foster respect for law itself, which is taken to be an authoritative set of rules for human conduct. If people actually know the rules and can predict their application, they are arguably more likely to follow them.

For these reasons, a practice has developed among common law courts that has been widely followed, especially in the centuries since judicial opinions have been published. That practice is called "stare decisis," literally meaning, in Latin, "stand on the decisions" or "stand on what has been decided." The practice of stare decisis might be said to create a presumption that an existing doctrinal proposition will be followed the next time it appears relevant to the decision of a case. Stare decisis does not mean that established doctrine absolutely must be followed; it is always open to common law judges to conclude that an established doctrine is not apposite to a particular case, or would yield an unjust result in that case, or even has outlived its usefulness and should be abandoned or overruled. But the practice does mean that it is very rare in common law fields for a case to emerge to which no established doctrine is applicable. And when an established doctrine is applicable, the courts usually follow it. When express overruling does occur, the courts tend to feel little or no need to stress adherence to established doctrine, and therefore less need to maintain continuity with the past. Overruling, even when it is articulated in the form of extending existing principles, ordinarily constitutes a sharp break with the past.

The accumulation of previous decisions that must be taken into account in deciding current cases necessarily introduces history into a court's decision-making process. Previous decisions stretching back in time are this "history." Moreover, it is incumbent on a court to consult that accumulation of decisions in deciding a current case, because it is the consultation of that accumulation of decisions—the current case's doctrinal framework—which signifies that a court is not simply wrenching a case out of the accumulation of doctrine arguably pertinent to it and deciding it afresh, as a matter of social policy. As Holmes once wrote, referring to judicial decision-making, "Continuity with the past . . . limits the possibilities of our imagination, and settles the terms in which we shall be compelled to think."[10]

History is thus an inevitable part of the process by which judges make decisions in tort cases. It is inevitable that changing public attitudes or experiences put pressure on the established rules and doctrines ostensibly governing them in the present. It is also inevitable, however, that judges deciding the cases need to consult those established rules and doctrines in the course of their decisions, and as such, "continuity with the past" serves to "settle the terms" in which judges "shall be compelled to think" about the cases. This is because, in deciding new common law cases, judges need to signal that they are mindful of their obligation to consult authoritative legal sources and be at least partially guided by those sources, as distinguished from merely deciding cases as matters of social policy.[11]

As we noted earlier, the most visible changes in tort liability over the last century have occurred in connection with tangible physical harm—bodily injury and property damage. There has been enormous growth in the number of suits seeking recovery for these forms of harm and in the amount of money spent litigating these suits and paying compensation to injury victims.[12] Expansion of tort *liability*, however, is not the same as change in tort *law*. There have been important changes in the law governing liability for tangible injury, but the law governing liability for intangible injury has arguably undergone even more change.

Moreover, many of the seminal decisions governing the former are fairly conventional examples of the dominant model of common law change in operation. For example, in *MacPherson v. Buick Motor Co.*,[13] the court held for the first time that a product manufacturer could be held liable to consumers for negligently caused injuries. But the court did this simply by enlarging the already-broad category of products that were dangerous enough to be subject to liability.[14] In *Summers v. Tice*,[15] the court adopted what has come to be called the "alternative liability" exception to the requirement of proof of causation. But it did this simply by applying an already-existing exception for defendants acting "in concert" to two individuals who were hunting together without being, technically, in concert. And in *Greenman v. Yuba Power Products, Inc.*,[16] the court adopted strict liability for product manufacturers for bodily injury caused by defective products. But it did this by converting what amounted to already-existing indirect strict liability for breach of warranty to direct liability without the fiction of a warranty.

MacPherson, *Summers*, and *Greenman* are tremendously important decisions from a substantive standpoint. But as examples of the way common law courts maintain continuity while expanding the scope of tort liability, they are not at all remarkable or distinctive. We need to look elsewhere to find different and more interesting ways in which the relationship between continuity and change is manifested in tort law, and especially to changes made in the law governing intangible injury since late in the nineteenth century.

Filtering and Cloaking in the Service of Continuity

It is often possible for the courts to accommodate continuity and change. This frequently happens through what we call "filtering." The accepted obligation of courts is to decide cases not merely on the basis of social policy considerations that might appeal to the preferences of judges deciding them but on an assessment of the relevant doctrinal framework in which cases are situated. That assessment includes a consideration of how far the framework might permissibly be modified to accommodate a decision in a new case. This results in any contemporary context associated with new cases, such as the extent to which they pose arguably novel questions of social policy or raise issues emerging from new features of contemporary life, being entertained by the judges deciding them within a received doctrinal apparatus. For example, we argue in chapter 5 that, when and if tort liability is expanded to apply to previously nonactionable forms of wrongdoing that have been called "sexualized misconduct," the courts will make a strong effort to fit the new liabilities within the rubric of already-recognized causes of action in tort, so that the expansion fits within an historically acceptable category and appears to be less radical than it may actually be.

Filtering is the process by which the contemporary policy implications of new cases, rather than being considered independently, are evaluated within established doctrinal frameworks to see where a new case with those policy implications fits within those frameworks. In this sense, *MacPherson, Summers,* and *Greenman* were garden-variety examples of judicial filtering. In cases in which a decision will not fit so comfortably within an existing doctrinal framework, more searching questions must be asked: Do the implications of deciding a new case in a particular fashion seem inconsistent with established justifications for doctrinal rules governing an area of tort law so as to undermine those justifications, thereby depriving the rules of much of their settled authority? Alternatively, are those implications rendered less compelling because of the disruptive effect they may have on established tort doctrines? Or does the recognition of the implications that follow from deciding a new case one way serve to promote a thoroughgoing reconsideration of a line of prior judicial decisions currently regarded as authoritative?

The filtering of the contemporary history of torts cases occurs, we are suggesting, in all common law torts decisions. And judicial filtering invariably reveals the pressures that outcomes in those decisions which embrace newly emergent attitudes and values, or recognize novel social contexts, place on established doctrine. Regularly, courts in torts cases face the question of how far established doctrinal frameworks need to be modified in order to make tort law responsive to new conditions and new attitudes. However attractive such responsiveness may appear to a court, it is inevitably accompanied by considerations of how much a modification may affect doctrinal stability and give rise to the inference that the court's decision is grounded on social policy rather than on law.

Judicial filtering, and the conflict between continuity and change in torts cases that filtering regularly reveals, precipitates another feature of judicial decisions in torts cases that we call "cloaking." Cloaking is the process by which newly emergent doctrine is described (cloaked) in the language of existing doctrinal principles, when in fact those principles have been modified in response to newly perceived policy considerations. Cloaking often occurs in the establishment of new torts. In chapter 3, for example, we show how three torts involving the protection of very different dimensions of privacy were established by the judicial treatment of the torts as consistent with, rather than distinct from, other forms of privacy that had previously been identified in the courts. The judges establishing those new torts thereby cloaked the extent to which their decisions were innovative. And in chapter 4 we show how the U.S. Supreme Court, in the course of extending the protection of the First Amendment from public officials to "public figures" in defamation cases, cloaked its holdings in a doctrinal framework that it had used to address the arguably different problem of public official plaintiffs. We do not contend, however, that judicial cloaking is usually disingenuous. On the contrary, it is a form of judicial reasoning that permits courts to construct doctrinal change by linking it with principles and values embedded in past decisions, even when doctrinal innovations extend, or even depart from, those decisions.

Contingency and Lost History

In contending that the role played by history in the development of tort liability has been inevitable, we do not mean to suggest that the particular changes that have occurred in tort law over a period of many decades were bound to happen. Most of these changes were, in the language of historians, "contingent." Describing legal changes over time as contingent has been a way of emphasizing their somewhat fortuitous nature, particularly when they represent the choice of one set of legal solutions to perceived social problems among several contemporary alternatives.

Contingency is sometimes an ingredient, perhaps even a cause, of what has been called "lost" history—the disappearance from memory of potential solutions to legal problems that were never adopted. John Witt, for example, has uncovered significant alternatives to workers' compensation, such as worker-centered mutual insurance, that were on the agenda before workers' compensation was enacted beginning around 1910.[17] And Risa Goluboff has unearthed a series of communications from African American agricultural workers to the U.S. Justice Department in the 1930s, revealing the slave-like conditions under which they worked. Goluboff shows that this was a pivotal point in civil rights history, at which the focus of civil rights protection might have developed a focus on employment rights and conditions.[18] Instead, however, racial inequality in education became the chosen object. In both instances, the approach that was ultimately taken was not inevitable but contingent. The contingent, unchosen solutions then disappeared from written history until those scholars rediscovered them.

We uncover several significant instances of lost history in this book, each of which has aspects of contingency, but each of which is consistent with our contention that history inevitably influences the nature of change in tort law. When we speak of history being "inevitable," then, we do not mean to imply that legal change is not contingent. Often it is precisely that. We simply mean that whenever a tort law change that was contingent materializes, the way it materializes and the way it is situated within a doctrinal framework is inevitably influenced by tort law's history.

How the Differences between "Internalist" and "Externalist" Legal History Do and Do Not Matter for This Project

Our approach to the relationship between law, continuity, and change should be situated within a current, and longstanding, debate among American legal historians about the causal relationship between law and its surrounding social context. We have a position within this debate, but the important point is that the analysis we undertake is not dependent on having any particular position. In the early twentieth century some legal historians treated what one called a "taught legal tradition" as the primary factor producing outcomes in cases, suggesting that events and attitudes in the larger culture were merely folded into that "tradition" by judges when they decided cases.[19] "Taught legal tradition" seems to have referred to what we have called the doctrinal frameworks in which both legal and cultural issues raised by cases were set.

That view of causal attribution seemed to assume that legal decisions existed largely independent of their cultural contexts, or at least that issues of social policy raised in cases were subordinated to issues of legal doctrine. By the 1960s those assumptions had largely been rejected by legal historians, who came to emphasize the extent to which interpretations of authoritative legal sources, such as provisions of the U.S. Constitution and common law rules, changed over time, and the recurrent existence of issues of social policy that seemed to be affecting the outcomes of cases.[20] By 1973 Lawrence Friedman was prepared to claim that "American law" was "not a kingdom unto itself, not [a] set of rules and concepts, not . . . the province of lawyers alone, but . . . a mirror of society." There was "nothing . . . autonomous" about legal decisions, Friedman maintained; they were "molded by economy and society."[21]

Friedman's "mirror of society" conception of the causal relationship between law and its cultural context was influential among American legal historians in the late twentieth century, but by the opening of the twenty-first century a number of historical and historiographical works had posed a challenge to it. One set of works served to resurrect the importance of legal doctrine and to complicate the relationship between legal decisions and their social, political, and economic contexts.[22] Another set suggested difficulties with perspectives that wholly rejected autonomous elements in legal decision-making, advancing the view that although "legal forms and practices" were "the product of political conflict," they tended "to be embedded in 'relatively autonomous' structures that transcend and to some extent help to shape the content of, the immediate self-interest of social groups." Legal decisions were, to an extent, the products of "independent variables" that "require study [of] their peculiar internal structures."[23]

By the first decade of the twenty-first century those differing perspectives on the causal relationship between law and its cultural context seem to have settled into two versions, which a forum in the *American Historical Review* in 2005 labeled "internalist" and "externalist." Both perspectives conceded that factors in the larger culture in which legal decisions were situated and the "relatively autonomous" forms and practices of legal discourse affected decision-making; the debate was about the respective causal weight of those factors. "Externalists" maintained that the political, social, and economic dimensions of cases were driving their outcomes; "internalists" suggested that the "peculiar structures" of legal decision-making were of greater causal importance than commonly understood.[24]

One way to understand the chapters on tort law in this book is to see them as exercises in fleshing out the ways in which the "legal forms and practices" of that area of common law, its "internal structures," have ended up influencing its content and scope. If one of the assumptions of "internalist" legal history is that those forms, practices, and structures should be afforded causal weight in describing the relationship of a common law field to its cultural context at various points in its history, it seems incumbent on those making that assumption to show how the residue of accumulated doctrine in which new tort cases are situated actually serves to shape the outcomes and the judicial reasoning employed in those cases. What we are seeking to do is to take a closer look at the ways in which the "relatively autonomous" dimensions of a common law field serve to affect judicial decisions made in that field. Although we reject the version of "internalist" legal history that claims that ideas and events in the larger culture are simply folded into doctrinal frameworks which are largely autonomous, our approach, viewed in terms of an internalist/externalist debate, is focused on the particular mechanisms that courts employ when the internal doctrinal structure of tort law must be modified, even when that occurs because of external forces.

The Plan and Place of the Book

We suggest throughout this book that the ways in which history inevitably functions in the judicial decisions of torts cases permit a generalized characterization of the judicial process in those cases. The process is about the role of law—in this book, judicially fashioned tort law—in preserving continuity and constructing change. For the reasons we describe, our coverage of issues in tort law in the book departs from what has been the central emphasis of torts scholarship during the twentieth and early twenty-first centuries, a focus on physical harm to persons or property.

We have adopted this emphasis not only because so many of the major decisions regarding physical harm constitute conventional examples of judicial filtering, or on occasion of express overruling of past precedents.

In addition, the issues we are taking up have been under-researched and not widely addressed in tort law scholarship. Moreover, the common law of tort liability for physical injuries to persons and property has been significantly affected by the twentieth-century emergence of liability insurance, whereas most of the issues associated with nonphysical harm have not.[25] Unlike liability for physical harm, liability for most of the intangible harms that we discuss has never been and is not now covered by liability insurance that is accessible to businesses or individuals. The growth of such liability, and the manner in which the courts articulate the change they accomplish, therefore have not been influenced or distorted by the availability of insurance to potentially liable parties.[26]

There has also been considerable tort law scholarship that seeks to conceptualize the tort system as a whole, either describing and analyzing its basic structure or by reference to tort law's overriding social goals. That work has sometimes combined descriptive and normative analysis, seeking to show how tort law has functioned to promote particular goals or why those goals should remain of paramount importance in its continued functioning. Some work has identified economic efficiency as the tort system's overriding goal.[27] Other works see corrective justice as the underlying principle at work.[28] Still others argue that the core of tort is "civil recourse," meaning the redressing of "wrongs" rather than "losses," which the first two conceptual theories emphasize.[29]

We do not intend this book to be seen as demonstrating the primacy of any of those conceptual approaches or the accuracy of any of their interpretations. The approaches operate at a level of generality (and sometimes abstraction) distinct from the level at which we are operating. We are not interested here in demonstrating why tort law should function in the service of particular social goals, or even how it has functioned to promote those goals. Instead, we are interested in showing, by examining a series of concrete episodes, how the construction of change in American tort law has occurred and how the inevitability of history has affected that process.

Our approach leads us to emphasize some features of tort law that we find to be deeply embedded in the field but which have not received much attention from historians. The successive chapters in the book seek to introduce those features and show how they have served to influence the content and growth of tort law. Among those features are the pre-1850 prohibition against testimony in tort cases by any party having a "pecuniary interest" in the outcome of the litigation, including the parties themselves (chapter 1); the persistence of a conceptual organization of tort law based on older forms of pleading, which served to determine whether a plaintiff had brought a viable tort action, long past the point where the "writ" system of pleading had been abolished (chapter 2); the inability of tort actions designed to protect "dignitary" interests to emerge as a unitary tort, notwithstanding a growing concern over the course of the twentieth century with developing remedies for assaults on and violations of "human dignity" (chapter 3); the longstanding assumption throughout most of the twentieth century—now possibly in question—that a number of activities with "speech" dimensions, such as warnings on product labels, fraudulent or negligent misrepresentations of the value of goods or services, and false and damaging statements about the performance of competitors' products, were actionable in tort without any attention to First Amendment concerns (chapter 4); and the very small number of "new" torts that have come into being over the last three quarters of a century, despite the presence of heightened attention to a variety of activities, ranging from sexual assault to breaches of confidential data, in which the victims of those activities can be subjected to physical and emotional damage (chapter 5). In a concluding chapter we attempt to develop some general insights that can be derived from our examination of the five episodes that comprise the core of the book.

In each of those chapters we identify attitudes and experiences in American culture that affected the developments we discuss. In that sense there are "externalist" dimensions to our analysis. But most of our attention is directed to showing precisely how "internalist" practices and features of common law decision-making have been employed in the judicial construction of change in tort law.

1

The Epistemology of the Civil Trial and the Rise of Modern Tort Liability

THE COMMON law of torts is constructed by courts. Sometimes change in the law of torts results from external social, cultural, or political pressure, such as concern about automobile accidents, dangerous products, or hazardous chemicals. The courts then adjust the substance of tort law doctrine to accommodate such concerns, in ways that we contend usually maintain continuity with the past. Sometimes, however, change in tort law occurs because the internal ground rules first have been altered, thereby facilitating change in the substantive law.

This chapter examines an episode in which that second form of influence occurred, in the middle of the nineteenth century, and then was lost to history. In this episode, evolution of modern attitudes toward the causes of events in the world enabled—arguably even required—a radical reconsideration of a central rule of evidence, resulting not only in repeal of the rule but also in the disappearance from legal consciousness of any awareness that the rule had ever existed. We uncover the lost history of this rule, which was well-known and not obscure in its time. Moreover, we argue, repeal of the rule was an essential ingredient in the transformation of tort liability in the second half of the nineteenth century, and in the rise of liability for intangible injury in the twentieth century. Yet the role played by repeal in the transformation has gone completely unrecognized in efforts to explain the rise of modern tort liability.

A Preview of the Story

The key feature of this transformation can be simply described. Before about 1850, the plaintiff, the defendant, and other "interested" witnesses were almost universally prohibited from testifying in civil trials. Although the prohibition was typically described as one against all "interested" persons testifying, "interest" was narrowly defined to mean "pecuniary" interest, and thus the principal effect of the prohibition was against *party* testimony. Even under that definition, however, the prohibition massively affected the state of civil trials: they were forums in which neither of the litigating parties could appear as witnesses.

The prohibition on party testimony bears emphasis because it is both so fundamental and so surprising: until the middle of the nineteenth century, neither the plaintiff nor the defendant was permitted to testify in a tort suit by the former against the latter. Add to this two other features of premodern evidence rules that contrast sharply with modern practice—hearsay was generally admissible but cross-examination was not routinely available as a means of assuring the ability of the jury to find facts accurately—and the distinctiveness of the premodern epistemology of the civil trial becomes even more evident.

Merely to state those forgotten rules of evidence is to highlight how different the premodern epistemology of tort trials was from their modern epistemology, which reflects much greater realism and transparency in the introduction of evidence and is a much more straightforward search for the truth. Testimonial prohibitions of various sorts were more common before the turn of the twentieth century. Before the Civil War, not only slaves but also free Blacks were prohibited from testifying in the South, as well as in a number of northern states.[1] Disputes over such testimony persisted even after the war.[2] And there was a near blanket prohibition on spouses testifying against each other.[3]

The prohibition on party testimony, however, was more fundamental than any of those other testimonial prohibitions. It was central to the way tort litigation worked. Without testimony by the parties, what the jury could "know" about the facts underlying a tort action would have been derivative and incomplete, like the reflection in a broken mirror. With the repeal of this limitation, the epistemology of the civil trial, including trials in which plaintiffs sought damages for bodily injury or property damage, underwent a transformation. Civil trials went from being premodern efforts to resolve disputes whose outcomes were affected by the spiritual weight assigned to oaths taken by witnesses and the social roles associated with judges and juries, to the searches for factual truths that we now (incorrectly) assume they have been for many centuries.

Under the old epistemology, moreover, it is no surprise that tort law was barely recognized as a distinct subject. It takes lawsuits to generate a detailed body of law. Many tort actions that could in principle have resulted in the imposition of liability prior to 1850, however, for practical purposes could not be brought because the only evidence available to the plaintiff was his or her own account of what had happened, and that was inadmissible. Without the plaintiff's own testimony, the action would fail. In contrast, once the old rules were repealed, victims of bodily injury were able to describe before juries the circumstances in which they had been injured. They were able to talk about what they had done, what the individuals and entities they were suing had done or not done, and how they had suffered. They no longer needed the fortuitous presence of third-party witnesses at an accident to elicit testimony about how they had been injured. The abolition of the prohibition on party testimony, in short, made it much easier to bring and to succeed in bodily injury lawsuits. With more suits, tort law was able to develop an identity.

No wonder many commentators have suggested that the tort law of the first half of the nineteenth century was stacked against plaintiffs. But those commentators have not fully appreciated exactly why and how this was the case. Modern tort scholars appear to have been completely unaware of the prohibition on testimony by the parties to a lawsuit, and have therefore failed to take it into account in the ways they write and teach about the development of tort law.[4]

It was not the repeal of the premodern rules of evidence, however, that installed a new epistemology in the civil trial. Rather, the emergence of a modern epistemology in the social and cultural world of the mid-nineteenth century generated dissatisfaction with those rules and led to their change. Only after new understandings of the causes of events in the world emerged was it possible for the rules of evidence to change. Moreover, this change could not have been harmonized with existing rules or practices. It therefore could not take place in the conventional fashion of common law decisions modifying legal rules that had come to be perceived as obsolete. Instead, the change was a sufficiently radical break with the way civil trials had been conducted until then that it had to come through legislation.

Repeal of the prohibition against the testimony of "interested" witnesses was a change in the general rules of evidence in civil trials, not a specific change affecting only tort litigation. But the former was a prerequisite to the latter. Without the transformation in the epistemology of the civil trial that enabled the parties and other interested witnesses to testify, restricted hearsay, and permitted cross-examination, other forces responsible for the emergence of modern tort liability could not have exercised the influence they did have. The transformation created the very conditions under which modern tort law could, and then did, emerge. Here is how that happened.

The Conventional Stories and Their Flaws

From medieval times onward, instituting a civil suit required the issuance of a "writ," which was available only for a distinct and limited number of "forms of action," essentially bases for the imposition of liability. As we describe in more detail in chapter 2, there were two forms of action employed in cases involving bodily injury and property damage. The first was "trespass," which required that injury to a person or damage to property have been direct and by force. Trespass was available only in a limited number of situations. Bodily injury and property damage along with other forms of loss that did not occur "directly" did not fall within the scope of the trespass writ. Another form of action, termed "trespass-on-the-case," became available in a residual category of situations, most commonly involving indirectly caused physical harm.

In the middle of the nineteenth century, after decades of severe criticism of the forms of action, reforms began to eliminate their substantive requirements, although the writs continued to have some procedural significance for several more decades. As the forms of action withered away, a general civil action for negligence in cases involving injuries not arising out of contract crystalized. Oliver Wendell Holmes, Jr., in three articles in the 1870s and 1880s identified tort law as a substantively distinct subject, divorced from its origins in the forms of action.[5] Others followed this view, and tort law came to be generally recognized as a separate subject.

There are currently three conventional explanations for this comparatively late emergence of tort law as a discrete common law subject and a basic field of legal study in the United States. In some respects the explanations significantly overlap; in other respects they diverge. Although their proponents do not necessarily offer them as only partial explanations, we think that most often they are understood this way. Because the explanations are not mutually exclusive, most torts scholars believe that the combination of explanations comes close to, or actually does, account for the emergence of modern tort law. But even a combination is only as strong as the sum of its parts, and in this case the sum is inadequate.

The first explanation is the longest established, dating back at least to the first edition of Friedman's *A History of American Law* and anticipated by earlier scholarship.[6] Friedman maintained that the proliferation of bodily injury cases in English and American courts in the last decades of the nineteenth century—a development that all legal historians writing on the topic agree occurred—was connected to the emergence in those decades of industrial enterprises, mines, railroads, and trolleys that either engaged in dangerous activities or carried passengers and goods at high rates of speed. Those developments, Friedman has argued, increased the chances that industrial workers and passengers would be injured in those activities and seek compensation for their injuries in tort suits.[7] Friedman believed, more generally, that law is a "mirror of society," so that causal influence runs virtually exclusively from social forces and context to law.[8] It follows from Friedman's hypothesis that had the transportation revolution and industrialization been delayed in England and America until, say, the early twentieth century, tort law would not have emerged as a separate field until then.

The second conventional explanation for the late emergence of tort law proposes a different model of historical causation. The explanation focuses on the relationship between the nineteenth-century developments in transportation and industrial enterprise that Friedman described and the persistence of the forms of action in England and the United States throughout the first half of the nineteenth century.[9] According to this explanation it was only when the forms of action were replaced by what was called the "unitary civil action" that a need to organize the common law into separate fields with their own doctrinal requirements surfaced. And once that occurred, doctrinal space for the "new" field of tort law was created into which the dramatic rise of late nineteenth-century bodily injury actions could pour. If the forms of action had not been abolished when those bodily injury cases were being brought, bodily injury actions might have proliferated, but they would not have been conceptualized as "tort" or "negligence" actions.

A third explanation, approaching conventional status because of its current resonance, has emphasized the evolution away from a premodern consciousness about the social significance of bodily injury.[10] Prior to the emergence of altered understandings of the sources of causal agency in the world that accompanied the advent of modernity in England and the United States, fortuitous injuries to individuals were thought of as "caused" by agencies, such as God, fate, nature, the cycles of history, and a social order with relatively fixed ranks, which were independent of human will and that determined the destinies of individuals and societies.[11] Being injured, like falling sick, was treated by this view of causal agency as the equivalent of "fate" or "God's will" or as a punishment for failing to conform to the conduct expectations associated with one's rank in the social order. Injuries were not thought of, in the main, as something for which a society had a responsibility to provide an avenue for redress. Individuals occupied social roles in which they cared for the sick and hurt, but the state, or society at large, was not regarded as having an obligation to compensate or provide injured people a means of obtaining compensation for their injuries. Some civil remedies existed for people who could trace their injuries to conduct of others that society deemed reprehensible, but such situations were regarded as unusual.[12]

According to this story, tort law did not begin to expand its ambit, nor develop doctrines that defined it as an independent legal subject, before modern understandings of the sources of causal agency in the world were in place. Those understandings emphasized the importance of human will and human power-holding in shaping the course of social events and the destinies of individuals. The understandings displaced premodern causal assumptions, which treated laws and policies fashioned by human beings as largely powerless to alter the course of history, the organization of society, or the destinies of individuals.[13]

We do not quarrel with those stories as far as they go. Tort law as we know it would not have emerged if those factors had not come into being. They are causal forces in precisely that sense. Indeed, each of the factors conventionally understood to have helped to generate tort liability can be seen as aspects of late nineteenth-century legal modernity; they are reflections of the evolution from the premodern to the modern stages of American legal culture during the nineteenth century.[14]

In other words, we believe that each of the conventionally accepted explanations contains more than merely a kernel of historical truth. But neither alone, nor all of them taken together, constitutes a largely complete temporal correlation to the emergence of tort law. For example, the growth of heavy industry and the shift away from an economy largely centered on agriculture was well underway in England as early as the 1820s, yet no English treatise on the law of torts appeared until after the 1850s.[15] Furthermore, the English treatises included coverage of material that would subsequently be regarded as within the common law fields of property, evidence, or damages.[16] In the United States, transportation-related tort actions had appeared before the Civil War, but the emergence of tort law as a discrete common law field did not occur then. And when tort law did emerge as a subject in the 1870s, that was more than a decade before bodily injury suits arising out of transportation accidents spiked in American courts.

Similarly, research on the forms of action in England has suggested that at least by the late eighteenth century it had become habitual for plaintiffs who could not meet the strict requirements of the forms to file bills in equity asking for relief, and for the chancery court to routinely assume jurisdiction over common law cases.[17] The common law forms of action may have been the equivalent of substantive categories of law, but the contours of the forms of action were apparently not as sharply etched as may first appear.[18]

It is thus hard to know why the forms of action would have had the effect of altogether suppressing the development of any common law field, including tort law. It is clear that there was a recognized common law field of contract law by the 1850s.[19] In contrast, tort law had not yet reached comparably distinct and recognizable status. Moreover, the emergence of tort law as a discrete field preceded in many American states and law schools the abandonment of the forms of action, a process that was not universally completed until the early twentieth century.[20]

Finally, even though the emergence of modernity, and modernist attitudes toward causal agency, can be observed in England as early as the 1830s and in the United States by the decade following the Civil War, there is not much evidence that a large number of inhabitants of the United States by the decades immediately following the Civil War had developed a consciousness that society bore some responsibility to alleviate the suffering and compensate for the losses of injured people, either directly or by providing an avenue of redress against private parties. Some private institutions were performing those tasks, and many family members may have done so, but the idea that the state should facilitate redress for injured persons, either through workers' compensation or other social insurance schemes, was not widely accepted.[21] On the contrary, for several decades after modernism was in place, a *laissez-faire* attitude toward the responsibility of the state and of business enterprises for misfortune prevailed. This attitude played a role in supporting certain nineteenth-century tort doctrines, such as contributory negligence and assumption of risk, that made it harder for injured persons to recover in tort suits. An altered "ethos of injury" in favor of compensation may well have facilitated the undermining of those doctrines in the twentieth century.[22] But this alteration does not explain the timing of the emergence of tort law as an independent common law field. When American torts treatises and casebooks first appeared and tort law became the subject of a basic course at some American law schools, the *laissez-faire* attitude prevailed. When tort cases began to explode around 1880, the twentieth-century ethos of injury was not yet in place.

In short, the conventional stories do not provide a full, or fully satisfying, explanation for the timing of the emergence of modern tort law and tort liability. We believe that the missing piece of the explanation for the development of modern tort liability is the transformation of the epistemology of the civil trial. To understand how that came about, we must first understand the origins and nature of the premodern epistemology that it displaced.

The Orthodox Anglo-American Civil Trial, 1600–1850

We can get only a limited glimpse of what took place in early English civil trials, and relevant information about trials in the United States until the twentieth century is virtually nonexistent.[23] But mid-nineteenth century commentary and brief passages in recent scholarship have made it plain that the witness disqualification rule was universally in place in England and the United States from at least 1600 to the late 1840s.[24]

Under the rule—and to a very real extent for a considerable period before it came into being—the function of the civil trial was more nearly dispute resolution than truth-seeking. Although to the modern observer truth-seeking may seem always to have been one of a trial's functions, the epistemology of the trial—the basis upon which truth was sought and found—was fundamentally different in the seventeenth, eighteenth, and early nineteenth centuries from the epistemology of the modern trial. At the center of this epistemological change was the jury, considered both as a legal and social institution.

Very early after the Norman Conquest in 1066, at least in criminal trials there was trial by ordeal—by water, fire, or battle.[25] The ordeal revealed God's truth. When the church forbade priests to participate in ordeals in 1215, jury trials developed. The loss of the divine verdict that was understood to be the product of the ordeal was replaced by testimony under oath. Because oaths were sacred and taken to God, the notion that truth came from God was not eliminated. Rather, the oath was a different source of God's word.

The exact role of the jury in civil cases around this time is not completely clear, in part because there are far more records of criminal trials. But certainly by the early thirteenth century, juries were at least partly self-informing, in both civil and criminal cases. They were chosen from men of the neighborhood who had either witnessed the relevant events themselves or spoken to those who had witnessed or knew about them. Jurors came to court at least as much to speak as to listen, although there was also testimony from witnesses.[26]

With the growth and dispersal of populations in medieval and Renaissance England, however, jurors became less likely to be familiar with or capable of making themselves familiar with the facts underlying lawsuits. Testimony from witnesses became more necessary, but the notion that trials sought God's truth did not disappear. Testimony under oath therefore became one of the principal means of arriving at that truth.

At least by 1600, civil trials in England employed an approach to oral testimony that centered on the witnesses' taking an oath. During the oath regime of civil trials, witnesses were expected to be facing God, as it were, by testifying in a fashion that would not damn them for eternity. Although modern trials equate that concern with an obligation to tell the truth, that was not quite the understanding in the oath regime. Instead, the understanding was that a witness's testimony would be approved by God's will, that is to say, testimony would be seen as reinforcing the natural order of things in society, which was, after all, God's handiwork.

There was thus another function of oath-taking, aside from truth-seeking, in the regime. It was to assure that a witness's testimony would not radically disturb the social hierarchies of the time. In a world in which social status was more than a badge of one's place in the world but rather the very essence of that place, and in which the "orders" of society were relatively fixed and perceived as ordained, one might think of oath-taking as a way of in effect saying, "I as a witness am not going to say something that will disturb the existing social order." This is not to say that there was no room for truthful testimony from a witness under the oath regime, or no concern with ferreting out false or self-serving testimony. The witness disqualification rule was partially concerned with doing just that. But it is important to understand that reaching the truth about contested factual issues, while a goal of the oath regime's epistemology, was not *the* goal. Truth was to be placed in spiritual and social contexts. As James Oldham has put it, the primary goal of trials was "peaceable, regulated dispute settlements"; searching out the truth, however desirable in the abstract, was secondary.[27]

Two other features of civil trials under the oath regime present a relatively stark contrast to the modern civil trial. First, the function of the judge was not quite that of a referee or umpire, seeking to ensure that a trial was fairly and accurately conducted and that the jury was not misled by the tactics or legal arguments of counsel. Instead, judges played a role somewhat analogous to that of squires in viva voce voting in eighteenth-century America. It was customary in some eighteenth-century American parishes for certain members of a squire's household, or certain artisans in the nearby township, to be eligible to vote. Although the franchise was limited, possession of freehold land, or even just the payment of taxes, was often a sufficient basis for eligibility to vote in local elections.[28] In this setting the squires of plantations or large farms would approach the ballot box and declare their preferences, and then, often in rote order, the members of their households and their "hired hands" would announce that they were voting "as the Squire does."

The assumption was that the squire, holding both superior social status and economic leverage over his "inferiors," could educate them about their political preferences. A like assumption seems to have been driving the early Anglo-American civil trial: the judge, being a person of high status and respect, could instruct jurors, drawn from the ranks of the community at large, about how witness testimony should be understood. In particular, once a witness had taken an oath and testified, the judge was at liberty to decipher the meaning of that testimony for the jury. Indeed, judges felt entitled, in both civil and criminal trials, to disregard a jury finding if it did not comport with the judge's sense of a proper outcome.[29]

Second, it followed from this conception of the role of judges under the oath regime that the jury's role would also have been understood as somewhat different from that in modern trials. Today we anticipate that a jury verdict is the equivalent of the truth about what happened. We allow for miscarriages of justice and even for corrupt or utterly incompetent juries, but we do that against a baseline that the jury is, as George Fisher has put it, a "lie detector." Under the oath regime juries were not so regarded. Although finding out "what happened" in a contested dispute was clearly their function, "what happened" meant as much "what was spiritually and socially appropriate" as "what was the truth of the matter."

With this epistemology of civil trials in place, we can readily understand how the witness disqualification rule emerged. Apparently in an effort to protect the sanctity of oath-taking, individuals with an "interest" in the outcome of litigation were precluded from testifying. The most-often quoted passage stating the rationale for the rule is from the eighteenth-century evidence scholar Jeffrey Gilbert: "Men are generally so short-sighted, as to look at their own private Benefit which is near to them, rather than to the good of the World that is more remote; therefore, the Law removes them from Testimony, to prevent their sliding into Perjury; and it can be no Injury to Truth, to remove those from the Jury, whose Testimony may hurt themselves, and can never induce any rational belief."[30] Thus, the rule minimized the risk of perjury and protected the legitimacy of oath-taking by preventing those thought most likely to commit perjury from doing so.[31] Moreover, since if the parties testified they might contradict each other under oath and thereby call into question the notion that God's word was revealed in testimony under oath, the rule avoided this kind of open contradiction.

The rule was carried over to the American colonies. In America the sole criterion for disqualification of a witness seems to have been a showing that the witness had a "pecuniary" interest in the outcome of the litigation. "Pecuniary" seems sometimes to have been defined narrowly, so that, for example, relatives or servants of parties to litigation might or might not be permitted to testify on a party's behalf. But quite early on the witness disqualification rule was understood to apply to both *parties* to a civil lawsuit. Over the centuries there also developed a series of rules detailing the way in which juries should deal with conflicting testimony—which was under oath and therefore answerable to God. The most notable such rule came from *Bethel's Case,* which dictated "that juries should call one witness mistaken before calling either witness a liar."[32] Similarly, in felony cases the defendant could "testify" but not under oath. Those rules preserved the legitimacy of the oath.[33]

Moreover, there seems to have been a tacit understanding in early Anglo-American civil trials, after the witness disqualification rules were in place, that the "best evidence" in those proceedings was written rather than oral evidence. If we think about the epistemology of the oath regime of civil trials, a preference for written over oral evidence might well comport with the tacit purposes of those trials. Only a very limited number of the members of the population could write, and such persons were overwhelmingly high status, being in the nobility, gentry, or clergy.[34] Thus, one can imagine, in a setting in which an important purpose of evidence at a trial was to instruct the jury as to the spiritually and socially beneficial outcome of the dispute, why evidence produced by persons of high status would have been preferred.

In accidental bodily injury or property damage cases there would rarely have been any written evidence. However, sometimes such accidents would have taken place in public, where evidence might have been available from disinterested, third-party witnesses. Indeed, a number of the canonical pre-nineteenth-century accident cases explicating the differences between trespass and trespass-on-the-case turn out to have involved exactly that: accidents that occurred in public.[35] That is probably why it was feasible for them to be filed at all—because the accidents occurred in public, there would probably have been nonparty witnesses.

It was only when Simon Greenleaf compiled and published his treatise on evidence in 1842, six years before Connecticut became the first state to partially abolish the rule, that the witness disqualification rule was given an extended treatment by an American commentator.[36] In addition to reviewing English cases and commentary, Greenleaf integrated early American decisions, virtually creating the field of evidence in American law. His treatise was in the tradition of Kent's *Commentaries on American Law* and Story's commentaries on multiple subjects.[37] It was to remain the authoritative work on American evidence law until the early twentieth century, when John Henry Wigmore, who had previously edited a portion of the last edition of Greenleaf's *Evidence*, published his own treatise.[38]

Greenleaf's treatise provides a snapshot of the state of the witness rule in the United States just at the point where its epistemological assumptions were about to be rethought. Greenleaf devoted 104 pages of his treatise to discussion of the rule, its permutations, and its exceptions.[39] His discussion and analysis does not reflect even a bit of dissatisfaction with or criticism of the rule.

Greenleaf described the rule as one that declared a class of persons "incompetent" to testify in civil proceedings. The principal application of the incompetency rule, Greenleaf said, was against persons "who are *interested in* [the] *result* [of a litigation]. The principle, on which these are rejected, is the same with that, which excludes the parties themselves, namely, the danger of perjury, and the little credit generally found to be due to such testimony, in judicial investigations."[40]

Greenleaf next turned to some common applications of the rule, one of which he summarized as follows: "If the witness believes himself to be under an *honorary obligation,* respecting the matter in controversy, in favor of the party calling him, he is nevertheless a competent witness . . . and his credibility is left with the jury."[41] Why should Greenleaf have regarded a witness who was "under an honorary obligation" to testify in favor of the party who called him as competent? It would seem that there was no plainer example of a "biased" witness. And yet, Greenleaf maintained, such witnesses typically were not, and should not be, disqualified: they should be allowed to testify and the jury should be allowed to assess the witness's credibility.

The "honorary obligation" illustration from Greenleaf reveals that premodern conceptions of "honor" (strong concern for the value of one's name, family heritage, class, and reputation) were continuing to be treated in early nineteenth-century America as significant constraints on perjury or other evasive conduct by witnesses in civil trials. Greenleaf, and many of his historical contemporaries, believed that the preservation of one's "good name" and social reputation was so important that interested witnesses should be permitted to testify because they were honor-bound to do so, whether or not that testimony was true.[42] Here we see, as late as 1842, the remnants of an older epistemology of the civil trial: an epistemology where the dictates of social class occasionally trumped the search for truth. Greenleaf did not assert positively that the jury should invariably believe the testimony of a witness who was honor-bound; he simply stated that it could weigh that witness's credibility.

Two other features of evidence law in early civil trials were allied with the witness disqualification rule. There was limited cross-examination of witnesses, and there were few restrictions on hearsay—testimony by a witness about what a third party, who was not also a testifying witness and therefore subject to cross-examination, had said to that witness. Cross-examination, and the related restriction on hearsay testimony, are so basic to contemporary civil litigation that it may be hard to imagine a civil trial without them. Yet their omission appears to have been conventional for much of the period when the witness disqualification rule was in place.[43]

Cross-examination is a method of impeaching a witness's testimony on behalf of one party in a litigation. Without it, a jury might be misled as to what actually occurred in a dispute because the testimony of a witness could not be tested through questioning by opposing counsel. As a consequence, the jury's ability to get at the truth would be hindered. Similarly, the hearsay rule prevents parties or their witnesses from bringing into court statements whose truth cannot be questioned by cross-examination because the maker of the statement is not present. Both cross-examination and the hearsay rule presuppose that the function of a civil trial is to discover the truth about a dispute.[44]

In contrast, within the epistemological assumptions of the oath regime a trial's primary purpose was somewhat different. It is not as if truth was not a concern of early trials, but truth was filtered through spiritual and social lenses. It is not as if the jury was ignored in its role as decision-maker, but the jury was less a lie detector than the voice of a community in which spiritual and social principles were taken to be foundational to that community's flourishing. When modern scholars look back at the oath regime, they have a window into a premodern sensibility that attributed causal control to God, the relatively fixed "orders" of society, and fate. Those causal agencies were to an important extent independent of individuals' free will and the human capacity to influence events. The oath regime reflected this sensibility.

Importantly, the effect, and in a sense the purpose, of this regime was to relegate many disputes to extra-legal resolution, or no resolution at all. It is commonplace today to think of civil litigation as an expanding method of dispute resolution whose trial procedures are designed to make it relatively easy to bring cases to court. Arguably the purpose of civil litigation under the oath regime was close to being the opposite. The witness rule functioned to ensure that only a special category of cases would be brought in the common law courts: cases where a clear showing of injury and damage had been made out, where the jury would not be distracted by perjured or biased testimony from "interested" witnesses, and where the courts would thus remain institutions that could resolve disputes without unduly upsetting the existing social and spiritual realms of life. When understood to be allied with the rigid limits of the forms of action, the effect would have been to make it difficult to succeed in a suit

seeking damages for bodily injury or property damage, and therefore un-
common for an injured party to bring such a suit.

It is true that, if a case in the common law courts was dismissed, the
plaintiff could sometimes repair to the chancery court for equity and cir-
cumvent the dismissal. But we do not regard this as inconsistent with
the oath regime. The concept of "chancery" began with the idea of the
king granting grace outside of strict legal rules. It had roots in medieval
England in the practice of permitting persons whose conduct subjected
them to punishment under the common law to take refuge in a church,
seek sanctuary, and remain outside the jurisdiction of the common law
courts. From those origins a system of "chancery courts" developed in
which the law of "equity" (a concept roughly equivalent to "God's justice
and the sovereign's mercy") emerged as an alternative to the common
law.[45] All this was consistent with the notion that a secular, temporal
search for the truth was not the principal aim of civil trials.

In short, both the evidentiary practices of the common law courts
and the discretionary availability of the chancery courts were reflections
of the epistemology of the oath regime. Both the oath regime's epistemology and the notion of equity in the chancery courts assumed that
there was a spiritual world that existed above and beyond the temporal
world of ordinary life. That spiritual world, and the presence of God and
his appointed human servants, were omnipresent in the temporal world.
Human beings thus needed to live their lives with one eye, as it were, on
their worldly affairs and the other on their prospective salvation or dam-
nation. Further, people needed to "know their places" in the temporal
world but also to recognize that it was a mystery as to whether they would
retain those places in the hereafter. The oath regime's practices and the
institution of chancery communicated each of those messages.

Repeal of the Prohibition

As the middle of the nineteenth century approached, a number of related
developments would lead to the repeal of witness prohibition, quickly in
England and over a period of decades, state by state, in the United States.
Cross-examination of witnesses had become a more common practice,
arguably lessening the concern that perjured testimony would be unchal-
lenged. In addition, something like the modern hearsay rule became a
regular feature of civil trials, replacing earlier practices in which there

were virtually no limitations imposed on evidence based on what witnesses recalled individuals absent from court to have said. Both of those
changes had epistemological roots and epistemological effects: civil trials
were becoming processes in which judges and juries were expected to assess critically the testimony of witnesses based on what they said, rather
than who they were or to whom they owed spiritual allegiance. Those
changes reflected a shift away from premodern epistemology. Criticism
of the witness disqualification rule was part of that shift.

As time went on, the tensions within the witness disqualification rule
became more evident as exceptions testing its coherence emerged. For
example, an anonymous 1841 English commentator considered the application of the rule to some tort cases. "It is said," he observed, "that if one of
several defendants in trespass allow judgment to go by default, he is not a
competent witness for the plaintiff, though he is for his co-defendants."[46]
In addition, "where one of several defendants suffers judgment by default in an action of tort, he is a competent witness for his *co-defendants*
to prove that he alone is liable."[47] The commentator then gave a rationale
for that treatment, which he apparently thought sufficiently unusual to
require explanation: "For though [the co-defendants] be acquitted, [the
defendant witness] would remain liable, and he is not necessarily liable
to the costs of the issue tried against his co-defendants."[48] But "Best,
C.J.," the commentator pointed out, "thought [in the case of *Mash v.
Smith*[49]] that a defendant in trespass who had suffered judgment to go
by default was not a competent witness for his co-defendants who had
pleaded, if the jury are to assess the damages against him, as well as
to try the issues against the other defendants; it was said that the proposed evidence would give a complexion to the case, and it might go to
reduce the damages against himself, and therefore he was not competent."[50]

Such cases seem to have presented courts with a conundrum when they
sought to determine whether a potential witness for the plaintiff or the
defendant was an "interested" party. It seems clear that by the early nineteenth century, English common law courts were defining "interest" as
limited to pecuniary concerns but at the same time were having difficulty
figuring out, at least in trespass actions involving multiple defendants,
where a potential witness's "interest" lay. A major reason for not allowing
witnesses to testify whose liability was no longer at issue because they
had defaulted (such as co-defendants) or whose sympathies with a party
for whom they were prepared to testify seemed obvious (as with servants

of masters or agents of employers) was that a judgment might eventually rebound on them. A defaulted defendant might want to impeach his co-defendant in order to avoid paying the full judgment. An agent or servant might want to aid the position of his employer or master in order to avoid their coming against him for damages.

But of course the "interest" of a prospective witness might line up the other way. A co-defendant in a trespass action might simply want to help the cause of his fellow defendants. A servant or agent might want to aid the cause of his master or employer. Indeed, it might be in the "interest" of such persons to do so because they wanted to preserve good relations with others who had been named defendants in a trespass suit, or because they wanted to maintain good relations with their masters or employers. In short, defining "interest" as a pecuniary interest did not necessarily make the witness rule easier to apply.

Other commentators also took aim at the rule. Jeremy Bentham, who had been called to the bar in 1772 but never practiced law and was a life-time opponent of the elaborate procedures in place in the late eighteenth- and early nineteenth-century common law and equity courts, attacked the witness rule in lectures as early as 1777, but not in print. In 1827 Bentham's *Rationale of Judicial Evidence* was posthumously published, and his arguments against the rule, which he had developed years earlier, were publicly disseminated for the first time. Bentham argued that the principal purpose of the rule, eliminating perjured testimony, was largely negated in criminal trials by the practice of cross-examination and in civil trials by the jury's awareness of any "interest" a disqualified witness might have had.[51] Trials should be searches for truth, Bentham believed, not vehicles for perpetuating spiritual and class attitudes. Although Bentham's critique of the witness rule was actually seven decades old in the 1840s, only in that decade did legal audiences become receptive to it.

All this culminated in England in Parliament's passage of Lord Denham's Act, which in 1844 abolished the rule with respect to nonparty witnesses in civil and criminal cases. The rule was abolished for all "interested" parties in civil cases in 1851.[52]

Similar tensions were brewing on the American side of the Atlantic. Although Greenleaf was not critical of the rule, his treatise described its complications. For example, he considered the application of the witness rule to cases in which a master was considering filing a trespass-on-the-case action against a servant to recover the damages the master incurred because the servant's negligence had injured a third party. Greenleaf believed that there were only "certain cases" in which the evidence of the servant's previous negligence could be introduced in that action. One was "where the servant or agent has undertaken the defence" and the other was where the servant was "bound to indemnify" the master or employer. In both cases the servant, Greenleaf concluded, "has been duly required" to assume an obligation to the master.[53]

Under such circumstances, when did the servant have an "interest" in the outcome? As time goes on, a rule like the witness rule is likely to generate complications such as these, and therefore to yield a complex set of subsidiary rules. That is why Greenleaf's treatise took 104 pages to cover the rule. Those kinds of difficulties increasingly came to be considered a cause for concern.[54] An article in the *American Law Register* in 1857 captured the point of view that was becoming dominant. "The only conceivable objection that can be urged against a repeal [of the witness rule]," the author argued, "is the pretended inducement to the commission of perjury it would afford." He then noted the growing number of exceptions to the rule and asserted that it "has worked much injury in past times to the rights of deserving men and has retarded the due course of justice." Perjury could be prevented by "cross examination—at once the most perfect and effectual system for the unraveling of falsehood ever devised by the ingenuity of mortals."[55]

Connecticut was the first state to abolish the witness rule in civil cases in 1848. Nine states followed in the 1850s, eighteen in the 1860s, and three in the 1870s. Others did so in subsequent decades. Repeal in criminal cases sometimes occurred simultaneously and sometimes at different points. By 1904 every state had abolished the rule in civil cases.[56] Astoundingly, Georgia was still adhering to the rule in criminal cases when, in 1961, its statute on the issue was ruled unconstitutional in *Ferguson v. Georgia*.[57]

Tracing the Effects of the Transformation

While witness disqualification was in force, it would have had substantial effects on what lawsuits were brought and how trials in the suits that were brought were conducted. After repeal, those effects began to disappear and, together with the other factors we have described as part of the conventional story, modern tort liability was free to develop. It is useful to identify the ways in which witness disqualification would have impeded the development of tort liability, in order to recognize the fundamental impact accomplished by its repeal.

First, there would have been fewer of what would eventually be termed tort suits, because sometimes the necessary testimony could only come from a potential plaintiff, whose testimony was inadmissible. In our view, this was the most fundamental, and also the least subtle, impact of the parties to a suit being disqualified from testifying.

Second, the eventual emergence of liability for negligence would have been impeded because of the greater evidentiary demands of suits sounding in negligence as opposed to trespass. Trespass actions involved direct, forcible injury, which could often have been witnessed by nonparties. The application of force, and injury, would usually be nearly simultaneous. Negligence also sometimes occurs immediately before it causes an injury and in the presence of nonparty witnesses, as when a coachman carelessly steers his wagon or a railroad fails to sound its whistle immediately before a collision with a vehicle crossing the tracks. But negligence sometimes occurs at a considerable remove from the time it causes injury, as when a drug is mislabeled or an engine part improperly installed. There are less likely to be nonparty witnesses to the latter kind of negligence. Cases involving this kind of negligence were therefore less likely to be brought, and the opportunity for the courts to develop a body of law governing negligence would have been correspondingly limited.

Third, the jurisprudence of damages in bodily injury cases would have been underdeveloped because of the difficulty of proving the plaintiff's subjective pain and suffering. Because the very party who experienced injury—the plaintiff—could not testify, there could be no testimony from the plaintiff about the nature, extent, and duration of his or her injuries. Evidence about the subjective experience of the plaintiff, which is the centerpiece of the damages element of modern tort trials, would have been mostly, or completely, missing.

Not only did the absence of such evidence mean that there were few cases that could serve as the raw material for judicial decisions about such matters as how to project future suffering, whether an unconscious person could "suffer," and what to instruct the jury about how to place a monetary value on physical pain and emotional suffering. Even more importantly, because the plaintiff could not testify about his or her pain and suffering, the monetary damages awarded in the typical case would have been disproportionately small as compared to cases brought post-repeal, thus impeding the bringing of suits and discouraging the development of the contingent fee system that emerged after repeal.

Fourth, as negligence emerged as a distinct concept and an independent basis of liability during the first half of the nineteenth century, it quickly became established that negligence was defined by what was termed an "objective" standard of reasonable care. The motivations and good faith of the defendant, his or her personal characteristics, and his or her state of mind were not relevant to the reasonable-care standard. But of course it could hardly have been any other way since the defendant could not testify. Adoption of the objective standard, so central a part of modern negligence law and so much the subject of modern scholarship and analysis, was in a sense made inevitable at the time of its creation by the witness disqualification rule.

Fifth, the central feature of the modern negligence suit—that it involves an "all things considered" determination by the jury—would have been missing because all things could not be considered. It was only after the witness disqualification rule was repealed that this formulation, and the admission of all sorts of evidence pursuant to the formulation, could make sense and generate the impact that it has had in making the modern negligence trial a potentially complicated, wide-ranging morality play.

Sixth, the capacity of modern appellate courts to make a judgment about whether justice was done at trial, and then, sub rosa, sometimes to implement that judgment in its doctrinal rulings, would also have been missing. No appellate court could have any confidence that the record of the trial painted an accurate portrait of the accident that had generated the suit because the parties to the suit had not testified. Without confidence that it could understand accurately how the accident that injured the plaintiff had actually occurred, such judgments could not be made, and appellate review would not have proceeded with the subtext of ensuring justice that we now think sometimes occurs on appeal.

Seventh, the centrality of the parties' testimony that characterizes modern negligence cases would have been missing, and consequently the modern truth-testing device of a jury's assessing the parties' credibility based on their testimony would not have been a feature of civil trials. But this would have tended to adversely affect plaintiffs more than defendants. This was because so many defendants in nineteenth-century torts cases were entities such as railroads, steamboat companies, and municipalities. In many states, employees of such entities were permitted to testify on their behalf, on the (sometimes fictional) ground that they did not have an interest in the outcome of a suit against their employer, at least when they had already been released from the potential liability to their employer.[58] When an employee had been a percipient witness to an accident, it would have been as if the defendant itself was testifying.

Consequently, trials in which the defendant was an entity—many, perhaps even most tort trials, judging from the admittedly limited data we set out below—did not consist entirely of secondhand testimony. Rather, they consisted of secondhand testimony on behalf of the plaintiff and firsthand testimony on behalf of the defendant. Over large numbers of cases it seems likely that this disparity in the immediacy of testimony worked in favor of defendants. A number of commentators have suggested that tort law was stacked against plaintiffs in the nineteenth century, and to some extent it may have been.[59] But we think that the impact of this evidentiary imbalance on plaintiffs' prospects of success may have been at least as much responsible for any bias against recovery in tort as were the substantive rules of tort law.

Eighth, because of the absence of party testimony, there may well have been fewer purely factual disputes.[60] Whereas most cases that come to trial today do so because of disputes about the facts, a larger percentage of cases before repeal of the witness rule would have involved disputes about the *significance* of the facts. Plaintiffs would have tended not to bring suit when the parties' versions of the facts clearly would differ and there was no way to prove the plaintiff's version. Moreover, when there was evidence introduced in early nineteenth-century American civil trials about a plaintiff's perceptions of how he or she had been injured, it would have been through testimony by a third party. This testimony would have been several steps removed from direct perception or firsthand recollection. It would have been what the witness remembered the plaintiff had told him or her, either about what the plaintiff had just experienced or what the plaintiff told the witness the plaintiff had just experienced.[61]

The suits that actually came to trial, therefore, would more often have been the ones in which the facts were not disputed. The contemporary two-step process of (1) determining what the defendant did and (2) deciding whether what the defendant did constituted a breach of duty would more often have been reduced to step two. With the facts less often at issue, the morality or reasonableness of the defendant's conduct might more often have been the central or exclusive issue.

Turning from witness disqualification alone to the interaction of this rule with the other evidentiary developments we have described yields further hypotheses. Langbein's study of the Ryder sources, previously alluded to, noted little concern with or exclusion of hearsay evidence in mid-eighteenth-century England, and other sources suggest that American courts were similarly willing to admit such evidence.[62] In the next century, however, hearsay restrictions took hold.

Both contract and tort disputes may have been affected by the new hearsay rules in ways that changed the epistemology of trials and led to pressure to repeal witness disqualification. Langbein has explained how, in the eighteenth century, disqualification of the parties powerfully reinforced the common law's preference for written testimony, encouraging "prudent transaction planners to attempt to channel significant matters in writing."[63] That may have worked for some parties, but if party disqualification gave those who made contracts the incentive to make them subject to writing, the increased velocity of commerce in the first half of the nineteenth century may have rendered this increasingly unrealistic and infeasible. It might well have been difficult to enforce typical informal contracts because of the inability of parties to those contracts to testify about their terms and alleged breaches.

Theoretically, if both "interested" witness and hearsay testimony were treated as inadmissible, the practice of cross-examination, still comparatively new in the early nineteenth century, would have had little subject matter in tort trials on which to operate.[64] But once other forces put pressure on the rules precluding party testimony, the availability of cross-examination as a preventer of perjury by the parties may have softened the concerns that had been preserving the disqualification rule until that point.[65]

As the witness disqualification rule was being abolished beginning in 1848, the formal requirements of the forms of action were coming under attack as well. The forms of action and the witness disqualification rule reinforced each other in a particular manner. Although each phenomenon inhibited suits for accidental injury, in combination they were all the more effective in doing so. The strict requirements of pleading under the forms of action forced plaintiffs to make an irrevocable choice as to the legal wrong alleged, with no possibility of amendment as the actual facts became known. With the near-simultaneous abolition of the forms of action and repeal of witness disqualification, civil trials could become more freewheeling efforts to determine the facts and identify wrongful conduct.

Rethinking the Conventional Story

If repeal of the witness disqualification rule removed the obstacles to the development of modern tort liability that we have just identified, then what is the evidence that repeal was a causal force in that subsequent development? The answer is in some respect obvious and indisputable. Without repeal, there would have been many cases in which only the plaintiff had been a witness to the defendant's alleged negligence, and that the case therefore would have failed. Similarly, without repeal of the witness disqualification rule, for example, plaintiffs could not have testified in tort trials about their own pain and suffering.

In other respects, however, the impact of repeal is less obvious. Certainly the effects of repeal on the doctrinal expansion of tort law, and on the escalation in the frequency of tort suits in the late nineteenth century, are not entirely self-evident. In theory we ought to be able to look at what happened in trials, and to some extent in appeals, after repeal to identify those effects. In particular, we ought to be able to see the parties—and especially plaintiffs—testifying at trials. And we ought to be able to observe a connection between the newly created opportunity for plaintiffs to testify and the expansion of tort liability.

THE REASONS FOR LIMITED TRIAL DATA

There is an enormous obstacle, however, to investigation of the epistemology of tort trials in the nineteenth century: very few trial records of the time contain accounts of the substance of the testimony given at trial. Detailed, direct evidence of the substance of trial testimony before the twentieth century is therefore extremely scarce. The microfilm copies of various local trial court records that we have been able to examine—often called "Order Books" and "Minute Books"—do not indicate much more than the nature of the actions, motions filed, orders issued, and judgments entered.[66] The modern practice of preparing a transcript of trials, whether in anticipation of appeal or for other purposes, was not adopted until decades after the developments we have described. Stenography itself was primitive until the 1880s.[67] In an earlier study we described at length the limited nature of the trial records that are available.[68]

In fact, transcripts of trials were taken only in exceptional instances. Perhaps the most studied law practice in all of the nineteenth century is that of Abraham Lincoln, who practiced in Springfield, Illinois, from 1836 to 1861. Books on Lincoln's law practice make almost no reference to testimony in the cases of Lincoln that went to trial. And the references that are included are citations to newspaper stories, not to transcripts.[69] The substantial online data regarding Lincoln's law practice indicates that he handled twenty-two cases during his career that are classified as involving negligence. Fourteen of these involved defendants that were stagecoaches, municipalities, or railroads. Eight involved bodily injury and fourteen involved property damage.[70] But that is the extent of the data.

The reason there is virtually no record of trial testimony in Lincoln's cases or more generally is that there were no transcripts. When an appeal depended on the testimony that had been given at trial, the relevant portion of the testimony was reconstructed from notes or memory, and an agreed-upon summary was prepared.[71] This required the preparation of handwritten narrative summaries until the introduction of the first commercial typewriters in 1874.[72] Thus, we have been unable to get a representative sense of how trials were conducted or what evidence was introduced in the periods in question, either from trial or appellate records.

Opinions in appellate cases are available and can tell us some things. The dangers of relying on appellate opinions as evidence of what was occurring at the trial level, however, are almost too obvious to state. Most importantly, the sample of cases that are appealed is not necessarily representative of the cases that are filed or the cases that are tried to a verdict. And the issues that are selected for appeal in any given case are not necessarily indicative of the character of the trial that occurred even in that particular case. Nonetheless, appellate opinions are what we have.

APPELLATE CASES

Consequently, because the kinds of trial records we would prefer to examine do not exist, we have behaved like the man who looks under the lamp post for his lost key because that is where the light is. We have done a qualitative assessment of appellate opinions in tort cases for a decade before and a decade after repeal of witness disqualification rules, in four states that repealed their witness disqualifications shortly after state-by-state repeal began: Connecticut (1848), Ohio (1853), Maine (1856), and Massachusetts (1857).

We begin by noting that tort actions in the mid-nineteenth century are not the rare birds that they are sometimes thought to have been. Langbein found an "absence of tort" in his eighteenth-century review of the Ryder sources, but that was a century earlier in England.[73] Friedman has said that "the law of torts was totally insignificant before 1800."[74] Fifty years later, however, tort suits certainly appear from our sources to have been meaningful in number. In Massachusetts, for example (allowing for differences in how one classifies certain actions), the Supreme Judicial Court wrote opinions in ten appeals of tort actions in 1849, nine in 1860, fifteen in 1861, and ten in 1862. If appeals are the tip of the iceberg, then tort actions were not rare, even if they were a tiny percentage of the number of actions that would be brought fifty years later. A very rough quantitative search that we conducted also appears to reveal a striking increase in the number of appellate opinions referencing testimony by the parties in the years immediately following repeal.[75]

As might been expected, the opinions do not clearly reveal or reflect a change in the epistemology of trials before and after repeal. Many of the opinions, and the syllabi that precede them, do not describe testimony in detail or at all, being often directed solely at doctrinal issues of law. Moreover, we suspect that within a decade prior to repeal, the adjustments made by the law to witness disqualification (permitting employees and spouses of parties to testify, for example) would have been maximized, and that trials immediately before repeal would more nearly have resembled post-repeal trials than would have been the case many decades earlier.

Undoubtedly the parties who had previously been barred from testifying began almost immediately to do so after repeal of witness disqualification.[76] But it probably would have taken some time before lawyers learned not only that testimony by plaintiffs could now include evidence of what the plaintiffs had directly perceived but also how to exploit the jury sympathy that such testimony could elicit. The factual richness of the modern negligence trial may not have been the immediate result of the repeal of witness disqualification, but witness disqualification was one of the necessary conditions to the eventual emergence of that kind of trial.

A second telling point is that, both pre- and post-repeal, defendants in the appellate cases in our sample typically were businesses or municipalities for whom the testimony of a servant or employee would frequently have been admissible even before repeal under the rule that an employee released from liability to his employer was not "interested." As a result, confirming what we suggested earlier, witness disqualification probably had much less impact on the ability of commercial defendants to stake out their positions. In Massachusetts shortly before repeal, for example, the Supreme Judicial Court finally held that testimony by a third party regarding the plaintiff's expression of present pain was admissible but that testimony by the same witness regarding the plaintiff's narrative describing his pain after the fact was not.[77] It is no surprise, therefore, that as late as the eighteenth century the rules governing damages for bodily injury seem to have made no express reference to this form of loss.[78] Thus, before repeal, it would have been difficult for plaintiffs in bodily injury cases to introduce testimony about the extent of their pain and suffering. After repeal, however, plaintiffs could testify and the opportunity to clarify the rules on this issue arose.

There are hints in the post-repeal cases of the ways in which repeal would come to affect testimony. In one Connecticut case the plaintiff and his wagon were thrown over a bridge onto the rocks below. The defendant objected to an instruction to the jury that, in the assessment of damages, it might consider "the peril and danger to which the plaintiff was exposed, by the accident which produced the injury complained of." The court held that the instruction was correct, indicating that actual injury "is not confined to wounds and bruises upon his [the plaintiff's] body, but extends to his mental suffering. His mind is no less a part of his person than his body; and the sufferings of the former are oftentimes more acute and more lasting than those of the latter. . . . The dismay, and the consequent shock to the feelings, which is produced by the danger attending a personal injury, not only aggravate it, but are frequently so appalling as to suspend the reason and disable a person from warding it off."[79]

There is nothing in this opinion suggesting that allowing testimony about pain and suffering connected to a physical injury was a new principle of tort law. But we found no cases addressing the issue in the ten years before Connecticut repealed its witness disqualification rule. The fact that the defendant raised the issue implies that it was not viewed as fully resolved at that point. At the least, repeal of the disqualification had made it easier for issues such as this to arise and be squarely resolved. A robust jurisprudence of pain and suffering damages could then develop.[80]

Similarly, in a Massachusetts case the plaintiff who sued for injuries suffered when he was struck by a train testified that

> in crossing the platform in going to the cars he did not go in a direct course, but a little obliquely, from Boston; that he looked to see where he should get into the cars, and as he was stepping from the platform he saw the train coming from Boston, and instantly after that the sound of the whistle struck his ear; that the train was then twenty or thirty feet from him, and he had not time to save himself; that he had no intimation whatever that the train from Boston was coming; that he did not recollect that he looked towards Boston at any time after he came out of the station, until he was stepping on to the rail of the track; and that on the outside of the platform he could see an approaching train at a distance of thirty or forty rods.[81]

We did not see this kind of granular, factual detail about plaintiff's perceptions in the opinions in cases decided before repeal. In rare cases before repeal it may have been possible to introduce this sort of perceptual evidence through another witness who had viewed the scene from the same standpoint as the plaintiff, but that would have been unusual. Once plaintiffs could testify, however, this sort of evidence could become routine. The tests for negligence, and for contributory negligence, could then become the under-all-the-circumstances notions into which they eventually developed.

Our review also revealed the significance of the transportation revolution for accident litigation in the middle of the nineteenth century.[82] Many—in some instances most—of the cases both before and after repeal involved railroad and highway accidents. Often the suits were based on breach of statutory standards creating maintenance and safety obligations on the parts of railroads and municipalities.[83] Both before and after repeal, cases involving property damage predominated, but after repeal there was a discernible increase in the number of appeals involving bodily injury claims. The absolute numbers, however, are too small to be statistically significant.

The expansion of the railroads in the 1850s surely helps to explain the frequency of railroad cases. Total railroad mileage expanded from nine to thirty thousand miles between 1850 and 1860.[84] An increasing number of suits involving encroachment on neighboring property or obstructions, as well as suits involving actual physical damage, would have been generated by this new construction.

An additional explanation for the property damage cases is that, in contrast to some situations that cause bodily injury, the conditions that give rise to property damage suits, especially those involving encroachment and obstructions, are durable. Witnesses other than the parties can observe and testify about those conditions without having been present at the scene at any particular moment. In contrast, the conditions that cause bodily injuries are more likely to be momentary—how a train was operated, how a victim behaved—and therefore less susceptible to proof on behalf of the plaintiff by third-party, disinterested witnesses. As a consequence, the percentage of bodily injury accidents that resulted in suits was probably lower than the percentage of accidents or occurrences involving property invasions or losses.

Taking Stock

To summarize, the factors conventionally associated with tort law's late emergence as a common law field in the United States had a complicated connection to the repeal of the witness rule and the consequent ability of parties to testify in tort cases. The transportation revolution and the associated emergence of industrialization in mid-nineteenth-century America enhanced the likelihood that people would be injured in transportation accidents, but those developments did not precipitate a spike in bodily injury suits for several decades. This was partly because the rate of accidents associated with these activities probably did not truly skyrocket until later. Important studies of late nineteenth-century tort filings in particular localities have revealed features of the rise of tort liability during this period. Those studies document substantial increases in tort filings, especially involving bodily injury, between 1880 and 1910.[85] But only one of the studies included data from the 1870s, and none included data for decades prior to that.[86] Even with the increases in transportation and industrial accidents it still was not possible in many jurisdictions to bring a modern tort suit. That could only happen after repeal, which had not occurred in a substantial majority of states until the 1870s. Therefore, it would be difficult to correlate in any systematic way the repeal of witness disqualification to subsequent increases in accident rates or tort filings.

The impoverished state of mid- and late nineteenth-century trial records leaves us, then, with hypotheses about the effects on American tort law of the witness rule, and its repeal, that remain strongly suggestive rather than capable of airtight proof. We assumed when we began to study the issue that sustained qualitative and quantitative analyses of cases and commentary on the witness rules, and on the routine disqualification of "interested" persons, would enable us to confirm or qualify the hypotheses with which we began the project. Most centrally, perhaps, we assumed that there would be ample sources for us to examine along the way.

Instead, we found a much more attenuated collection of relevant sources than we had anticipated. Although there was some discussion of the witness rules by eighteenth- and early nineteenth-century commentators, there was less than we expected, particularly in America. And although there were obviously a large number of cases in which the rules were in place, there was very little *comment* on the rules by courts or litigators. Nor did we find any precise descriptions of how civil trials were conducted with the rules in place, or how the process of a civil trial might have been altered as jurisdictions began to repeal the rules. The only descriptions we did find suggested that the epistemological assumptions of those involved in civil trials with the rules in place were quite different—arguably radically different—from modern epistemological assumptions about the primary purposes of a civil trial. The witness disqualification rule had seemingly led us to a world—we have called it a premodern world—in which the participants in a civil trial—judges, juries, litigants, witnesses—were thought of as engaging in something different from the conventional "search for truth" associated with modern civil trials.

We therefore have little documentation to support our hypothesis that repeal of the witness disqualification rule had a significant and unrecognized impact on the development of modern tort law. Nonetheless, if repeal of the witness disqualification rule were removed as a causal agent in the late nineteenth-century emergence of tort law, we would be left with an unexplained puzzle. With repeal understood as a causal agent, the data can be more fully explained.

Industrialization was well underway in the United States in the decades prior to the Civil War, and yet a spike in bodily injury lawsuits did not take place until the 1880s or later. If the forms of action alone had functioned to limit the number of bodily injury actions that could have been brought in the early nineteenth century, the rigors of that system had broken down by the middle of the century, and yet bodily injury actions were still comparatively rare. And if an altered ethos of injury, in which public institutions were expected to take a greater share of responsibility for alleviating the costs of injuries to individuals, was partly responsible for the advent of such early twentieth-century social programs as workers' compensation, there is no evidence that such an ethos had surfaced when bodily injury actions began to proliferate in the 1880s. Further, there is some contrary evidence, such as Holmes's famous statement in *The Common Law* that the then "prevailing view" was that losses from bodily injury should lie where they fall, in the absence of strong reasons for state intervention to shift them elsewhere.[87]

The most persuasive support for our hypothesis that the witness disqualification rule retarded the emergence of bodily injury actions in American courts, and that repeal of the rule contributed to that emergence, is thus the historical logic of the hypothesis. With industrialization and the associated growth of modes of transportation, more accidents allegedly connected to the negligent conduct of factories, railroads, and streetcars occurred. Eventually many of those accidents spawned bodily injury lawsuits, resulting in a noticeable spike in those lawsuits in urban centers in the years between 1880 and 1920. But the major spike in bodily injury claims did not take place contemporaneously with the growth of railroad networks, or even with the emergence of streetcar lines. It began to occur approximately one or two decades after railroads and streetcars had become the dominant modes of urban transportation. The suits were typically actions for negligence and frequently included damages for pain and suffering, an element hitherto lacking.

We are thus confronted with a historical scenario in which one set of phenomena (industrialization and the consequent growth of railroads and streetcars as ubiquitous modes of urban transportation, resulting in more persons being exposed to the risks of railroad and streetcar travel) might have been expected to cause a proliferation of bodily injury suits

from injured railroad and streetcar passengers but did not, at least initially. In the time period in which a growth in those suits did not occur,
another phenomenon (the witness disqualification rule) was in place.
Then, in the next two decades, many jurisdictions abolished their witness disqualification rules, and a spike in bodily injury actions in those
jurisdictions began. Moreover, in the limited number of such cases that
we were able to recover, plaintiffs were able to testify about their injuries.

It thus seems probable to us that the abolition of the witness rule was
a causal agent that, when added to the dramatic increase in the number
of people exposed to the risks of railroad and streetcar travel, helped turn
the option of seeking civil redress for injuries suffered from that travel
from an unlikely to a more likely possibility. This was because injured
passengers were now able to describe, before juries, the circumstances
in which they had been injured. They were able to talk about what they
had done, what the entities they were suing had done or not done, and
how they had suffered. They no longer needed the fortuitous presence
of third-party witnesses to elicit testimony about how they had come by
their injuries. The abolition of the witness rule, in short, made it much
more likely that they would consider filing bodily injury lawsuits.

Why This History Was Lost

The existence of the witness disqualification rule has been lost to history,
and especially to the history of tort law, for over a century. We have found
no mention of the rule or its repeal in early twentieth-century torts scholarship. It is not mentioned in any of the work of Francis Bohlen, the Reporter for the first *Restatement of Torts.* The first edition (1941) of *Prosser
on Torts,* the foremost torts treatise of the period, contains no mention
of the rule.[88] Nor does the competing Harper and James treatise, published in 1956.[89] Nor does any of the other torts scholarship of the second
half of the twentieth and the first part of the twenty-first century, including our own previous work, recognize the existence of the rule, or its effects, or the effect of repeal on the development of tort law.[90] It is as if the
rule never existed.

If the existence of the witness disqualification rule and its repeal were
important causal factors in the timing of tort law's emergence as a discrete common law subject in the United States, then why has no attention been paid to it in conventional accounts of the history of American

tort law? Obviously, awareness of the rule was not lost immediately upon repeal. It took decades before it was repealed everywhere. The multiple editions of Greenleaf's evidence treatise, for example, which addressed the rule at great length, were consulted throughout the second half of the nineteenth century. Then why, although awareness of the witness disqualification rule, and of its ongoing repeal, must have been pervasive during this period, was that awareness lost once the twentieth century began? We can offer two possible explanations.

Disbelief

The first possible explanation is that a radical change in the worldview of legal scholars made the history of the witness rule unrecognizable. There may well have been a shift in consciousness among twentieth-century legal scholars about the very conception of a civil trial, along with accompanying conceptions about the nature of the human condition and the purpose of resolving disputes through trials, that rendered the history of the witness rule invisible to them. That shift may have been sufficiently powerful and broad-ranging to "wipe out" awareness of and interest in the previous, arguably irreconcilable sets of cosmic attitudes. Given the idea that the purpose of a trial is something like an empirical search for the truth, it would have made no sense at all to a twentieth-century torts scholar to disqualify the parties from testifying, since their testimony is essential to the truth-seeking, adversarial process. Since the witness rule would have made no sense, the notion that it existed for at least two and a half centuries would simply have seemed incredible.

That is actually the first reaction that we have encountered on bringing this lost history to the attention of many of our colleagues—total disbelief. Indeed, that was our first reaction as well. We are speaking of disbelief not only in the abstract but also accompanying discomfort at the prospect that the pre-1850 cases that we and our colleagues have been reading all of our professional lives now had to be re-understood as taking place in a world in which neither the plaintiff nor the defendant could testify. That kind of discomfort could well have generated enough cognitive dissonance among early twentieth-century scholars that they shied away from any mention of the witness rule, which after all was no longer in effect anyway. Once that generation of torts scholars ceased to mention the rule, it was lost to future generations.

Here we encounter one of the endemic difficulties of doing scholarship in legal history. How should the historian react when evidence from the past seems to reveal that past actors held a set of meta-theoretical beliefs about the human condition, the role of social organization, even the meaning of existence, that are no longer held by most people in the twenty-first century? How can historians of law prevent themselves from recoiling from the meta-theoretical beliefs of past actors if they seem so alien as to nearly lack credibility?

The beginnings of the transition from disagreement to disbelief are evident in the last prominent reference to the rule that we have found. It came from the great evidence scholar John Henry Wigmore, who had been the editor of the sixteenth edition of Greenleaf's treatise, published in 1899. Five years later, Wigmore published his own multivolume treatise of the Anglo-American system of evidence in common law trials. In the course of that work Wigmore noted the existence of the witness disqualification rule and its widespread repeal, criticized it, and sought to confine it to oblivion.

Wigmore has been properly criticized for supporting rules of evidence that reflected nineteenth-century male conceptions of honor, but his attitude toward the witness disqualification rule would have been very much in the mainstream for that period.[91] Wigmore's attitude reflected the modern worldview that had by then totally replaced the premodern view which lay behind the witness rule. He was determined to demonstrate that the adoption of the rule in England and America had been seriously misguided. First, he suggested that the rule's existence had been anomalous originally: "The result, then, may be summed up in this way: That the party's oath was necessarily excluded in jury trial; that when modern witnesses came into vogue in the 1400s and 1500s, the party was naturally deemed incapable of being such a witness; that otherwise no rule or disqualification for interested persons was recognized in the earlier days of witnesses; and that finally, after Coke's time and probably under the influence of his utterances, the rule for a party was extended by analogy to interested persons in general."[92] The fact that Wigmore completely ignored the premodern epistemology that the rule reflected, and was either not clearly right or was in fact wrong on every conclusion he drew from his historical survey, did not deter him from proceeding to the next step in his attack on the witness rule.[93]

This step began with a quotation from *Starkie on Evidence*, one of the principal expositors of the witness rule.[94] "This rule of exclusion," Wigmore quoted Starkie as saying, "considered in its principle, requires little explanation. It is founded on the known infirmities of human nature, which is too weak to be generally restrained by religious or moral obligations, when tempted and solicited in a contrary direction by temporal interests. . . . The law must prescribe general rules; and experience proves that more mischief would result from the general reception of interested witnesses than is occasioned by their general exclusion."[95] Wigmore responded to Starkie's arguments by treating them as unsound policy. As Wigmore put it, "The answer to this syllogism is merely that both its premises are unsound—that pecuniary interest does not necessarily raise any large probability of falsehood, and even if it did, the risks of false decision are not best avoided by such testimony."[96] In other words, the syllogism was unsound because Wigmore said it was. But Wigmore was not content with that assertion; he next summoned up a series of commentators, beginning with Bentham, who advanced arguments against the witness rule.

Having quoted not only from Bentham but from an 1853 English commission and the 1848 report of the New York Commissioners on Practice and Pleading, Wigmore was ready to sum up.[97] And sum up he did, relegating the witness rule to obscurity:

> It is not easy nowadays to appreciate why these plain objections remained so long without recognition: (1) One reason, certainly, is found in the much stronger influence, up to the 1800s, of the emotional element in human conduct. . . . Speech and action were more passionate and violent: witness . . . the enormous excess of libel actions over their present number, as well as the extremities of abuse that were indulged in by gentlemen. . . . Eventually the influence of scientific research and of industrial invention and organization made for a more rational and less emotional life. . . . Thus with the diminution of the control of mere emotion and partisanship over conduct and opinion, the rules of law which were natural enough while that domination existed ceased gradually to correspond to the facts of life and survived as anachronisms.
>
> (2) A second reason perhaps is to be found in that "dead weight of an oath" which in popular probative notions prevailed from primitive times and still is so difficult in some communities to make weigh against.[98]

Here Wigmore felt he had unearthed a truly significant feature of his project for modernizing Anglo-American evidence law, so he spelled matters out. Wigmore believed that "cross examination is the greatest legal engine ever invented for the discovery of truth."[99] Consequently, the witness disqualification rule became superfluous once cross-examination became prevalent:

> As long as juries were inclined to give a numerical value to witnesses . . . to believe that ten witnesses were ten times as probative as one witness, and to treat a sworn assertion on the stand as being good for so much testimony, irrespective of the witness' personal credit, so long might a legislature well hesitate to admit to the stand persons who in their credit would certainly be weaker than the normal witness and would yet be indiscriminately counted as good witnesses by the jury.
>
> [Nowadays] . . . the tribunal's opportunity for a careful weighing of a witness' measure of credit, and the means afforded for doing so by cross-examination and the like, form the safeguards which induce us to take the risk of introducing interested witnesses. . . . If [during the time the witness rule was in place] the tribunal [would have been] apt to ignore those safeguards, the reason for admission [of "interested" persons would have been] much weaker.
>
> Perhaps the two foregoing considerations sufficiently explain why the [legislation abolishing the witness rule] dates no earlier than the second half of the 1800s.[100]

Wigmore had consigned the witness rule to history. It was "unscientific," inconsistent with "modern" procedure in evidence cases, an anachronism. Yet Wigmore had himself been anachronistic at every point, either ignoring or being unaware of the cultural and social significance of oaths and witness testimony during the period when the rule was in force. In his historical and policy analyses of the witness rule this not only had not troubled him; it had very likely not troubled his early twentieth-century legal contemporaries either. He was so successful that his 1904 treatise on evidence marked the stage at which the witness rule passed out of modern memory. Thus, the earlier regime of conducting civil trials, with its earlier epistemology, was not merely dismissed as wrongheaded. It was literally lost from consciousness because its assumptions seemed so alien that they could not be imagined, let alone painstakingly recovered. That is one of the ways that the phenomenon of "lost history" occurs.

Doing legal history is arguably all about such complicated interactions with the past. And sometimes, as in this instance, the "lessons" to be drawn from a historical inquiry are not those associated with a putatively authoritative "explanation" for a historical phenomenon. Instead, we associate them with a "solution" to a "mystery," a mystery about how so arguably important an episode in the Anglo-American law of evidence, procedure, and tort law could have largely passed from the consciousness of contemporary lawyers and scholars. The solution for us does not just lie in a suggestion about why tort law was late to emerge in America. It lies in the discovery of a different epistemological universe of civil trials that has mainly been forgotten.

THE SUBSEQUENT PREOCCUPATIONS OF TORTS SCHOLARSHIP

The second reason the witness disqualification rule became lost to history, we think, was that the effects of its repeal were simply not high on the agenda of tort scholars in the second half of the nineteenth century. These scholars were undoubtedly aware of the rule, and its repeal, but that is not what primarily concerned them. The rule and its repeal were the province of the law of evidence, and they affected all civil trials, not merely trials in tort cases. In addition, the rule was something from the past, and they were interested in the present. So those scholars did not write about it. And when early twentieth-century scholars went to read what their predecessors had written, the witness disqualification rule was not mentioned. It was lost to history because it was not a part of anyone's scholarly agenda.

The reason for what was and was not on the scholarly agenda is that, at roughly the same time the repeal of the witness disqualification rule began to occur, abolition of the forms of action also began. Although the witness rule had been a fundamental feature of civil trials for a long time, there had been far more preoccupation with the scope and nature of the forms of action during the same period. All common lawyers had spent much of their apprenticeships learning about common law pleading, at the center of which were the forms of action. Judicial decisions addressing which form of action would "lie," that is, be appropriate under different factual circumstances, abounded. When the forms of action were abolished, centuries' worth of case law central to most lawyers' work was set aside.

For torts scholars, then, the witness disqualification rule faded into the background and was eventually forgotten. Torts scholars working in the period after abolition of the forms of action would have been understandably much more preoccupied with the significance of this development than with the witness rule's repeal because abolition of the forms of action led to the very recognition of tort law as a separate subject. Once tort law was a separate subject, torts scholars' principal challenge was to define tort law's scope and nature. Well into the 1920s, such scholars had their hands full attempting to meet this challenge. As it turned out, conceptualizing tort law has been a continuing challenge. Part of the reason is that the forms of action may have been abolished but their underlying structure has continued to influence tort law's structure and organization. Thus, although the forms of action were abolished, they have not been fully escaped. As the chapters that follow demonstrate, modern tort law still must deal with their inevitable influence.

IN TURNING from the abolition of the witness disqualification rule to other episodes in the history of American tort law, we are devoting more attention than we have in this chapter to judicial decisions about doctrinal frameworks, containing an accumulation of prior cases and rules, in which tort cases tend to be set. In this chapter we have seen that a long-established rule in civil trials, in place for centuries, was suddenly eradicated through legislation because premodern epistemological assumptions about the conduct of civil trials had been abandoned. Repeal of the witness disqualification rule represents an unusual instance in which evolving modern attitudes about the proper function of civil trials strongly implicated an existing doctrine that was so fundamental that the doctrine could only be abolished by legislation. We have also seen that once the rule was abolished it was quickly lost to the consciousness of torts scholars, primarily for the same reason: the rule seemed incompatible with modern conceptions of the civil trial as a search for truth and was thus discarded as reflecting alien, outmoded conceptions.

The combination of attitudes about the proper conduct of civil trials and estrangement from premodern conceptions of the function of those trials that produced the abolition of the witness disqualification rule and its being "lost" to the consciousness of post-repeal commentators serves as an illustration of the capacity of changing cultural phenomena—in this instance changes in epistemological attitudes and assumptions—to serve as powerful forces fostering changes in the law. To the extent that those changes can be associated with particular historical eras—here the recoil of mid-nineteenth-century actors from the epistemological assumptions of the oath regime of civil trials—they provide evidence of one way in which history "inevitably" affects the development of law. But, as we will see, that is only one dimension of the interplay of law, continuity, and change. The other dimension involves the ways change is affected by another "inevitable" form of history: the established doctrinal frameworks in which common law cases are situated. We now turn to some episodes in which the power of those frameworks to affect legal change are prominently featured.

2

Conceptualizing Tort Law—the Continuous (and Continuing) Struggle

TORT LAW, as we saw in chapter 1, emerged as a separate field of law in the 1870s. As we suggested in the introduction, it was very much the tort law of the nineteenth century. The test for negligence, for example, was whether an individual had behaved as a "reasonable man," apparently even when the individual was a woman, with all the subtle and not-so-subtle implications about women that accompanied this formulation. That test would not be changed for decades.

In any event, tort law got off to a rocky start. In 1871, for example, the young Oliver Wendell Holmes, Jr., asserted that "Torts is not a proper subject for a law book." The basis of his comment was the absence of any "cohesion or legal relationship" among the topics grouped under the heading of "torts."[1] Holmes soon changed his mind, and within a decade had famously organized tort liability around the standards of conduct that governed different torts.[2] In the twentieth century the newly founded American Law Institute (ALI) took up the challenge, preparing the first set of its important "Restatements" of the law, including the *Restatement of Torts*. The *Restatement* achieved consensus, but like its nineteenth-century precursors, it did not achieve coherence. Nor have its successors. Tort law remains to this day a fragmented, conceptually disorganized field.

The primary reason, we think, is that tort law is the prisoner of its traditional, and inevitable, disorganization. It has never been able to escape the received doctrinal structure that is an essential part of its history. When tort law changes, it must accommodate itself to that doctrinal structure. Today, for example, all tort lawyers, scholars, and teachers, following Holmes (whether they know it or not), understand that there are three bases of liability in tort: intent, negligence, and strict liability. That is ordinarily how we think about tort liability and how we organize tort law in our thinking. But that way of thinking actually does not capture, and has never captured, all of tort law.

This may be one of the reasons Holmes originally had doubts about the viability of tort law as a legal subject. A quick look at any of the successive *Restatements of Torts,* or at the leading treatises and casebooks, reveals that his tripartite division is only partly reflected in their organizational structure. Many torts typically are treated in piecemeal, atomistic fashion, as if they fall outside of this tripartite structure of organization altogether. In addition, very different matters are addressed under the three divisions: sometimes full-blown torts (such as battery) are discussed, but sometimes only the nature of an abstract standard of conduct (such as negligence) is the focus.

Something else, or something additional, is going on in tort law, but exactly what is not clear, and never becomes clear. What is actually going on in tort law, we argue, is that for 150 years the choice has inevitably been between engaging in the overgeneralization that produces an artificially organized presentation of the subject and reproducing the "chaos with an index" that replicates what tort law was even before it had that name.[3]

This chapter explores the reasons this is the case. The chapter is intended as an illustration of how the received doctrinal framework of a common law subject can serve to affect efforts to reconceptualize that subject, to the point of making a thoroughgoing reconceptualization impossible. It is also another effort to uncover an episode of lost history, this time in the archives of the ALI. Our inquiry reveals how the drafters of the first *Restatement of Torts* first attempted, but then largely abandoned, an effort to develop a new, coherent organization of tort law. Instead, they adopted the fragmented organization that has served as the model for subsequent torts *Restatements* and for most contemporary surveys of tort law. The first *Restatement*'s inability to meet the challenge it perceived is emblematic of everything that has come after it.

Abolition of the Forms of Action

In the preceding chapter we introduced the prohibition against "interested" witness testimony, which was in place for at least three centuries before it was repealed in both England and the United States, beginning in the mid-nineteenth century. When the witness prohibition rule was in existence, it was accompanied by a system of pleading in civil cases that emphasized the matching of civil actions to what were termed "writs," literally pieces of parchment that were filed as part of a plaintiff's case.

For more than half a millennium, the writ system and its accompanying "forms of action"—the technical procedural pigeonholes into which lawsuits were required to fit—governed civil actions at common law.[4] Instituting a civil suit required a writ, which was available only for a distinct and limited number of "forms of action."[5]

There were separate forms of action associated with what would later become separate subject matter fields. Debt, covenant, and assumpsit would eventually merge into contract, for example. There were two forms of action employed in cases involving bodily injury or property damage not arising out of breach of contract.[6] The first was "trespass," which required that injury to a person or damage to property have been direct and by force. In fact, when trespass was brought for causing bodily injury, it was denominated trespass *vi et armis*—"by force of arms"—even if weapons had nothing to do with it.[7] Early on, the availability of a damage remedy in the common law courts for conduct that met the trespass requirements seems to have signaled that the conduct was socially disapproved of (conduct that precipitated actions in trespass was ritualistically described as a "breach of the King's peace"), and that a damage remedy was being employed as a preferable alternative to a violent reprisal by the injured party.[8] Those historical features of trespass slowly faded away even while it was still in force, but they were part of its origins and influenced its development.

Trespass was available only in a limited number of situations. Bodily injury and property damage that did not occur directly, and other forms of loss, did not fall within in its scope. Another form of action, termed "trespass-on-the-case," or just "case" for short, became available in a residual category of situations, originally involving indirectly caused physical harm.[9] Eventually trespass-on-the-case was the form of action also employed for slander, libel, deceit, and certain forms of negligence.[10] Another form of action, "assumpsit," which was available for certain other forms of misfeasance, grew out of trespass-on-the-case.[11]

Because of the differences among them, the choice of a form of action could be dispositive:

> To a very considerable degree the substantive law administered in a given form of action has grown up independently of the law administered in other forms. Each procedural pigeon-hole contains its own rules of substantive law, and it is with great caution that we may argue from what is

found in one to what will probably be found in another; each has its own precedents. . . . The plaintiff's choice is irrevocable; he must play the rules of the game that he has chosen. . . . Lastly he may find that, plausible as his case may seem, it just will not fit any one of the receptacles provided by the courts and he may take to himself the lesson that where there is no remedy there is no wrong.[12]

Some of the forms of action imposed what amounted to strict liability (liability even in the absence of blame or fault), while others did not. For example, proof of intent to cause harm was not required in trespass actions. Since battery, assault, and false imprisonment were actionable in trespass, it follows that those "intentional torts" were not intentional at common law, although they frequently would have been accompanied by intent to cause harm. Over time, the fact that the actions brought in trespass often involved some purposive conduct on the part of defendants, and that those brought in case involved conduct which typically was accidental or inadvertent, would be emphasized by scholars conceptualizing and organizing the law of torts in treatises and casebooks. But even at the end of the era during which the forms of action governed, there was no established classification of different forms of tort liability based on varying standards of conduct. In fact, there was no established classification of tort law at all.[13]

There was increasing dissatisfaction with the forms of action as the nineteenth century proceeded. Dissatisfaction stemmed from their tendency to privilege procedural technicalities over substantive rules and principles. Speaking of this tendency in one of the more striking images in the history of legal scholarship, Sir Henry Maine observed that the forms of action were so dominant in the early years of the common law that "substantive law has at first the look of being gradually secreted in the interstices of procedure."[14]

Francis Hilliard, who published the first American torts treatise in 1859, wrote in his preface to that work that "by a singular process of inversion . . . *remedies* [the procedural requirements of the forms of action] have been substituted for *wrongs* [the substantive elements of tort actions]. To inquire for what injuries a particular action may be brought, instead of explaining the injuries themselves," he felt, "seems to me to reverse the natural order of things."[15]

Similarly, as we noted above, Holmes initially concluded that "Torts is not a proper subject for a law book" because its various causes of action lacked "cohesion" or a proper "legal relationship."[16] He attributed that in part to the failings of the forms of action, which did not "embod[y] in a practical shape a classification of the law, with a form of action to correspond to every substantial duty" but were "in fact so arbitrary in character, and owe their origin to such purely historical causes," that "nothing keeps them but our respect for the sources of our jurisprudence."[17]

Another factor contributing to support for abolition of the forms of action was the changing nature of the bar as the nation grew, demographically and geographically. The American population and the territory of the United States expanded dramatically in the three decades beginning in the 1830s, with an increased number of immigrants from Europe coming to America, and the United States acquiring a vast amount of territory west of the Mississippi.[18] Developments in transportation, including the emergence of canals and railroads, facilitated the movement of populations westward and resulted in many new states entering the Union as their populations reached sufficient numbers. Those states needed lawyers, and the bars of those states welcomed them: in many new states in the 1830s, 1840s, and 1850s it was not necessary for an applicant to the bar to have graduated from a law school or served as an apprentice to a law office.[19] The result was an influx of new lawyers in new states whose training was rudimentary. In that setting, few lawyers could be expected to know the intricacies of the forms of action and writ pleading; they probably were often ignored.

At the same time, a movement emerged in some states to "codify" the law. This meant replacing the common law with a state-enacted comprehensive code, modeled on those of European nations that had established civil law systems. The expectation was that codes would have far more detailed doctrinal rules than those supplied by judges in deciding common law cases. This would result in ordinary people having a better understanding of their legal rights and responsibilities, and in the reduction of judicial discretion to make law. Proponents of codification also expressed dissatisfaction with the dominance of English common law doctrines in the United States and with the technicalities of the forms of action.[20]

When the 1848 Field Code in New York became the first to abolish the forms of action and substitute a "unitary civil action," it was made available as a template for procedural reform.[21] California abolished the forms of action three years later.[22] In all, twenty-three states or territories adopted versions of the Field Code in the two and a half decades after 1848, fifteen of them states that entered the Union after 1850.[23] Additional states followed thereafter. The forms of action were disappearing. The question was what was taking, or would take, their place.

The Resulting Conceptual Challenge

Abolition of the forms of action moved substance to the foreground. But this posed a problem. Previously, procedure was the dominant means of providing a semblance of conceptual order to the law governing civil actions. That would not now suffice; indeed, it would be misleading. A half-century of intellectual struggle to provide conceptual substance ensued, through scholarly efforts to identify what the law of torts consisted of and then to classify the constituent parts of that body of law. Classification was thus the central preoccupation of the torts scholars who worked after the forms of action were abolished.

Two surprisingly different products of this impulse toward classification emerged. Treatises on the new subject of torts published in the second half of the nineteenth century took on the challenge of classification. They attempted simultaneously to transcend the now-abolished forms of action and to paint a picture of tort law as it stood at that time. But they were not very successful in producing coherent portraits of tort law. In contrast, for reasons we indicate, casebooks used in law schools—sometimes written by the same author who had published a treatise—stayed much more anchored to the forms of action that had dominated the past.

The opinion of the scholars who began working on tort law after abolition of the forms of action was that the forms had been an obstacle to understanding tort law on the basis of substantive principles. Holmes suggested, for example, that, had the forms of action employed in tort actions corresponded to "every substantial duty" in the field, a "practical" "classification" of tort law would have been accomplished.[24] If such a correspondence had been achieved, he intimated, the forms of action would have been the equivalent of substantive doctrinal categories. But they were not: they were "arbitrary," sometimes owing their contours to "purely historical causes" rather than efforts to match them up with particular doctrinal principles.[25]

It was not as if prominent torts scholars such as Hilliard and Holmes did not know the sort of conduct that was actionable in tort. Many forms of tort liability were of ancient origin: assault, battery, false imprisonment, trespass to real and personal property, slander, libel, and deceit had been actionable for centuries. Moreover, those actions were perceived as qualitatively different from actions in contract and actions affecting real or personal property; they were brought under the distinctive forms of action of trespass and case. But the grouping of tort actions around forms of action employed to successfully bring them into court rendered uncertain what they had in common, or what their subject matter identity was composed of, except for being civil "wrongs."

For this reason, a common goal of torts treatises in the late nineteenth century was to classify tort causes of action based on their substance rather than on the now-abolished forms of action. But why did some form of conceptual ordering of the field of torts, based on some general understanding of what tort actions were, what they had in common, and how they were distinguished from other common law actions, seem an imperative for late nineteenth-century scholars? The answer, we think, is that this was a period when American intellectuals were embarking on an epistemological search for order, seeking to organize and classify fields of knowledge on the basis of common, foundational principles.[26] Both this search, and the change in the epistemology of the civil trial that we described in chapter 1, were features of the modernism that was taking hold at the time.

The search-for-order impulse has been linked to two phenomena that defined the experience of many post–Civil War Americans: the collapse of religious-based explanations for the course of human events in the wake of pressure from secular-based explanations such as Darwinian theories of natural selection, and the enthusiasm for "scientific" organization of fields of knowledge along the lines of the natural sciences, which had begun to feature the classification of fields on the basis of common characteristics and governing principles.[27]

This was a preoccupation in law as much as in other fields. When Christopher Columbus Langdell published the first casebook on contract law in 1871, in the preface he urged students "to select, classify, and arrange all the cases which had contributed in any important degree to the growth, development, or establishment of . . . essential doctrines."[28] Thus, the idea of arranging and classifying common law subjects around their fundamental principles was not merely a response to the fact that any conceptual order the forms of action had supplied for those fields could not be expected to survive their replacement by the unitary civil action. It was also part of a general interest in finding or fashioning conceptual order within fields of knowledge. And of all the common law subjects, tort law posed the greatest organizational and conceptual challenges because the field appeared to be something of a default category, a set of private wrongs that were not crimes and did not arise out of contract but had little else in common.

For this reason, late nineteenth-century torts scholars wanted to go further. They aspired to show, in the words of Hilliard, that tort law "involve[ed] principles of great comprehensiveness."[29] However, those scholars turned out to have enormous difficulties achieving this goal. They had to arrive at an organization of tort law that was not based on the forms of action but that revealed a coherent set of substantive principles. What they were actually able to produce was not coherent; it was a fragmented organization, if it can be called an organization at all.

TREATISES

Hilliard's 1859 treatise was the first significant work published on torts after abolition of the forms of action had begun ten years earlier. He indicated that although he had "entire confidence" that the fundamental principles of tort law could be identified, he had "much diffidence in the *execution*."[30] By "execution" Hilliard very likely meant offering an arrangement or classification of tort law that would reveal the "principles of great comprehensiveness" which supposedly characterized the field.

He was right to be diffident. The two volumes of his treatise addressed a grab-bag of subjects, including some that would not today be included in tort law at all.[31] Some chapters were devoted to individual tort actions such as assault and battery, which were combined in a chapter entitled "Torts in the Person."[32] That was at least a start at conceptual classification. But other causes of action that would subsequently come to be thought of as "intentional" torts, such as false imprisonment, malicious prosecution, and conversion, were covered in separate chapters.[33] Still other chapters were not about causes of action at all but the *duties* of categories of individuals or entities, including husbands, wives, parents, corporations, and railroads.[34] And although there was a chapter on nuisance, and one on "injuries to property," there was none on negligence, despite Hilliard's having chapters about other duties.[35] For some reason Hilliard seems not to have recognized that although trespass-on-the-case no longer existed, the types of negligence liability that had been subsumed under that form of action still did.

The core of the problem Hilliard and subsequent scholars faced was explaining not only what tort liability there was but why liability was not imposed when it could conceivably have been. The common law of the time had a term for conduct that caused harm but was not actionable—*damnum absque injuria*—which roughly translates as loss without a legal remedy. Hilliard made reference to the term in his treatise, as did other late nineteenth-century commentators on tort law.[36] In discussing the doctrine of *damnum absque injuria* in treatises and casebooks in the 1870s, several commentators gave explanations for it that appear circular. Charles Addison maintained that when an injury was the result of "a lawful act, done in a lawful manner," there was "no legal injury" and hence "no tort giving rise to action for damages."[37] Thomas Shearman and Amasa Redfield, who published a treatise on negligence in 1869, stated that as long as someone was "engaged in a lawful business," he or she was "not responsible for an injury caused purely by inevitable accident."[38] And Thomas Cooley, in his 1879 treatise on tort law, maintained that actors who did what was "right and lawful for one man to do" could not be accountable if their actions injured others, because what they were doing was a "proper exercise . . . of [their] rights" and thus could not inflict legal wrongs.[39]

All of those explanations, however, begged the question of what was "right and lawful." Saying that there was no liability because no right had been violated was circular in the same way as saying, twenty years earlier, that there was no liability because no form of action was available under the circumstances. The notion of *damnum absque injuria* was simply a placeholder for the reason, whatever it was, that there was no liability. Only Holmes seems to have advanced a substantive, noncircular reason why many acts that injured others did not give rise to tort liability: "The general principle of our law is that loss from accident must lie where it falls" because it was expensive and time-consuming to enlist the cumbersome machinery of the state in the effort.[40]

But for scholars who did not simply accept Holmes's explanation, some other organizational principle was necessary. Late nineteenth-century torts scholars experimented with two thematic organizations, one substantive but circular and the other merely taxonomic. The first centered on efforts to identify "rights" that, when "invaded" by certain conduct, resulted in the imposition of tort liability for the harm which resulted. The other was based on the standards of conduct associated with tort liability. Neither produced more than a semblance of conceptual clarification.

Thomas Cooley's 1879 treatise on tort law succeeded in transcending the forms of action. The writ of trespass-on-the-case was not even an entry in the index to Cooley's treatise. In addition, he made a concerted, but not entirely successful, effort to get beyond Hilliard's grab-bag listing of tort actions. The principal device Cooley employed to achieve conceptual ordering was borrowed from Blackstone, who had identified civil "wrongs" that were invasions of "rights."[41] Cooley placed assault, battery, and false imprisonment in a category of "wrongs affecting personal security," which also included malicious prosecution.[42] This organization suggested that Cooley was attempting to classify torts based on the rights they invaded.[43]

Such an approach had been foreshadowed by Hilliard's treatment of assault and battery as "Torts in the Person." Cooley's was the first sustained effort by an American torts scholar to invoke what we call "interest" analysis, a classification of tort actions in terms of the rights or interests of the plaintiff that have been invaded or interfered with by the defendant's conduct. As we will see, efforts to organize tort law around the invasion of interests would become more frequent in the early twentieth century, as commentators became more convinced that a central function of tort law was identifying interests worthy of protection and determining under what circumstances they should be protected. Other late nineteenth- and early twentieth-century torts treatise writers thereafter adopted versions of Cooley's organizational emphasis on the invasion of "rights" whose invasion produced civil wrongs.[44]

But Cooley's effort to classify different tort causes of action based on the "rights" against whose invasion they provided protection did not extend much beyond his "wrongs affecting personal security" category. Although he included chapters on "injuries to family rights," "wrongs with respect to civil and political rights," and "invasion of rights in real property," each of which pointed in the direction of "interest" analysis, his treatise also contained chapters that made no explicit reference to rights.[45] Those included slander and libel, fraud, nuisance, master and servant, "wrongs from non-performance of conventional and statutory duties," and "injuries by animals."[46] Whereas Hilliard had not addressed negligence at all, Cooley included negligence in the chapter on wrongs arising from nonperformance of duties.[47] Like Hilliard, then, Cooley was not only attempting to conceptualize the constituent parts of tort law; he was also struggling to define its boundaries and scope.

Other scholars moved in a different organizational direction. Some of their names are more familiar to us—Holmes, Frederick Pollock, Wigmore—partly because their approach ultimately became more widely adopted. But we should not think that the ultimate success of the approach indicates that it was immediately accepted. How to conceptualize and organize tort liability was very much open to debate in the late nineteenth and early twentieth centuries. Four important writers on tort law explored the possibility of a tripartite organization of the field based on standards of conduct.

Holmes wanted to show that tort liability, even when it exposed defendants to liability at their peril, had almost always been based on "fault" of some sort, either of the intentional or negligent variety, and that in the "great mass" of modern torts cases, negligence cases, "fault" was a legal rather than a moral concept. Of the common law tort actions, however, only malicious prosecution, abuse of process, and possibly conspiracy had required culpability, in the form of "malice." The other actions brought under trespass or growing out of trespass on the case—assault, battery, false imprisonment, deceit, slander and libel, and trespass to real and personal property—had not embodied a culpability requirement.

Holmes dealt with this difficulty for his theory by limiting his discussion of "intentional torts" to deceit, defamation, malicious prosecution, and conspiracy, and equating "intent" with malice.[48] In so doing, Holmes created a category of tort actions that differed from actions resting on act-at-peril liability or negligence. He was content to classify the intentional torts as a subcategory of "fault" actions, lumping them together under a somewhat contrived culpability standard. However, Holmes had not shown what else the torts based on "fraud, malice, and intent" had in common, and he conveniently omitted from his classification the long-established torts of assault, battery, and false imprisonment because they had not required intent when the forms of action were in force. What he did was to suggest that a salient organizing principle for tort actions was the standard of conduct they applied.

In contrast, in 1878 Melville Bigelow published a torts treatise beginning with the insight that "torts spring, not from a common centre, but from a series of different centres. . . . Each [tort action] has its peculiar rules of law . . . and the same is true of all other branches of the general subject. There is, then, no such thing as a typical tort."[49] A scholar holding this point of view—correct though it may have been—was bound to face challenges in organizing a treatise.

The organization that followed was based partly on a classification of duties.[50] Bigelow acknowledged that this organization was repetitive in that most of the topics he was addressing fell into one division. At the same time, however, Bigelow identified another way of classifying tort causes of action. That was to classify causes of action based on "a peculiar *animus* (intent) . . . essential to a right of redress for the alleged breach of duty," causes of action in which "the existence or non-existence of the *animus* is immaterial," and causes of action where "the breach of duty consists in damage caused by a failure to the care or diligence or skill observed by prudent men."[51] Although all the causes of action arose from breaches of general or specific "duties," what distinguished them was the standard of conduct that applied.

Bigelow then grouped causes of action into those three divisions. He placed deceit, slander and libel, malicious prosecution, and conspiracy in a group requiring "animus" to make out a successful action.[52] He placed nearly all the remaining torts—assault, battery, false imprisonment, trespasses to real or personal property, infringement of patents and copyrights, violation of water rights, nuisance, damage by animals, escape of dangerous elements or substances, and enticement and seduction—in a group in which a showing of "animus" was immaterial because "the law conclusively presume[ed] that the act complained of, if proved, was intended."[53] He placed negligence in the third group.[54]

That organization, which would somewhat resemble Holmes's in *The Common Law,* had some obvious difficulties. Slander and libel were described as torts requiring a showing of intent to be actionable, which was clearly not the case. Although assault, battery, false imprisonment, and trespass to real and personal property would subsequently come to be characterized as "intentional" torts, they had certainly not been historically actions in which "intent" was immaterial because "the law had conclusively presumed" it. And there was every indication that nuisances, actions involving damage by animals, and *Rylands v. Fletcher*–type actions, were act-at-peril torts in which neither intent nor negligence was required. So perhaps the most that can be said for Bigelow's organization was that it unconsciously served to demonstrate the accuracy of his opening insight that there was no such thing as a typical tort.

Over the next fifteen years two other important scholars concluded that organizing tort law based on the tripartite standards of conduct would be fruitful. In 1887 the English torts scholar Frederick Pollock made it a basis for organizing his torts treatise.[55] In the introduction to the 1887 edition of his torts treatise, Pollock stated that now that the English common law was "independent of forms of action," it "would seem . . . that a rational exposition of the law of torts" based on "general principles of duty and liability" might be possible.[56]

Pollock's organization would end up being congenial to other scholars seeking to classify the law of torts in two respects. It emphasized that most of the ancient tort actions, whether originally brought in trespass or in case, required some showing of "intent." Because many of those actions were the result of intentional or reckless conduct, and the requirements of the forms of action, such as "direct" or "indirect" injury, were no longer relevant, placing most of the ancient actions in the category of "intentional torts" seemed to make intuitive sense. And Pollock's classification scheme significantly narrowed the category of act-at-peril torts, resulting in either intent or "fault" being a prerequisite for recovery for most tort actions. Pollock's scheme suggested that the most relevant feature of tort actions was not the "rights" they invaded or the "duties" whose violation they were based on but the standard of conduct with which they were identified.

The other important scholar to adopt the tripartite conceptualization did not do so in a treatise, but he is sufficiently important in his own right to warrant mention. John Henry Wigmore, who figured in chapter 1, was the foremost evidence scholar of his time, but he also was an important torts scholar who would publish a prominent torts casebook as well.[57] Wigmore published four articles on tort law in the *Harvard Law Review* in the single year of 1894.[58] In one of those, commenting on the "general analysis of a Tort," he noted that tort liability may be based on conduct taken "designedly . . . negligently . . . [or] at peril" and elaborated on the point.[59] In this he obviously was aligning himself with Holmes, Bigelow, and Pollock. Together with those scholars, then, Wigmore helped to establish the organization of tort law based the tripartite standards of conduct as one of the principal possible bases for conceptualizing the field.

In summary, the legacy of the treatise writers was to make available two distinct schemes for classifying tort actions, one emphasizing rights—in what respect the plaintiff was adversely affected by particular forms of conduct—and the other emphasizing the standards of conduct to which tort defendants were held. Taken together, the two schemes revealed that classifications of tort actions around the forms of action were no longer necessary. But a difficulty remained for the late nineteenth-century scholars, and their early twentieth-century successors, in the production of casebooks on tort law. This was the very limited amount of necessary raw material for a casebook in the new era—cases decided after the abolition of the forms of action.

CASEBOOKS

By the last decades of the nineteenth century, the forms of action may have ceased to be a feature of modern tort actions and may not have been perceived as helpful classification devices. Nonetheless, as a practical matter, most collections of tort cases still would have had to include a majority of cases employing the forms of action because little else was available. Suits in tort had for centuries been brought into court under trespass and case. Only in the most recent decades had tort suits not been brought in this manner. There simply had not been enough time yet for post-abolition appellate cases to accumulate addressing the myriad of different issues that arise in tort cases. Consequently, in whatever way a casebook author might wish to conceptualize the subject of torts—around substantive principles, rights, or standards of conduct—most of the cases that could be included in the casebook would have been decided in the era of the forms of action. A case would therefore begin with reference to the form of action under which it was brought and might be decided in language making reference to issues associated with that form of action. The result was that it was more awkward to organize a casebook based on rights or standards of conduct than to organize a treatise around these concepts. Casebook authors in the late nineteenth and early twentieth centuries thus did not emphasize the approaches to organizing tort law that were appearing in torts treatises in that time period.

The first casebook on tort law to be published in the United States was James Barr Ames's *A Selection of Cases on the Law of Torts*, which appeared in 1874.[60] It was closely followed by Bigelow's casebook the next year.[61] An additional casebook was published by Francis Burdick of the Columbia law faculty in 1891 and had gone through three editions by 1905.[62] Between 1892 and 1915 nine more casebooks on tort law were published.[63]

None of those casebooks organized the presentation of cases around invasions of rights or standards of conduct. Rather, each employed an organization that combined classifying tort actions in connection with the forms of action and miscellaneous presentation of cases representing different torts but decided under the forms of action. Escaping the gravitational pull of the forms of action was obviously more difficult to do than might otherwise have been expected.

We can only wonder how confused late nineteenth-century law students must have been in torts courses that used those casebooks. The casebooks were anchored in and at least partly organized by reference to the forms of action, which had been abolished decades earlier. But torts treatises, to the extent students consulted them, were organized partly thematically, by reference to rights, standards of conduct, or both, along with discussions of atomistically presented miscellaneous torts. To the law student, and subsequently to the lawyer embarking on a career in practice between roughly 1870 and the early decades of the twentieth century, all this would have given the appearance of enormous conceptual confusion, with little means of clarification available. Law students and lawyers would have had no reason to suppose that tort law was anything other than a disorganized, fragmented, not-very-coherent field.

This situation did not improve as the twentieth century proceeded. In 1915, for example, Francis Bohlen published a torts casebook.[64] Bohlen's casebook is important for our purposes in two respects. First, Bohlen was a prominent torts scholar on the faculty of the University of Pennsylvania Law School who would eight years later be named by the newly formed American Law Institute as the "Reporter"—principal drafter—for the *Restatement of Torts*. In that capacity he would make an attempt to reconceptualize the field.

Second, Bohlen's casebook, and the dilemma it reflected, was representative of the state of the field at that time. Bohlen began the preface to his casebook by stating that "the preparation of a collection of cases on the law of Torts has certain difficulties peculiar to itself" because "in perhaps no other branch of the law is there so little agreement . . . as to how [the subject] should be classified and arranged."[65] Bohlen then introduced his own approach to classification by noting that "the method of the older text writers was to adopt a purely procedural classification," emphasizing "the form of action appropriate for the redress of particular wrongs." Because that approach treated "principles which determined the liability in a particular tort action . . . as distinct from those applicable to any other tort action," it made "little or no effort to ascertain the fundamental principles underlying the law of Torts as a whole."[66]

Bohlen maintained that "this method, still used by many able text writers," was "entirely opposed to the trend and spirit of the modern study of law," which was concerned with classifying legal subjects around their fundamental principles. The reader of those passages would have been justified in thinking that Bohlen was going to introduce the "fundamental principles underlying tort law" and adopt an approach consistent with the "trend and spirit of the study of modern law."[67] But that is not at all what his casebook did.

Abandoning the old method altogether posed difficulties, Bohlen said. One was that "even among modern students of the law of Tort there is little or no unanimity as to the proper way of arranging the subject so as to best present to the student its underlying principles and philosophy." Each writer on tort law needed to "adopt his own arrangement."[68] The other difficulty was that "while classification solely in accordance with the forms of action is undoubtedly unscientific and unsatisfactory," it was still embedded in "the mind of the legal profession."[69] For this reason, Bohlen believed, casebook editors had to reckon with the fact that they were preparing students for law practice, where they would be encountering senior members of the bar and judges in courts, all of whom had been taught and continued to understand tort law through an emphasis on the forms of action. Bohlen felt that a "law teacher [who] commits himself to teaching the student any revolutionary view of his subject or adopts any personal arrangement of it entirely contrary to that adopted by the profession . . . must be very sure of his ground."[70] And apparently Bohlen was not.

Consequently, Bohlen explained, he was not planning any "revolutionary" or even "novel" framing of the cases he had collected. He retained the "old division into actions . . . whenever helpful to explain the historical development of general principles" or "whenever the subject matter is so distinct" that an emphasis on the forms of action served to illuminate controlling doctrines.[71] Of the three "Books" into which his casebook was divided, Book I was "devoted to a rather elaborate scrutiny of the various formed actions in Trespass" and of "the writ of Disseisin and . . . the action of Trover, closely akin in scope and content to trespass to real and personal property."[72] This "cleared" the "way" for Book II, by far the largest in the casebook, in which Bohlen took up negligence cases as well as handful of cases "which show a survival of the primitive idea that one doing harm must make it good, although free from personal fault," and "a persistence of the equally primitive idea that no actual harm is required if the plaintiff's personal interests are directly and intentionally invaded."[73]

Bohlen did observe that "the tolerance of harmful acts because of their social convenience" was an emerging "principle," which he labeled "modern." That new rationale for refraining from imposing liability for some harmful acts, Bohlen thought, "reflects a change in philosophic thought, a revolt from . . . extreme individualism."[74] Indeed, as early as 1911 Bohlen had employed the term "interest" in discussing whether the strict liability principle of *Rylands v. Fletcher* should be limited in a society whose increasingly industrialized and urbanized character had resulted in numerous socially useful but dangerous activities being part of the experience of modern Americans.[75] By 1915, then, Bohlen seems to have been poised to advance a conception of tort law as evolving from a series of actions designed to protect individuals from being injured to one emphasizing the social "interests" at stake in tort cases, interests that went beyond the rights and duties of individuals in an action in tort.

But Bohlen did not take the next step and adopt that approach in his casebook. Either he felt that his audience was not ready for it, or his thinking had not developed to the point at which that approach could be the basis for his reorganizing all of tort law. Instead, Bohlen's organization was nominally based on the forms of action. But then midway into the material even that organization broke down, with separate chapters on particular causes of action (such as deceit and defamation), particular duties (such as those of landowners, manufacturers, and suppliers of chattels), and particular tort doctrines, such as contributory negligence and assumption of risk.[76] In many respects Bohlen's 1915 casebook did not look very different from those published by Ames in 1874 and Bigelow in 1875.[77]

The Saga of the First *Restatement of Torts*

The principal impression we derive from our examination of the late nineteenth- and early twentieth-century treatises and casebooks is of the absence of any consensus during this period regarding the proper way to think about the law of torts. There was recognition that the now-abolished forms of action were an inappropriate basis for organizing the subject, though the fact is that most scholars still could not completely transcend them. There were halting but incomplete and unsuccessful efforts (such as Cooley's) to organize tort law on the basis of rights or interests protected. And there were a few prominent figures who had talked about tort law differently—in terms of the three standards of conduct. But among the most prominent, neither Holmes nor Wigmore had written an entire treatise, Pollock had done so but was English, and the tripartite division was not then the dominant framework that it would become a half-century later. Rather, tort law was only partly organized, treatises and casebooks employing various combinations of the forms of action, rights-based analysis, and division by reference to standards of conduct. And whatever combination was employed, the presentation invariably included a miscellany of freestanding torts that seemed to have little in common. The field was conceptually unorganized.

It would not be surprising, then, that when Bohlen, the Reporter for the *Restatement of Torts,* began preparation of the project in 1923, he would seek to surmount the organizational difficulties that had challenged torts scholars for the past fifty years but end up reflecting those difficulties. Try as he might, Bohlen found that he could not easily escape the gravitational pull of the past.

The American Law Institute (ALI) was founded in 1923 with the aim of organizing and improving the law. It was a blue-ribbon organization of prominent lawyers, judges, and law professors. The method it adopted was to prepare a series of "Restatements" of the law, which were to "present an orderly statement of the general common law."[78] The need for such an effort was recognition of the "increasing volume of decisions" and "the numerous instances in which the decisions are irreconcilable," which were "rapidly increasing the law's uncertainty and lack of clarity."[79] The first *Restatements* that the ALI undertook were on contracts, torts, and conflicts of law. There soon followed ones on agency, business associations, property, and trusts.[80]

It is obvious from the ALI's stated aims that its founders thought those subjects were susceptible to "orderly statement," and that their "uncertainty" and "lack of clarity" could be remedied. But whatever may have been the case for the other subjects of the first *Restatements*, torts posed a special problem. As we have just seen, what we now call tort law had until recently been a set of largely procedural pigeonholes embedded in the forms of action and the writ system. Tort law became a distinct subject only in the second half of the nineteenth century, after the forms of action were abolished and substance took priority over procedure. Not only, however, was the subject of tort law new. In addition, and more importantly, what made it a distinct subject—aside from the fact that it involved civil liability but not for breach of contract—was not immediately clear. It certainly had not thus far been amenable to easy systemization.[81]

Yet, as it emerged, the *Restatement* paradigm involved not merely stating the law so as to reduce its "uncertainty" and enhance its "clarity." To present an "orderly statement" also meant organizing, or conceptualizing, the field being restated. In each field there tended to be an overall organizing concept. In contracts, the concept was promising. In property, the concept was the nature of rights to or in a thing—about which there were rules to be restated or around which a conceptual structure could be built. In contracts, for example, this meant setting out the core rules governing promising—contract formation, consideration, the rights of third parties, assignment, interpretation, breach, and remedies.[82] In property, this meant dividing up the subject of ownership into the law governing freehold estates, future interests, restrictions on the creation of property interests, and servitudes.[83]

In contrast, there was no analogous organizing concept available in tort law; the subject was not coherent in any obvious way. It is impossible to review the drafts and final version of the first *Restatement*, and especially the material on intentional torts, without being simultaneously impressed and bemused by the efforts to meet the challenges it faced. The first draft was a heroic effort to organize tort law in a way that improved on the efforts of the late nineteenth- and early twentieth-century scholars to get beyond the now-abolished forms of action. But in retrospect, certain features of that first effort seem almost quaint. And the vision of a new structure reflected in the first draft quickly faded away. Subsequent material on negligence, other bases of liability, and other torts did not reflect this vision, and eventually even the later drafts on the intentional torts largely dropped the initial vision without substituting a different, coherent one.

Bohlen had arranged his 1915 torts casebook by reference to the forms of action, noting that there was no "unanimity as to the proper way of arranging" the subject of torts, and that each author therefore had to "adopt his own arrangement."[84] Bohlen's thinking had evidently evolved during the ensuing ten years, for his initial draft for the *Restatement* departed dramatically from the organization of his casebook.

Bohlen clearly understood the challenge he faced. Speaking to the ALI's second Annual Meeting, at which a first draft[85]—addressing only battery, assault, and false imprisonment—was presented to the membership, he said,

> There seemed to be only two possible ways of going about it. One was to accept the classification, if it may be so called, that one finds in the earlier textbooks, and to deal with the various named torts themselves, which is usually nothing more than describing the content of some particular form of action. . . .
>
> As an alternative we have adopted a novel approach. First of all, we have dealt with the legal consequences of certain conduct. We have approached it primarily from the standpoint of the effect which the defendant's conduct has had upon the plaintiff. . . . Now, I agree that to the person not used to this method of approach there may be some difficulty in understanding exactly what we, the Reporter and his Advisers, are attempting to lay before you.[86]

The approach Bohlen described may have seemed "novel" to the lawyers at the ALI Annual Meeting, many of whom would have been educated during the first years after the forms of action were abolished. But the approach actually was not completely unprecedented. "The effect which the defendant's conduct has had upon the plaintiff" to which Bohlen referred sounds a lot like what a number of the late nineteenth- and early twentieth-century treatise writers had flirted with in focusing on the rights protected by some of the torts they discussed.

The First Draft

The first, partial draft of the *Restatement* confirmed that this sort of rights analysis was precisely what Bohlen had in mind, although we think that he was probably thinking of "interests" even when he used the term "rights" in Tentative Draft No. 1.[87] The opening, general heading was "Conduct Violating Rights of Personality."[88] The rights of personality were listed as the rights to freedom from "bodily harm," from "offensive bodily touchings," from "apprehension of a harmful or offensive bodily touching," from "confinement," and from "disagreeable emotions" (though it turned out there was almost no protection of this right).[89] Aside from this list of rights, however, what the "right of personality" consisted of was not specified. There was no description or account of what a "right of personality" was, nor did any description appear anywhere else in the first draft. Perhaps Bohlen intended to elaborate on the meaning of the notion in a later draft, but that never occurred.[90] Nor did Bohlen elaborate on what the phrase meant when he presented the draft to the Annual Meeting.[91]

As other scholars have shown in recent decades, it is clear that, whatever a "right of personality" was, some people's interests were excluded from it. What would today undoubtedly count as "offensive" bodily touching or a "disagreeable emotion" was more narrowly understood at the time.[92] As we show in chapter 3, for example, the result was that women traveling on railroads and elsewhere were subjected to indignities at the hands of conductors and other men but received little or no protection against these wrongs from tort law. And even when the rights of women or African Americans were protected, their losses were undervalued and the damages they recovered were reduced accordingly.[93]

In the paragraphs that follow we describe Bohlen's organization and assess its significance. But the reader can best appreciate what we contend Bohlen was attempting to do by reading the relevant portion of his draft, which we set out verbatim in a note.[94] The first subdivision of the material on rights of personality addressed "Conduct Violating the Right to Freedom from Bodily Harm." This subdivision began with a section entitled "General Principles," which listed the bases of liability for violating the right to personality by causing bodily harm: (1) acting with the "intention of bringing about bodily harm"; (2) acting under circumstances that "a reasonable man would recognize as creating" an undue probability of harm; (3) acting in "breach of duty" to protect another from bodily harm; and (4) acting under circumstances that are "at the risk" of the actor.[95] All this material—basically referencing the different standards of conduct that could be breached and give rise to liability for bodily harm—preceded reference to any particular torts.

Only then did there follow what amounted to a sub-subdivision, on intentional violation of the right to freedom from bodily harm—battery. This sub-subdivision contained a number of sections and looked very much like the *Restatements* we recognize today. Then, in due course, there were two separate series of sections on "Conduct Violating the Right to Freedom from Apprehension of a Harmful or Offensive Contact [Assault]" and "Contact Violating the Right to Freedom from Confinement [False Imprisonment]."[96] There was no equivalent to section 1—"General Principles," setting out the different bases of liability for causing bodily harm (intent, negligence, etc.)—at the beginning of the material addressing assault and false imprisonment, however, for the obvious reason that there was (and is) no liability in negligence, or strict liability, for those harms.[97]

Clearly, then, Bohlen was presenting the material on the intentional torts as part of what would be a larger body of material on the protection of the general right of personality and as part of a sub-right of the right of personality to freedom from bodily injury, the latter through the imposition of liability for intentionally, negligently, or non-negligently causing bodily injury. Battery, assault, and false imprisonment were not presented as freestanding torts; they were nested within this structure, first by reference to the interest ("right") they protected and only then by reference to the standard of care that triggered liability under these particular torts—the intent to cause harm.

The logic of this organization—and its only possible purpose, really—would have been to signal that there were rights other than the right to personality that were protected by other torts and bases of liability; that when it came to the right of personality, there were other torts and bases of liability that protected the right of personality and its sub-right to protection against bodily harm; that some of those other torts were actionable without intent to cause harm (and indeed without negligence), though battery, assault, and false imprisonment were actionable only on proof of intent to cause harm; and that the law governing the other forms and other bases of liability for violation of the right to personality, and of other rights to be specified, was to be addressed within this overall structure in later drafts. If all of this were not the case, then it would have sufficed to present battery, assault, and false imprisonment not as having the particular place within this overall structure that they had been given, but simply as three torts that had in common the requirement of intent to cause bodily harm or a bodily effect—that is, the way those three torts are presented in the more recent *Restatements.*

Thus, it appears that Bohlen was thinking of organizing the *Restatement* in terms of (1) the nature of each right a tort protected, and only then (2) subdividing based on the standard of conduct that applied to that tort. That is why the right to freedom from bodily harm, whether caused intentionally, negligently, or without fault, was addressed in a framing section (section 1, "General Principles") before taking up battery—intentionally caused bodily injury—in the sub-subdivision that followed. The remainder of the *Restatement,* if this basis were followed, would have been organized through an analogous set of sections next addressing negligently caused interference with the right to freedom from bodily harm, and strict liability for it, which would follow down the road. Then, having completed the material on the right to freedom from bodily harm, there could have been sections addressing other rights or interests—first identified and then subdivided into material addressing intentional, negligently caused, and strict liability causes of action for invading those other rights or interests, to the extent that those causes of action were available.

Bohlen was off to what must have seemed to be a good start toward achieving the goal he disclosed to the Annual Meeting, that the *Restatement* would be organized from "the standpoint of the effect which the defendant's conduct has had upon the plaintiff."

THE FINAL VERSION

But it did not turn out that way. Little of the material that Bohlen subsequently prepared followed the rights-based approach that seemed to dominate the first draft. An entire volume's worth of material on negligence that came next completely ignored rights-based analysis. And when the first draft's material on intentional torts was eventually revised, "rights" were called "interests," and interest-based analysis now took a distinctly back seat, even in that material. Finally, a whole series of other torts were treated as freestanding causes of action not linked to any other torts protecting the same interest, and in most instances there was no reference at all to the interest they each protected individually. The apparently unified vision of tort law foreshadowed by the first draft had given way to fragmentation.

After completing drafts on the intentional torts, Bohlen turned to negligence. Like the material on bodily harm in Tentative Draft No. 1, his earliest draft on negligence also began with a heading labeled "General Principles."[98] But in contrast to what Tentative Draft No. 1 had done for battery and presaged for negligently caused bodily injury, the negligence material made no reference, in the General Principles or in any subsequent section, to the right of personality, to the right to freedom from bodily injury, or to the interest or interests protected by liability for negligence.[99]

The initial material in the draft was about the nature of negligence, not the rights that liability for negligence protects. Nor did anything in the final version of the negligence material, which occupied the entirety of volume 2, make reference to any interest protected, until chapter 18 (of nineteen), on "Negligent Invasions of Interests in the Physical Condition of Land and Chattels."[100] Even here the reference appears to be to the notion of ownership "interests," such as fee simples and easements, rather than to substantive interests such as an interest in enjoyment or use of property. The entire structure that the first draft adopted had disappeared, as if it had never existed.

Not only did the entire volume on negligence ignore rights analysis. The next time the material on battery, assault, and false imprisonment was presented, the rights analysis it previously contained had been sharply reduced. This was when the material came before the 1934 Annual Meeting for final approval in revised form. In the revision there was still brief reference to the protection of interests—in fact, for the terms "right" and "rights" that had been used in Tentative Draft No. 1, "interest" and "interests" had been expressly substituted.[101]

But the interest analysis that remained was a pale shadow of the interest-based organization that had dominated Tentative Draft No. 1. No longer was there an opening umbrella heading referencing the general right to protection against conduct violating rights or interests of personality. No longer was there a separate framing section (what had been "General Principles") referencing the three standards of conduct as the possible bases for protecting the right of or interest in freedom from bodily harm. Rather, there was merely a brief mention in an "Introductory Note" that the interest in freedom from bodily harm was also sometimes protected against negligent invasion and against invasions caused without negligence.[102] There followed a heading entitled "Intentional Invasions of Interests in Personality and Property."[103] The material straightforwardly addressed the three intentional torts, as well as trespass to land and chattels, indicating which interest each protected.

In presenting this material to the 1934 Annual Meeting, Bohlen said that "chapter 2 of this division [chapter 1 now contained definitions] . . . deals with intentional invasions of interests of personality and includes actions of trespass for assault, battery, and false imprisonment. . . . [It] is really a condensation of Tentative Draft No. 1 [1925]. . . . Here again there is so far as the first Restatement goes substantially no material change."[104]

Bohlen's statement was literally true. There had been "substantially no material change" in the material that expressly addressed battery, assault, and false imprisonment. There had, however, been a substantial change in the framing and apparent conceptualization of that material. The intentional torts were no longer part of a larger heading under which all invasions of the interest in personality, or in which all freedom from bodily harm or effect, were or would be addressed. The intentional torts now simply stood on their own, rather than being part of any larger category. And there would be nothing in the remainder of the Restatement labeled anything like "Nonintentional Invasions of Interests in Personality." In fact, the interest in personality was never again mentioned.

Whether Bohlen really believed that the change in the headings and framing of the intentional torts he presented in 1934 was not a substantial change from his first draft we cannot say. He had spent the previous nine years preparing other material that did not follow the initial rights-based organization or its framing. For him that original approach may have been something left behind long ago and therefore mainly forgotten. We have found nothing in the ALI archives reflecting his thinking about the matter or indicating when his conception had changed.[105] At the very least, we can say that continuation and extension of the earlier rights-based approach in the material that he went on to draft after 1925 did not occur.

Nor did the Restatement go on to classify groups of any of the other torts based on some distinctive and generalized conception of their effects on the plaintiff or the interests they protected, as it had originally attempted to do with invasion of the interest in "personality." Instead, the Restatement would end up being a mixture of unanalyzed interest identification organizing the intentional torts and a few others, abstract material on negligence making no reference to interests protected, and piecemeal treatment of the other torts, not indicating what they may have had in common with each other and with little or no reference to the interests they protected.

The *Restatement* was more orderly than many of the nineteenth-century treatises we surveyed above; it was not the grab-bag that they were. But it was not significantly more organized conceptually, as the first draft seemed to promise it would be.[106] The first two and a half volumes addressed liability for intentional torts, negligence, and absolute (i.e., strict) liability, with the minimal interest analysis that we have discussed associated with the first, and virtually no such analysis applied to this other material. The second half of volume 3 and all of volume 4 took the piecemeal approach, separately addressing deceit, defamation, disparagement, unjustifiable litigation, interference in domestic relations, interference with business relations, and invasions of the interest in land other than by trespass. Except for interference with business relations, there was no significant classification of any torts in combined analytical or interest-based categories, and there was little reference to interest protection in the piecemeal discussions of each tort.

Further, the superficiality of the interest analysis that did appear was evident. For example, final versions of a few chapters referred to an "interest" protected—the material on trespass, for example, referred to the "interest" in the exclusive possession of land, and the material on defamation carried the subheading "Invasions of Interest in Reputation"—but most did not.[107] And in any event, those references were not part of a classification system but merely synonyms describing the freestanding torts of trespass and defamation.

The result is that when it occurred at all, the *Restatement* approach of classifying based on the effect of the defendant's conduct on the plaintiff was, in effect, merely tautological. False imprisonment distinctively involved unlawful confinement of the plaintiff; defamation distinctively involved a communication to a third party that injured the plaintiff's reputation. Sometimes the classification was even expressly tautological. For example, trespass to personal property and conversion were addressed under the headings "The Interest in the Retention of the Possession of Chattels" and "The Interest in the Availability of Chattels to Possession."[108] What defined each tort was what determined its "classification." But since something different defined each tort, except for the linkage of battery, assault, and false imprisonment, there really was no interest-based *classification* at all, just a list of torts that were not classified but simply introduced by reference to the interest each tort protected.

We will never know exactly what went through Bohlen's mind as he continued to work on the *Restatement,* unless records of his thinking that we doubt exist are discovered.[109] One possibility is that Bohlen never had a systematic organization of the *Restatement* in mind. In that view, his thinking did not change. Perhaps when he told the 1925 Annual Meeting that he had organized his first draft based on the "effect of the defendant's conduct on the plaintiff," he had only the intentional torts in mind. The argument for this interpretation is that the second edition of Bohlen's casebook on torts was published in the same year as Tentative Draft No. 1, and the overall structure and organization of that casebook—which of course covered all of the subject, not just intentional torts—does not reflect a new vision of tort law.[110] It was a striking blend of the various classification schemes employed since Cooley, including over seven hundred pages on "The Development of Tort Liability by the Action of Trespass on the Case," which looked backward rather than forward to the ultimate organization of the First *Restatement.*[111]

This seems the more likely possibility. What may have happened, we think, is that Bohlen and his advisors recognized, as the *Restatement* project proceeded, that interest analysis was not as promising a method of organizing or conceptualizing all of tort law, and particularly of grouping torts together, as they had originally hoped, and that subdividing everything that involved protection of a particular kind of interest by reference to the tripartite standards of conduct would not be sensible either. Rather, a combination of the tripartite division of tort law based on standards of conduct, and the fragmented legacy of the forms of action, took over the reorganization of the project—starting first with the intentional torts, then negligence, then strict liability, then all the remaining torts. The titles of the four volumes that comprised the final version themselves reflect this transformation: *Intentional Harms* (vol. 1); *Negligence* (vol. 2); *Absolute Liability, Libel, Deceit* (vol. 3); *Miscellaneous Tort Defenses, Remedies* (vol. 4).

The challenge of drafting material on negligence—which Bohlen first did between 1925 and 1928—could easily have caused such a change of approach. Negligence is both a standard of care and, in connection with bodily injury and property damage (and sometimes other forms of loss), a cause of action—a separate tort, really. Framing the material on negligence with the notion that the right to personality, and its sub-right to freedom from bodily injury, were protected through imposition of liability for negligence would have treated negligently caused bodily injury as a tort, and would have carried forward the approach he had taken with battery, assault, and false imprisonment. But it is not at all clear that liability in negligence for causing bodily injury would have fit comfortably within the notion of protecting the right (or interest) in "personality." It might have been necessary to identify a different general right (or interest) within which to fit this form of protection of the right to freedom from bodily injury. Doing that might have seemed both complicated and potentially peculiar.

Since those were the difficulties that Bohlen faced, perhaps he simply decided on the approach that required him to forego framing negligence as a cause of action that protected the rights to personality and freedom from bodily injury, in order to minimize complications and to ensure that the concept of negligence as a standard of care received proper explication. Then, when he went to draft the material on the remaining torts, he may have found that those torts were not amenable to any sort of classification that treated some of them together, and that interest analysis applied to them individually was mainly tautological. This is why he would have deemphasized his original vision in his presentation of the intentional tort material—in order to avoid its contrasting so starkly with an overall product that now contained little interest analysis and nothing about the right to personality. What had started out as a new conceptual scheme ended up as an organization that was more modern than that developed by previous scholars but not much more coherent or cohesive.

Replication of the First *Restatement*'s Organization in Modern Tort Law

Once the *Restatement* was completed, it might have appeared to be a transitional document, using a modest amount of interest analysis and partial classification based on the tripartite standards of conduct as a bridge between the disjointed organizations adopted by the late nineteenth- and early twentieth-century scholars, and some form of future conceptualization that would be less rooted in the past and more coherent.[112]

But in the years after the First *Restatement* appeared in 1934, there was no further transition. The approach taken by the First *Restatement* is essentially the approach that has come down to us today. The leading treatises and casebooks that have subsequently been published have replicated the *Restatement*'s structure with only the barest discussion of their conceptual organization.

William Prosser's "handbook" on tort law, first published in 1941, is the most prominent example. The first edition of Prosser's treatise began with chapters on intentional interference with the person and intentional interference with property. The former addressed battery, assault, and false imprisonment, just as the *Restatement* had done.[113] This was interest analysis in precisely the same form that Bohlen had adopted, though with no reference to "rights" or "personality." Then followed multiple chapters on negligence, three on different forms of strict liability, and freestanding chapters providing atomistic treatment of products liability, misrepresentation, defamation, and other separate torts. Buried in the interior of Prosser's treatise was the statement that "for no other reason than that the author finds it most convenient for what he has to say, the general plan of this book is the same as that adopted by the *Restatement of Torts*."[114]

Fowler Harper's far less well-known treatise, which actually predated final publication of the *Restatement* by a year and publication of Prosser's "handbook" by eight years, contained the same organization and sequence.[115] Prosser's subsequent editions of his treatise,[116] and of a casebook,[117] never departed from this structure.[118] Other major casebooks and treatises did the same. Charles Gregory and Harry Kalven's casebook, first published in 1959, divided the subject of torts into three parts, addressing physical harms, harm from insult, indignity, shock, and tort law in the marketplace, but otherwise duplicated the First *Restatement*'s approach.[119] Nor have there been major changes in the organization of torts treatises. The present-day treatise by Dan Dobbs, effectively the successor to Prosser, contains a slight modification, dividing itself into two major parts based on interests protected—physical interference with person and property, and economic and dignitary injury. Within the first part, Dobbs employs the tripartite standards of conduct as the basis of organization but not within the second part. The treatment there is an atomistic approach to separate torts.[120]

Moreover, the Second and Third *Restatements* have largely employed the First *Restatement*'s conceptual organization. The Second *Restatement* continued to address the intentional torts under the heading "invasion of interests in personality" but then addressed negligence, strict liability, and the other torts without reference to interest analysis. Even when any of this modern work employs the simple interest-based classifications to which tort liability is susceptible—such as Dobbs's breakdown into physical, economic, and emotional interests—they do not reveal very much. Similarly, classification based on standards of conduct—using the tripartite division—tell us only one of the things that is relevant to analysis of the differences and similarities among the various torts. In effect, neither interest analysis nor the tripartite division do very much beyond providing a seemingly logical basis for organizing a table of contents for a *Restatement,* treatise, or casebook. The only way to grasp tort law "as a whole" at any level of detail is to study the different torts individually. A classification scheme does not do that.

From the time of the First *Restatement* through at least the 1950s, the focus of most tort scholars was on individual torts or doctrines, although there was a growing concern, beginning in the 1940s, with the question whether liability for accidental bodily injury should be based on negligence or be "strict."[121] A considerable amount of tort scholarship addressed this question, as the issue arose in products liability, in auto liability, and for some scholars, across the board.[122] Debates about negligence versus strict liability tended to have little to say about intentional torts, because those torts did not involve accidental bodily injury.

It is no surprise, therefore, that beginning in the 1960s the concerns of torts scholars began to move beyond what was reflected in the structure of the *Restatements,* treatises, and casebooks. But new theoretical approaches to tort law did not usher in a new conceptual organization of the subject. The work of Guido Calabresi and Ronald Coase introduced economic analysis of tort law, and within a decade others—Richard Posner and Steven Shavell, for example—were engaged in this form of analysis.[123] Most of the work of scholars informed by economic theory centered on accidental injury, although Posner had something to say about intentional torts as well, so initially the new theoretical literature on tort law was directed at only a portion of the field. But when, partly in reaction to economic analysis, philosophically oriented scholars such as Ernest Weinrib and Jules Coleman developed a conception of tort liability as corrective justice, and John Goldberg and Benjamin Zipursky offered a contrasting but also deontological conception, civil recourse, the intentional torts fit comfortably within those approaches.[124]

For our purposes, however, the common feature of the theoretical contributions to modern tort law is that they involve conceptualization without classification. They make no effort to locate all the different torts within a detailed conceptual scheme, or to subdivide them into categories. They implicitly accept the proposition that tort law appears to be a disparate array of causes of action, linked only by the classic definition of tort law—a set of civil wrongs not arising out of contract. They then seek instead to make sense of all, or major portions of, tort law, from a different perspective entirely, fitting it into a single descriptive or normative conception—welfare maximization, corrective justice, or civil recourse. Such conceptions float above the messy details of the different torts that *Restatements* address and that we have been discussing. The post-1950s theoretical literature therefore stands to one side of the central concerns of this chapter.

The Classification Problem in Tort Law

All this brings us to the present. The century and a half of struggle that we recounted above has not yielded anything like a coherent conception of tort law. On the contrary, tort law is about as fragmented as it was a hundred years ago. The odyssey of the *Restatement (Third) of Torts* recapitulates the condition of its subject. Preparation of this *Restatement* has occurred in a series of separate projects, both because no single Reporter or small group of Reporters would dedicate themselves to preparation of the entire *Restatement* for as long as that would take, and because it simply was not necessary for Reporters to have a view of the entire subject while restating its parts. Why else would it be feasible first to restate the law governing apportionment (essentially contributory negligence, assumption of risk, and problems of multiple causation), then turn to the law of products liability, and then turn elsewhere?[125] The *Restatement* is a collection of independent modules, because that is what much of tort law is.

Even the last module in the series, "Concluding Provisions," which will include medical malpractice—certainly a form of liability for physical harm that would have fit comfortably in the "physical and emotional harm" category—reflects the difficulty of classification and the legacy of the category of miscellaneous torts that has been with us since the treatises of the late nineteenth century.[126] In short, there is nothing obviously wrong with the organization of the Third *Restatement* because there is no obviously right alternative organization.

With a full picture of this fragmentation in view, it is time to ask why this is the state of contemporary tort law. What is it that has prevented the subject from becoming increasingly coherent? Why is tort law so resistant to coherent classification? In our view there are three main reasons, the same reasons that have accounted for this fragmentation for the century and a half we have been discussing.

The Lack of a Unified Substantive Theory of Liability

The torts scholars of the late nineteenth and early twentieth century felt an understandable impetus to classify tort law. One of the reasons for this impetus is that, with the abolition of the forms of action, the dominance of procedure in tort law waned and substance came to the forefront. But what substance? Those scholars wanted to understand the basis or bases for the imposition of liability.

Much of their organization of tort law reflected their efforts to find the themes that were common to the different forms of liability. But their efforts always had a "connect-the-dots" quality: the scholars tried to find what linked together different causes of action. One of the reasons we have identified for their lack of success was that the different torts had less in common than the scholars supposed might be the case.

There was another reason for their lack of success, however, that was in a sense even more fundamental. Those scholars, and their successors to this day, never developed a theory that explained why there was no tort liability when there was not. Why did some conduct intended to cause harm, some negligent conduct, and some non-negligent conduct result in liability, while some such conduct did not result in liability? Nineteenth-century commentators had attempted to capture that phenomenon through the maxim of *damnum absque injuria,* but that maxim was conclusory, simply stating that sometimes the legal system had no remedies for civil injuries. Without a theory explaining why tort liability ensued in some situations and not in others, whether the characteristics that certain torts seemed to have in common were actually their operative characteristics could not be determined for certain. Why, for example, was intent to cause bodily injury actionable but intent to cause emotional harm not actionable? Whatever factor or factors distinguished those situations could be one of the bases for organization, but without an explanation of those factors tort law would only consist of formal categories, not substantive ones.

There have been some attempts to develop general theories of tort liability in the years since the first treatise writers addressed this problem, but those efforts have not provided a detailed enough basis for the organization of all of tort liability. The claims that tort law is principally concerned with corrective justice, civil recourse, protection of individual liberty, or optimizing welfare, whatever their accuracy, do not come down close enough to the ground to explain why there is and is not liability in different, related situations. Those claims therefore cannot be a basis for organizing the various forms of liability. Indeed, they place all of tort law under a single heading, without providing any subheadings or any way of developing them.

In short, the very idea of a unitary tort law is inconsistent with tort law as we know it. Thus, a first reason for the fragmentation of tort law has been the absence of a comprehensive substantive theory that serves to explain why some activities producing physical, emotional, or economic injury are actionable and others not.

Limited Practical Payoff

The conceptual organization of tort law can have a number of uses. It guides scholars, it enables students to place what they are studying in perspective, and it can give practicing lawyers a sense of the relationship among different causes of action. But conceptual organization of tort law is the least useful for the practicing bar. Beyond providing practicing lawyers a table of contents, the organization of tort law simply does not matter much to the practicing lawyer.

Most potential tort actions fall squarely (if at all) within the confines of a particular tort and only that tort. Plaintiffs' lawyers know which tort that is. Their first concern is whether the elements of that particular tort are satisfied. Defendants' lawyers have the same concern, though they hope for a different answer. It makes little difference to either plaintiffs' or defense lawyers whether the tort alleged in a suit bears a family relationship to another tort or protects a similar interest. Only in the occasional appeal posing a cutting-edge issue or involving a set of facts right on the border between two different torts does conceptual organization come into play.

The result is that there has never been any pressure from the practicing bar for torts scholars to develop a better or more insightful conceptual organization of tort law. Treatises are highly useful because they provide a source for black-letter rules and a soundbite's worth of analysis. But as long as the subject a lawyer wants to find in a treatise is readily findable, that is all the practicing bar needs.

A case in point is Prosser's "handbook," probably the most successful torts treatise of all time, published in multiple editions between 1941 and 1984. This work adopts just about the most atomistic organization possible. The book contains only two chapters discussing more than one tort. Every other cause of action is addressed in a separate chapter, with no umbrella or organizing headings other than the names of the causes of action themselves. Practicing lawyers obviously had little difficulty finding what they needed to find in Prosser's treatise, despite the absence of conceptualization, or it would not have been as successful as it was for many decades. Prosser's table of contents is essentially a list of all the torts, nothing more.

If Prosser's atomistic organization of tort law had served to prevent effective litigation of torts cases, there would undoubtedly have been demands from the practicing bar for treatises whose organization was more helpful. But in fact atomistic organization captures the essence of tort law. Some clusters of individual tort causes of action may have common features. That was undoubtedly why late nineteenth- and early twentieth-century scholars experimented with classifying intentional torts with respect to the common interests they protected or the standard of liability they seemed to require. But we have shown in this chapter that torts scholars, in seeking to establish some conceptual organization of the field, have repeatedly run up against the disparate character of tort causes of action, each with its own doctrinal requirements that appear to have little in common with other torts. Given this feature of tort causes of action, arguably the most important dimension of them for practicing lawyers, and the most accurate description of them for scholars, is their doctrinal elements. And since those elements differ radically from tort to tort, perhaps the most coherent organization of tort law is an atomistic one. Such an organization, of course, serves to reinforce the fragmented character of the subject.

The Accuracy of Atomism and the
Legacy of the Forms of Action

Whatever its flaws, no superior alternative to the fragmented organization of tort law that has come down to us has ever been developed. And the reason why no superior alternative has ever been developed is that fidelity to the actual nature of tort law precludes it. The great historian of the common law Frederick William Maitland said that we may have buried the forms of action, but that "they still rule us from our graves."[127] We think that, although this is no longer as true as it may have been in Maitland's time, some of the same imperatives that gave rise to the forms of action still operate and influence the conceptual organization, and fragmentation, of tort law.

This is because the exigencies that gave rise to the forms of action have not disappeared. Like our forebears hundreds of years ago, we still think that some kinds of harms should be actionable and that some should not be, and that the degree of blame attributable to the party causing the harm may be relevant, but that this relevance may vary, depending on the kind of harm or other circumstances in question.[128] As long as these things are true, then something like the forms of action—separate causes of action with distinctive, mandatory elements—is inevitable because some circumstances will qualify for tort liability and others will not.

It is true that, although separate causes of action with distinctive elements are inevitable, in principle it still would be possible to show that many separate causes of action nonetheless have common characteristics. Bohlen appears to have thought at the outset of his work on the First *Restatement* that all the torts would fall into groups based on the interests they protected, though the only general interest he identified before changing his mind was the right of personality. In chapter 3, we suggest in this vein that a number of torts could be understood to protect dignitary interests, although the burden of our argument is that dignity is so general a concept that it could not do much work beyond providing a label for several distantly related causes of action that are themselves the products of history.

Beyond such categories as the general interests in physical, emotional, dignitary, and economic well-being, however, the different torts do not hang together very much. This is a contingent fact, not a necessary one, but it has turned out that the kinds of wrongs deemed actionable in tort simply do not have much more than actionability in common. The intentional torts of battery, assault, and false imprisonment turn out to be the exception rather than the rule. They require intent to interfere with bodily security.

But there is another reason that those torts hang together. Battery, assault, and false imprisonment each were actionable under the writ of trespass *vi et armis,* whereas the other torts that require intent to cause harm were not. The first three involved direct, forcible injury (or bodily interference) that fell within the core of this form of action because, originally, they involved breach of the king's peace. They were the three torts that Blackstone mentioned in his discussion of trespass *vi et armis.*[129] They were the same torts (along with malicious prosecution) that Cooley classified together as involving the protection of "personal security."[130] And they were the first three torts that Ames and Smith addressed in their casebook.[131] So it is no surprise that Bohlen would also see the three torts as related.

But it is ironic, nonetheless. Bohlen's effort in the *Restatement* to escape the gravitational pull of the forms of action began by replicating important aspects of trespass *vi et armis.* This organization not only places the classic intentional torts together and has continued to do so until this day. In addition, the organization places the torts that require intent to harm but that were not actionable in trespass *vi et armis* elsewhere, and it turns out mostly outside of any organization. Fraud and malicious prosecution, for example, just stand on their own in most organizations of tort law, as if they were separate forms of action. At least in part because of the legacy of the forms of action, then, the other intentional torts are treated in piecemeal fashion.

The alternative, however, would have been even more unsatisfying and formalistic. Placing all the intentional torts together would effectively have adopted an organization based entirely on the tripartite division of standards of conduct. It would then have been necessary to place all the torts that were actionable on the basis of negligence in a second category and all the torts actionable on a strict liability basis in a third. This classification based on standards of conduct would have been a mere taxonomy that revealed nothing about the reasons the different torts were subject to different standards of conduct.

In short, the more we seek some comprehensive organization of tort law, the more we run up against endemic characteristics of the field that stand in the way of such organization: the absence of a substantive theory that can explain, across a range of diverse tort actions, why some civil conduct producing injury generates actions in tort and other conduct does not; the limited practical utility to be gained from a stronger organization of atomistic torts, even if it could be achieved; and, perhaps most fundamentally, the inherently fragmented character of the field itself, resulting in the only fully accurate characterization of tort law as consisting of (some) civil wrongs not arising out of contract. Prosser's typically exaggerated cynicism about conceptual order in tort law seems a good place for us to end. "There are many possible approaches to the law of torts, and many different arrangements of the material to be considered have been attempted," he said. "Other than mere convenience in discussion there is no inherent merit in any of them."[132]

After 150 years of conceptual struggle, the organization and classification of tort law, and of the individual causes of action of which it is comprised, is only slightly more orderly than it was at the outset. We have tried to show why this is the case. The late nineteenth- and early twentieth-century scholars sought to transcend the legacy of the forms of action but were only partly successful in doing so. And the various organizations of tort law that they developed in place of the ancient forms were disorderly. Bohlen's First *Restatement* was an advance over these early efforts, but he abandoned his apparent ambition to provide a conceptual reorganization of tort law, falling back on a mix of interest analysis, organization based on standards of conduct, and atomistic presentation of separate causes of action. The treatises, casebooks, and *Restatements* that followed have not departed substantially from the approach taken by that First *Restatement*.

There are a number of reasons, we have argued, why all this has occurred. The absence of an accepted comprehensive theory of the purposes underlying tort liability has contributed, as has the lack of a practical payoff that could be obtained from a new conceptual organization of tort law. The principal reason, however, lies in the inevitable influence of tort law's history: the subject of tort law is not amenable to any such organization. Although tort law can be ordered in a taxonomic sense, at its heart tort law is a series of causes of action—the classic set of fragmented "civil wrongs not arising out of contract" that it has always been. Any effort to make it more than that, except at the most general level, is bound to fail.

3

The Problem of the Dignitary Torts

WE CONCLUDED the last chapter with the observation that, at its heart, tort law is a series of different causes of action—a fragmented set of "civil wrongs not arising out of contract"—that defy fully coherent classification and organization. This chapter tests that observation by examining the nature, development, and relationships among what are sometimes called the "dignitary torts."

Tort liability is imposed not only in order to protect against and compensate for bodily injury, damage to property, emotional distress, and economic loss. In addition, certain forms of tort liability protect individual dignity of various sorts and compensate for invasions of different aspects of individual dignity. Contemporary treatises and casebooks repeatedly make reference to and categorize a distinct set of torts this way, with little explanation of what may or may not be significant about the categorization. And there were focused, but unsuccessful, efforts a half-century ago to bring those torts under a single doctrinal umbrella. So there is reason to examine this purported categorization. What does it mean to say that there is a *category* of "dignitary torts?" It means less than might be thought, we argue, for the reasons we have been emphasizing already. In tort law the influence of history is inevitable, and that history tells us that those torts simply do not have enough in common— in origin, purpose, or scope—to permit treating them as part of a single generic category.

This chapter examines the concept of dignity, the history of torts that can be said to at least partially protect dignitary interests, the development of two new such torts in the twentieth century, and the unsuccessful efforts of some prominent scholars during this period to achieve what we call "unification"—the treatment of several torts under the umbrella concept of dignity.

The ultimate result was that the "dignitary torts" remained, and continue to remain, individual actions in which a concern for the protection of human dignity may figure but cannot be said to fully define the action. The current "dignitary torts," in fact, look very much like tort actions generally, each with specific doctrinal requirements that sometimes overlap with, but often remain distinct from, one another. We seek to explain why this has come to pass through an analysis of what we are calling the "incomplete coincidence" of interests implicated in dignitary torts.

The emergence of "new" torts partially protecting dignitary interests—intentional infliction of emotional distress and invasion of privacy—came about in part because of two developments in the late nineteenth and early twentieth centuries. One development was altered attitudes about the cognizability of emotional injury itself, emanating from advances in the mental health professions that resulted in emotional injuries being conceived as "real" and capable of being analyzed and treated.

Those developments served to elevate emotional harm from the realm of elusive idiosyncrasy to that of something tangible and observable: something that courts and juries in torts cases could grapple with. The result was that when plaintiffs brought actions seeking damages for emotional harm, their damages were treated as comparably credible to damages for physical harm. As we show, the plaintiffs in the groundbreaking lawsuits establishing those torts were disproportionately women. The courts seemed to think that emotional suffering had a gendered aspect that rendered its recognition more palatable. There may also have been stereotyped judicial attitudes about women that, ironically, inclined late nineteenth- and early twentieth-century courts to be more sympathetic to what they regarded as "hysterical" women than they were to men who had suffered emotional distress.[1]

But the courts were ambivalent, repeatedly imposing serious limits on the extent to which women could recover in such cases. A number of the dignitary torts require that a defendant's conduct not only be wrongful but also be "highly offensive" to the reasonable person. And the courts were frequently prisoners of their own bias. For example, Martha Chamalas and Linda Kerber uncovered an episode in which the expert testimony of a male physician that "normal people do not suffer injury from fright" was for a time a significant impediment to the development of liability for this form of loss.[2]

Clearly there was no corresponding sympathy for or ambivalence about African Americans, who undoubtedly were also being systematically subjected to racist conduct that intentionally caused them emotional harm. As we indicated in the introduction, there are virtually no reported cases in which African Americans brought torts suit for this form of harm until well past the period when the tort was being established. For practical purposes they lacked meaningful access to the courts. And because the law required conduct that was "highly offensive" under "extreme and outrageous" circumstances, racial wrongdoing that resulted in emotional injury had little prospect of satisfying these requirements when they would be applied by white judges and juries.

The second development influencing the rise of the dignitary torts was the spread of mass media and associated developments in technology, such as improvements in transportation and communication, which made the nationwide transmission of instantaneous information about individuals, products, and services basic features of the American economy. Those developments greatly expanded the capacity of the media, and the advertising industry, to intrude on the private lives of individuals. Media could easily publish photographs of private citizens; advertisers could readily use the names or likenesses of people in commercial advertisements; people could use telephones, cameras, and recordings to interfere with the seclusion of others or intrude into their personal spaces. In sum, the capacity of the media and others to "invade the privacy" of individuals was dramatically increased.

The "new" torts of intentional inflection of emotional distress and invasion of privacy can be seen as responses to those developments. However, as we seek to show, although those torts had in common a concern with protecting different types of assaults on individual dignity, they did not become unified in a generic category of "dignitary torts." Instead, they emerged as discrete causes of action, with different specific requirements, even though they overlapped in some respects. Over time they very much came to resemble other tort actions generally, being defined by particularistic doctrinal elements in a manner somewhat resembling the older forms of action. In the end the dignitary torts were folded into the doctrinal apparatus characteristic of American tort law. This chapter describes how this came about.

Dignitary Torts: A First Look

There are five torts that involve liability for invasion of or interference with different aspects of the dignity of the individual. In the course of our examination of those torts, we show how three of the torts are of ancient lineage, while two others came into being in the twentieth century; how the courts, with the active aid of the celebrated torts scholar William Prosser, were able to cloak their recognition of the two new torts by asserting the continuity and consistency of the torts with tort law's past; and how and why the five torts have resisted unification under the umbrella concept of dignity.

Far from embracing the idea that the five torts have in common a unitary concern with protecting dignity, neither tort liability nor tort theory has ever developed very far in that direction, for two reasons. First, the concept of dignity is not sufficiently specific to ground the very different protections that would be encompassed within a unified cause of action for invasion of dignity. This is because, as we demonstrate, the interests protected by the torts that can be considered "dignitary"—offensive battery, false imprisonment, defamation, intentional infliction of emotional distress, and invasion of privacy—are very different from each other, and reflect very different dimensions of individual dignity.

Second, the doctrinal development of those torts has not simply been a function of changing attitudes toward the interests potentially being protected in tort suits. If that were the case, there are cultural reasons why this series of torts, perhaps still grouped under disparate doctrinal categories, might have readily been understood as essentially concerned with the protection of individual dignity. In keeping with its historical structure, however, the common law of torts separately specified the distinctive elements of several of those torts, and thereby determined the structure of tort liability for the wrongs they redressed, long before the general idea of dignity was ever thought to link them together. The resulting substantive and structural separation of the dignitary torts from each other rendered unification an impossibility. The history of the dignitary torts determined the form in which we have inherited them.

THE CONCEPT OF DIGNITY

By the late eighteenth century, the capacity of individuals to reason and to exercise free will had been secularized, most notably in the writings of

Immanuel Kant.[3] Kant did not often refer expressly to dignity, and there is some debate about whether the German term he employed (*wurde*, roughly equivalent to "worth") should be understood as the equivalent of dignity.[4] Most scholarship on Kant nonetheless associates him with two claims about dignity: that human worth should be understood in itself and not simply as a means to glorify God, and that human worth depends on autonomy, the capacity of people to choose and reason for themselves.[5] This conception of dignity is centered on the intrinsic qualities of human beings rather than in rank or status.[6]

The core meaning of dignity is composed of three elements.[7] The first is "that every human being possesses an intrinsic worth, merely by being human."[8] Here we see the "inner transcendental kernel" inherent in human existence.[9] The next element of dignity is "that this intrinsic worth should be recognized and respected by others."[10] It follows from that proposition that "some forms of treatment by others are inconsistent with, or required by, respect for this individual worth."[11] A third "core" element of dignity is the "claim that recognizing the intrinsic worth of the individual requires that the state should be seen to exist for the sake of the individual human being, and not vice versa."[12] The content of this third element, "the detailed implications . . . for the role of the state vis a vis the individual" of accepting the first two elements of dignity's "core meaning," remains uncertain.[13]

Despite the growing importance of individual dignity over the two centuries, exactly how to define this value has received little self-conscious or express attention in tort cases or torts scholarship. Separate aspects of dignity have received considerable attention, but the overall concept has not. Although there are frequent, passing references to the "dignitary torts," the references often are made without further explanation. The term "dignity" in passages referring to a sometimes unspecified set of torts appears to us to be a placeholder for an inchoate but unarticulated idea.[14] This is the notion that some tort actions are available when a person has been offended, embarrassed, ridiculed, or mis-portrayed by the words or actions of another, in a way that does not respect the intrinsic worth of that individual. There has been virtually no analysis, however, of the nature or scope of this interest in dignity, or of the ways that the often-unnamed dignitary torts protect this interest.

A quick review of the five torts that have from time to time been considered at least in part to protect individual dignity reveals an important division among them. Three of the torts—offensive battery, false imprisonment, and defamation—are of ancient lineage. They were firmly in place before the modern era. In contrast, two of the torts—intentional infliction of emotional distress and invasion of privacy—emerged late in the nineteenth century at the earliest and were recognized as distinct causes of action only well into the twentieth century.

This distinction between the "older" torts and the "newer" torts enables us to analyze both what they have in common in protecting interests in dignity and what is different about the new torts—how and why they came into being, virtually in living memory. Our analysis of the way the new torts were created identifies the particular relationships between tort law's past and the processes that led to the creation of those torts.

The "Older" Dignitary Torts

In the following paragraphs we describe the nature and elements of the three older dignitary torts. At this point we are making only summary reference to the nature of the dignitary interests the torts protect because we address those interests in detail toward the end of the chapter, when we analyze the question whether the notion of a unified dignitary tort holds up to scrutiny. The older torts came into existence long before tort law was a separate field, through a combination of recognition of the values they were seen as protecting, the ancient common law process of elaborating the scope of the writ of trespass (in the case of battery and false imprisonment), and the reception of a cause of action that previously had religious overtones (defamation) into the common law arsenal of civil actions.

OFFENSIVE BATTERY

Battery is an ancient tort with roots in the common law writ of trespass *vi et armis*.[15] Battery constitutes making, or causing, intentional contact with the body of another person. Many batteries cause physical harm, and in such instances this is the principal injury that liability redresses. Intentionally interfering with another person's bodily security is also a dignitary invasion, however, because doing so interferes with an individual's bodily autonomy. Even when there has been no physical injury, intentionally making physical contact with another person without express or implied consent amounts to a dignitary injury. By interfering with an individual's right not to be touched, touching or physical contact with another is offensive in itself.[16] This form of "offensive" battery is therefore mainly concerned with dignity, broadly conceived.

False Imprisonment

False (i.e., wrongful) imprisonment is also a linear descendant of the old action of trespass. False imprisonment is the intentional and wrongful restriction of an individual's freedom of movement. Confining an individual in a closed room or space, or detaining an individual in a retail store on suspicion of shoplifting, may constitute false imprisonment. Like offensive battery, false imprisonment is actionable on its own, even when confinement has not caused the plaintiff physical harm. Rather, confinement itself is a discrete form of interference with bodily autonomy and therefore an interference with the confined individual's dignity.

Defamation

Actions for defamation—for slander (oral) or libel (written)—were originally subject to the jurisdiction of the English ecclesiastical courts, but by the seventeenth century had become lodged in the common law courts.[17] Common law defamation amounts to strict liability for publication (communication to a third party or parties) of false information that is damaging to a person's reputation. The common law seems to accord no particular value to a statement that is damaging to another's reputation. Truth may be a defense, but prima facie the defendant speaks or writes at his or her peril.

Liability for defamation, however, is subject to a conditional privilege for information that furthers a purpose as to which the defendant and others with whom the defendant has communicated have a common interest. This privilege can be defeated by a showing that the statement about the plaintiff was made with malice—that is, with a desire to harm the plaintiff's reputation. And the privilege can be defeated in some jurisdictions even in the absence of such "common law malice" if the defendant knows the defamatory statement to be false or recklessly disregards whether it is true or false.[18]

Liability for defamation protects against the harm that results from having one's good name, one's reputation, diminished. The tort is not actionable in the absence of falsity; diminution of one's good name through the statement of false facts interferes with an individual's dignity by diminishing his or her standing in the community, or the view others have of the individual's character, personality, or actions.[19]

The "Newer" Dignitary Torts and Their Process of Creation

In contrast to the older dignitary torts, which have their roots in the inter-action of concern with preventing violence and vengeance, the technicali-ties of the forms of action, and beliefs and values held in high regard in medieval England, the origins and bases for establishing the two newer torts are less shrouded in the cloudy history of many centuries past. The impetus for the creation of the newer torts was rooted in social and cul-tural changes that created pressure for the recognition of new causes of ac-tion for intentional infliction of emotional distress and invasion of privacy.

The method by which those new torts were created consisted of in-cremental steps, beginning with courts providing redress against some conduct not previously regarded as tortious, then moving to the implied establishment of a new tort in extremely narrow circumstances, then to a broadening of those circumstances, and finally to open acknowledgment of the existence of a new tort. That incremental process was facilitated by the state-centered nature of American tort law, in which one state court's decision to provide tortious relief for conduct not previously treated as actionable not only provides a precedent within that state for further expansion of the relief but serves as a nonbinding guide for other state courts to consider following.

In the particular case of the two newer torts, however, there was an ad-ditional development furthering their emergence. This was the strategic intervention, in the form of scholarly observations in his torts treatise, of William Prosser. With characteristically camouflaged exaggeration, Prosser named the two new torts, delineated their putative contours, and gave them his imprimatur. Recognition of the torts was probably inevi-table in any event, but Prosser's intervention both accelerated and solidi-fied their emergence.

INTENTIONAL INFLICTION OF EMOTIONAL DISTRESS (IIED)

By the turn of the twentieth century the common law of torts had come to recognize a number of causes of action that sometimes awarded dam-ages for intentional infliction of emotional distress, as a kind of side ef-fect of the imposition of liability for other tortious wrongs: assault (for threatening physical harm), battery, false imprisonment, and the now-obsolete tort of seduction. All those torts typically involved emotional injury, among other things, and awarded compensation for it. But at that point courts were reluctant to recognize a freestanding cause of action for emotional distress because of concerns about encouraging much more frequent litigation, and because of the supposed difficulty of distinguishing between genuine and fraudulent claims.

A number of early twentieth-century developments combined to cause a few courts to relax the restrictions on recovery. One such development was society's increased willingness, in part because of the emergence of the fields of psychiatry and psychology, to take emotional harm more seriously. The professionalization of specialists in mental health made emotional harm more diagnosable and treatable, and also made it possible for expert witnesses in torts cases to quantify the costs of treating emotional harm.[20] As a consequence, the perceived difficulty courts were thought to face in identifying feigned or fraudulent claims and avoiding massive litigation came to be seen as less threatening. Emotional injury was then understood as more "real" and less idiosyncratic than in the past.[21]

Another important development was the increase in rail travel by women traveling alone or with children. The railroads during the late nineteenth and early twentieth centuries were not the comparatively luxurious means of transportation they became later in the twentieth century. Women traveling alone on railroads or streetcars faced special challenges, both from male passengers they encountered and in getting on and off trains. Women travelers often wore long skirts and shoes with high heels, carried packages, and were accompanied by young children whose behavior they sought to control. The result was to expose women passengers to a series of vulnerabilities: harassment by other passengers, the risk of falling while trying to board or exit trains, and the risk of injuring themselves while trying to manage young children.[22]

Railroads and trolleys, along with innkeepers, were classified as "common carriers" by the law of torts and therefore owed their customers a higher duty of care than ordinary defendants. The heightened standard of care for common carriers became a feature of negligence suits against railroads and streetcar companies for bodily injuries women suffered on trains and trolleys.

There were a lot of mixed results in bodily injury cases; female plaintiffs were by no means the automatic favorites of the courts. Nonetheless, in part because of the growing number of suits for bodily injury, when additional suits were brought by women who had not been physically injured while traveling but had been subjected to outrageous, sexually harassing, or verbally abusive behavior at the hands of a railroad employee or by another passenger, the courts already knew a bit about what women faced when they traveled. A few courts, in cases in which female plaintiffs had not quite been assaulted, battered, or improperly confined, permitted recovery of damages that consisted mainly of compensation for their mental suffering in the face of extreme behavior by the defendant.

In the earliest cases involving emotional distress suits by female passengers on railroads or streetcars, courts relied on the fiction that the terms of the plaintiff's contract with the carrier required it to protect the plaintiff from abusive behavior, either from another passenger or from an employee. In *Gillespie v. Brooklyn Heights Railroad Co.*,[23] for example, the plaintiff asked for her fare to be returned. The defendant's conductor leveled a stream of verbal abuse at her, calling her a "deadbeat and a swindler" in front of other passengers. The court held that she stated a cause of action because there had been "a breach of the defendant's contract and of its duty to its passenger."[24] The defendant's refusal to return the fare, the court held, was a "tortious act upon his part." The plaintiff "suffered insult and indignity at the hands of the conductor, was treated disrespectfully and indecorously by him under such circumstances as to occasion mental suffering, humiliation, wounded pride, and disgrace."[25]

Other early cases followed the same pattern, holding that when a railroad or trolley employee behaved abusively, there was both breach of contract and tortious conduct, without clearly identifying or separating the former from the latter.[26] Cases involving innkeepers reflected the same pattern.[27] To the extent that breach of contract was a fiction (and we think it was), this was a form of cloaking. As time went on, however, cases in which there was no conceivable contract, and therefore no conceivable breach of contract, were brought. Here, the abusive conduct had to be classified as either tortious or not actionable at all. And the courts held that some of the cases were actionable. Foremost among those were cases involving particularly malicious practical jokes.[28]

Significantly, there are few cases involving African American plaintiffs, whether male or female, during this period. Important studies of the legal system's treatment of race and gender during this period seem to have discovered almost no such cases, and neither have we. Thus,

Barbara Welke's work on the railroad revolution, and Martha Chamalas's and Jennifer Wriggins's work on race and gender in tort law, identify no significant litigated cases involving dignitary injury suffered by African Americans during the period when this tort was developing.[29] To continue what we hypothesized in the introduction, we think this is evidence that, whatever protections tort law was beginning to extend in theory, in practice the system was not hospitable to claims by African Americans that their "dignity" had been invaded. It was white women who received those protections, and whose cases established precedents recognizing the new tort. Indeed, in one noteworthy 1905 case, a white woman recovered from a railroad on the ground that it had permitted an African American ladies' attendant to treat her in an offensive manner.[30]

There are two important additional points worth making here. First, the reported cases that seemed to fall in the general category of intentional infliction of emotional distress were limited in number—at most, there were several dozen over a period of forty years. Second, the courts deciding the cases engaged in cloaking of the significance of their decisions by not acknowledging that they were creating, or recognizing, a new tort. They often cited earlier cases, simply asserting that what they were doing was nothing new. They cloaked their decisions in the earlier, inapposite precedents. In fact, as far as we can determine, no one during the period between the turn of the twentieth century and the late 1930s claimed that there was a whole new tort in the making. In 1934 the *Restatement of Torts* identified the "Special Liability of Carrier for Insults by Servants," but that obviously was not the recognition of a whole new tort.[31]

Then along came William Prosser. For nearly fifty years *Prosser on Torts* was arguably the leading single-volume treatise in American legal scholarship. Generations of law students used it, generations of lawyers consulted it, and generations of courts cited it as authority. The first edition was published in 1941.[32] It met with nearly universal praise.[33]

With the publication of his treatise Prosser quickly became a trusted authority on the entire law of torts. He introduced material on intentional infliction of emotional distress in the first edition of his treatise, in a section of the chapter labeled "Intentional Interference with the Person," which also included material on battery, assault, and false imprisonment. Prosser entitled the IIED material "Words and Acts Causing Mental Disturbance."[34] The section was thirteen pages long and contained eighty-eight footnotes.

The section started with a black-letter statement of the law, beginning, "In recent years the courts have tended to recognize the intentional causing of mental or emotional disturbance as a tort."[35] Two years before Prosser had published an article on the subject,[36] and he indicated at the outset that the substance of the section had appeared in that article.[37] But the article had opened by saying, "It is time to recognize that the courts have created a new tort."[38] The treatise contained no such statement. Indeed, judging by his black-letter statement, Prosser seems to have decided to go further and assert that recognition of the new tort had already "tended" to occur.

It took Prosser five of his thirteen pages of coverage of intentional infliction of emotional distress to introduce what might be called "weight-bearing" material, actual precedents recognizing the new tort. That material consisted of only three paragraphs, each containing a bit of categorization. The cases, Prosser said, concerned practical jokes; oppressive conduct on the part of those "in a special position to inflict" mental distress, such as common carriers, innkeepers, evicting landlords, schools, and detectives; mishandling of dead bodies; and technical trespasses on land with accompanying objectionable behavior.[39]

Most often, as we have noted, the plaintiffs in these cases were women, probably for a number of reasons. First, they were more likely to be treated offensively than were men. Second, the allegations that they had suffered enough offense to warrant an award of damages were more likely to have been taken seriously by juries. Third, for this reason women would have found it easier to get a lawyer to represent them on a contingent-fee (percentage) basis. Finally, appellate courts, which had the final say about establishing the new tort, were more likely to be sympathetic to claims of offense taken by women than by men.

The material on intentional infliction of emotional distress Prosser introduced in his treatise was not exactly misleading, but it was presented in a way that did not give the reader a context for judging the degree to which Prosser might have been regarded as overgeneralizing. Setting aside the common carrier cases, the dead body cases, and the other cases that sounded in contract rather than tort, Prosser cited twenty-one weight-bearing cases decided by courts in the United States that directly supported his assertion that there was an independent tort of IIED.

Five of those twenty-one cases involved innkeepers, whose liability was not encompassed in the existing *Restatement* rule regarding the passengers of common carriers but who traditionally had been considered another enterprise subject to greater common law duties than most other defendants.[40] That left sixteen other "weight-bearing" cases, a number of which involved insults by owners of premises that Prosser acknowledged "cater to the public—theaters, amusement parks, a circus, a telegraph office, and a dancing school."[41] This acknowledgment was unexplained, but it was obviously an implied admission that the defendants might also be something like common carriers or innkeepers.

This was hardly a substantial body of case law support for Prosser's assertion that the courts "have tended to recognize" IIED as a separate tort. Overall, of the 118 cases cited in the section, only sixteen directly supported the (at least implied) contention that the tort of IIED went significantly beyond what the *Restatement* had already said.

In the end, Prosser concluded, "So far as it is possible to generalize from the cases, the rule that seems to be emerging is that there is liability only for conduct exceeding all bounds usually tolerated by society, of a nature which is especially calculated to cause and does cause mental damage of a very serious kind."[42] It is impossible to know how cagey Prosser intended this statement to be. The statement invited a reader to believe that generalization about intentional infliction of emotional distress cases was possible, and that the most accurate generalization was that the rule emerging in tort law imposed liability whenever conduct exceeded all bounds usually tolerated by society. But it is difficult to see how Prosser could justify that generalization on the basis of the evidence he had provided earlier in the section. The three paragraphs actually addressing the cases imposing intentional infliction of emotional distress liability almost entirely involved defendants in a special position to inflict mental distress (common carriers, landlords, schools, detectives), plus those involving mishandling dead bodies, a few other "trespassers," and two non-U.S. decisions imposing liability for cruel practical jokes.[43]

The upshot of all this is that, although establishment of the tort of IIED in the United States was not Prosser's invention, IIED owes a lot to him. He named the tort, he asserted that it already existed in what quickly became the most prominent torts treatise in the United States, and his endorsement gave the tort respectability. And then, as the Reporter for the *Restatement (Second) of Torts*, he again endorsed and this time specified the elements of the tort. IIED is actionable, the Second *Restatement* provided, when the defendant "by extreme and outrageous conduct intentionally . . . causes severe emotional distress."[44]

Prosser accomplished all this through a combination of skepticism about and respect for the history of tort law. The established common law of liability for emotional distress, he suggested, had been too restrictive and was being modified. But although he said that there was case law supporting his contention that a new tort had already come into being, in fact there was a lot less case law than he implied. On the surface his analysis of intentional infliction of emotional distress cases appeared to have followed the convention that history, in the form of precedent, constrained, even determined outcomes in tort law, but his reading of the relevant history relied on an aggressive, arguably misleading interpretation of precedent.

INVASION OF PRIVACY

Emergence of the tort of invasion of privacy followed a pattern similar to IIED. Beginning around the turn of the twentieth century, developments both threatened privacy to a greater degree than in the past and placed an increased value on certain aspects of privacy. The courts then gave limited recognition to causes of action in tort for invasion of those different aspects of privacy. But the story here is a bit more complicated than it was for IIED because the tort of invasion of privacy actually became four different torts. As with IIED, however, it was Prosser who most prominently and aggressively identified the new tort. He was also the first to tease out the four different features of the tort.

DISCLOSURE

One development in the broader culture as the twentieth century approached was the rise of "publicity" given to the private lives of some individuals. The emergence of publicity was a product of the dramatic growth of the newspaper industry as a mass-market phenomenon in the late nineteenth and early twentieth centuries. When newspapers first emerged in the United States, they were largely read by elites, but by the late nineteenth century improvements in transportation and communication made it possible for some newspapers and magazines to cater to mass audiences. Competition among newspapers stimulated what came to be called "yellow journalism," featuring "sensational" stories designed to cater to less-educated readers. By the early twentieth century most large cities had multiple newspapers, appearing in both the morning and afternoon. The publicity generated by newspaper and magazine outlets was accentuated by the development of photography, with newspapers regularly employing photographers who accompanied journalists in their efforts to develop stories. Hand-held cameras made it much easier for photographers to take pictures of people in public settings, often without their consent.[45]

Samuel Warren and Louis Brandeis's famous law review article "The Right of Privacy," published in 1890, lamented the growth of "publicity."[46] The article was allegedly generated by Warren's indignation at the publication in a Boston newspaper of a picture of his sister at the time of her wedding.[47] Eventually the unauthorized publication of private, embarrassing facts about a person, or a reproduction of that person's likeness, were recognized as actionable under the torts of disclosure and appropriation.

But there were really no direct precedents for the cause of action Brandeis and Warren proposed. When the courts did establish the tort, they sometimes did so through forms of cloaking that involved heroic interpretation of precedents addressing other issues. For example, in Kentucky the tort of disclosure was first recognized in 1927 in Brents v. Morgan,[48] a case in which the defendant posted a notice on the window of the plaintiff's garage indicating that the plaintiff had not paid a bill for veterinary services. As precedent for its decision permitting recovery, the court cited its 1912 decision in Douglas v. Stokes,[49] maintaining that Douglas "could have been put on no ground other than the unwarranted invasion of the right of privacy."[50] But Douglas held only that a man had a property right in letters to his deceased wife. It was a case about copyright, not disclosure. Douglas provided a fig leaf of support in service of the court's effort to portray as continuity what was actually innovation.

Disclosure of facts concerning another person's private life became actionable if it would be "highly offensive to a reasonable person" to have the matter publicized and the matter was not of "legitimate concern to the public."[51] As a practical matter the two prongs of this test were often related because the disclosure of private information is most likely to be highly offensive when it has no legitimate news value.[52] And as Anita Allen and Erin Mack have forcefully argued, often it was highly offensive because it violated both men's and women's sense of what women's "modesty" required. That is how this form of invasion of privacy "got its gender," or at least part of it.[53]

INTRUSION

Another, related effect of the enhanced interest in "publicity" in the early twentieth century was the ability of people seeking information about others to violate private spaces through the use of technology. Cameras that could take pictures from long distances, the growth of telephones, and the development of electronic devices capable of surreptitiously recording private conversations made it far easier for "peeping Toms" and other unauthorized persons to intrude on the solitude of others. Cases imposing liability for this form of invasion eventually supported recognition of the tort of "intrusion."

As was the case with the establishment of liability for disclosure, the courts sometimes cloaked what they were doing, either by citing the general right to protection against invasion of privacy or by citing precedents establishing one privacy cause of action in support of the establishment of a wholly different cause of action. Whether this cloaking was conscious, or the result of confusion that required the clarification which Prosser would provide a few years later, is uncertain. In *Rhodes v. Graham*,[54] for example, defendants had tapped the plaintiff's telephone wires and listened to his phone conversations, employing a stenographer to record the conversations. In the course of allowing the plaintiff to recover, the court maintained that an action for invasion of privacy had been established in Kentucky, citing, among other cases, *Douglas v. Stokes*.[55] But that case (as we indicated earlier), if it was a privacy case at all, involved disclosure, not intrusion.

Intrusion on a private space or conversation became actionable when the intrusion was "highly offensive to a reasonable person."[56] The paradigm cases involved eavesdropping or other sorts of unauthorized recording of private information, but some cases held that actually accessing the information obtained by the invasion was not required to make out an intrusion.[57] The core interest protected by the tort was clearly that of keeping others from witnessing, hearing, or viewing what was reasonably understood as "private" information about a person.

The requirement that the intrusion be highly offensive might in theory sometimes turn on the method of intrusion but instead almost always turned on how a "reasonable person" would perceive the intrusion's character.[58] Spying on a family at its breakfast table would tend to be judged less "highly offensive" than recording what transpired in a family member's bedroom. Nonetheless, an intrusion might be "highly offensive to a reasonable person" not because the information revealed was embarrassing but simply because it was confidential. Looking over the shoulder of someone withdrawing money from a bank would be an example.[59]

APPROPRIATION OF NAME OR LIKENESS

A third aspect of invasion of privacy was connected to the dramatic rise of the advertising industry in the early twentieth-century United States, another side-effect of the ability of newspapers and magazines to reach mass markets. As manufacturers of products came to realize that the same advances in transportation and communication which enabled newspapers to distribute their editions would make it possible for them to widely publicize the existence and availability of their merchandise, they realized that the most efficient way to achieve that publicity was often through advertisements in the mass media. Their growing interest in developing advertisements for their products led to the creation of a cottage industry of advertising agencies.[60] Often ads for products featured photographs or the names of famous individuals who endorsed a product, and occasionally manufacturers used the images of celebrities, or simply those of private individuals, who were said to endorse their products without securing the authorization or consent of the individuals in question. This led to the use of a person's name or likeness for commercial purposes without consent becoming actionable in a number of states soon after the turn of the twentieth century.[61]

The seminal case recognizing the cause of action was *Pavesich v. New England Life Insurance Co.*[62] *Pavesich* is a long opinion that acknowledges the absence of direct precedent to support it. But the court recognized that it needed some other form of continuity to support what it was doing, and it found that support in a variety of sources. In support of its assertion that the right of privacy was "no new idea in Georgia law," the court cited an 1894 decision holding that a statute requiring railroad and telegraph companies to give employees the reasons for their discharges, and to be subject to civil fines for failure to do so, was unconstitutional as a violation of "the general private right of silence" as part of the "liberty of speech and writing secured by the Constitution."[63] There was nothing in that case about a right of privacy. But *Pavesich* went on to say, citing many different sources of authority, that "the right of privacy is embraced within the absolute rights of personal security and personal liberty," and that "personal liberty includes not only freedom from personal restraint, but the right 'to be let alone': to determine one's own mode of life, whether it be a life of publicity or privacy; and to order one's life and manage one's affairs in a manner that may be most agreeable to him."[64]

For the most part the tort of appropriation protects commercial and economic interests rather than the intangible interest in dignity.[65] But in some instances, especially in the early cases addressing the issue, the interest the plaintiff asserted was the right not to be associated with the defendant's business or to be portrayed in a manner that was embarrassing or humiliating.[66] Instead, the plaintiffs in such cases were concerned about a false impression that reflected poorly on them—the impression that they had consented to the use of their names or likenesses. In those situations the appropriation tort could be said to have been furnishing protection against the presumed or anticipated diminution of respect for the plaintiff that might result from the plaintiff's having been thought to be voluntarily associated with the defendant's commercial activity.

FALSE LIGHT

A fourth tort involving the invasion of privacy was yet another result of the rise of modern media. It involved depiction or description of an individual, usually in the media, that misrepresented him or her in some way without actually diminishing his or her reputation. The tort had emerged in situations such as *Time v. Hill*,[67] where *Life* magazine published an account of a family's being held hostage by convicts who had escaped from a nearby prison. The plaintiffs claimed that the story misrepresented interactions between the prisoners and family members, creating false impressions about the behavior of the latter. The account neither met the standard of "extreme and outrageous" conduct for IIED nor contained sufficiently damaging false allegations to make out a defamation. But it was clear that the family had not welcomed the publicity about their situation or taken any steps to publicize it, and that false statements had been made about members of the family, even though the statements were not necessarily ones that would cause others to think less of them. In one respect *Time v. Hill* was about the intrusiveness of media into the private lives of ordinary citizens in a setting in which many people could be expected to resent publicity, particularly misleading publicity, about themselves, but existing tort actions did not seem to provide relief.

Other cases imposed liability when defendants publicized matters that placed plaintiffs in a false light that would be highly offensive to the reasonable person and knew of that risk or recklessly disregarded it.[68] In *Cantrell v. Forest City Publishing Co.*, for example, the wife of a victim when a bridge collapsed was described in an article about survivors of the disaster as "wearing a mask of non-expression" and living under conditions of poverty. The author of the article had not interviewed the woman at all.[69] Once again the facts of the case suggested that neither claims in IIED nor defamation would be actionable, but a suit in false light was upheld on the ground that the author of the article had been recklessly indifferent to the truth of what had been reported about the plaintiff and had thus acted with "malice."[70]

BUT VIRTUALLY all of this was still in the future as of 1941. At that point there was only a small legal literature on the "right to privacy" and a handful of cases imposing liability for those different forms of invasion, interference, or wrongdoing. Prosser took note of those cases by including a section labeled "Right of Privacy" in the last chapter, "Miscellaneous," of the first edition of his treatise. Unlike what he did with IIED, Prosser did not engage in aggressive interpretation of the case law. But he did resort to powerful generalizations on the basis of a very limited set of cases. He did not create the impression that legal doctrine was remaining consistent with established doctrinal propositions when it in fact was departing from them but rather that doctrinal rules were solidly in place—in this instance rules recognizing the existence of common law privacy actions—when they had only appeared in a few jurisdictions, and in some cases in a form that did not necessarily suggest a new cause of action was being created.

At the outset of his "Right of Privacy" section in the 1941 edition of his treatise Prosser set out in black-letter form what he had found: "The majority of courts which have considered the question have recognized the existence of a right of 'privacy,' which will be protected against interferences which are serious and outrageous, or beyond the limits of common ideas of decent conduct."[71] The black-letter material then recited three of the four now-familiar, separate privacy torts: public

disclosure of private information, intrusion, and commercial appropriation of elements of an individual's personality.[72] Only false light was
not mentioned.[73]

The text of the section then began the stage-setting that Prosser so frequently employed. In this instance, this consisted of discussion of the famous 1890 article on privacy by Warren and Brandeis,[74] the subsequent,
highly prominent rejection of a common law cause of action for commercial appropriation by the New York Court of Appeals in *Roberson v.
Rochester Folding Box*,[75] and its acceptance in Georgia two years later.[76]

The Georgia decision, said Prosser, has been "followed by the majority
of the courts which have considered the question," and he cited eight states
(following Georgia) recognizing the "common law right" (of protection
against commercial appropriation), with either three or four denying it,
and "indications that it will be accepted" in five others (as well as in the
District of Columbia).[77] Prosser then argued that, although the right of
privacy had "commercial aspects," it was only a "phase of the larger problem of the protection of the plaintiff's peace of mind against unreasonable
disturbance." Therefore, the "great majority" of privacy cases were likely
to be "absorbed into the new tort of intentional infliction of mental suffering once it received recognition."[78] As it has turned out, this prediction regarding the growth of the new tort of IIED was overly optimistic, to
say the least.

After making the prediction, Prosser turned to the two other privacy
torts, intrusion on solitude and public disclosure of private facts. Each
of those torts was discussed in a single paragraph. He noted that intrusion on seclusion had resulted in recovery in "a few cases."[79] He certainly
was right about that: he cited only three cases that directly supported
recovery for intrusion on seclusion, two of which were from the same
jurisdiction.[80]

Turning to public disclosure, he had slightly more support for this privacy tort. Here Prosser was able to cite eight cases that directly supported
him, although two of the eight applied California law, and another two
involved disclosure that constituted a breach of confidence and which
might therefore have been distinguished on that basis.[81] A conservative
estimate would therefore be that Prosser had produced six cases in five
jurisdictions which had adopted the full public disclosure tort.[82] The remainder of the section—more than half of it, in fact—turned back to analyze the tort of commercial appropriation and the limitations on recovery.

In view of what Prosser had (and had not) demonstrated with this material, his black-letter statement at the outset that the "majority of the courts which have considered the question have recognized the existence of a right of 'privacy'" must be considered another overgeneralized formulation.[83] He did show that a majority of states that had considered the tort of commercial appropriation had adopted it. But that was a majority of nine out of only twelve states. Most states had not addressed the issue at all.

More importantly, a quick reading of the privacy section, beginning with the opening statement about the "majority of courts," could easily have led the reader to conclude that the majority of courts had already considered the right to privacy more generally, and that the majority of courts had adopted all three privacy torts wholesale. But Prosser's text provided no support for such a reading and did not attempt to do so.

By the time of the second edition (1955), the law had moved in Prosser's direction, and his contention that the tort of invasion of privacy existed in the three forms he had earlier identified was better supported. In the first edition, privacy was a section in a "Miscellaneous" chapter. Now it was a chapter of its own. Prosser said, probably accurately, that "after a half a century the opposition to the tort has all but disappeared."[84] He was able to cite more than a dozen new cases involving intrusion or disclosure, as well as a substantial number of additional cases involving commercial appropriation. And he observed that the tort "appears in reality to be a complex of four different wrongs, which have little in common except that each is an interference with the plaintiff's right 'to be let alone.'"[85] The most noteworthy change in the second edition was that it contained Prosser's first identification of the fourth privacy tort, which he would eventually call "false light."[86]

THE SIMILARITIES between Prosser's treatments of IIED and privacy are striking. In the first edition the material on each subject contained an ambiguous generalization on which a reader consulting a treatise to ascertain the state of the law on the subject would likely focus. The reader of those generalizations could easily have concluded, incorrectly, that there was more case law to support the generalization than a close reading would disclose. Yet in each instance the generalization was literally accurate. Prosser had given himself what we would now call "plausible deniability."

Second, in each instance the weight-bearing material consisted of surprisingly limited nuggets of text and only partially supporting case law, nested within much longer discussions about context and "limitations on recovery," the latter supported by extensive, often string-citing footnotes. Setting aside commercial appropriation, which (despite what Prosser contended) essentially protected a commercial property interest, in his discussion of privacy there were only two weight-bearing paragraphs; in intentional infliction of emotional distress there were only three. The overall impression conveyed to a casual reader was that there existed a substantial body of case law on each subject, and that it supported Prosser's generalizations. In fact, however, the case law was far more sparse than that, and it did not always support Prosser as squarely as he implied.

Prosser and his treatise have long been the subject of anecdotal legend. Over the years, in conversations and elsewhere, we have heard it said that he benefited from what might be called "bootstrapping"—asserting doctrinal propositions based on scant authority, being cited by subsequent courts, and then citing those courts to prop up his earlier assertions.[87] It has also been said that he had a tendency to see "trends" in the law of torts that had surfaced more in his own mind than in the case law.[88] In fact, however, the courts in cases decided in the fifteen years after publication of the first edition of Prosser's treatise rarely cited it. So he really had little opportunity to engage in bootstrapping. In general, his influence, at least in connection with IIED and privacy, was more evident in the academic literature than in the courts.

In light of the dearth of evidence that Prosser had a direct influence on courts deciding IIED and privacy cases during the decade after the treatise was published, the fact of the matter has to be that Prosser simply had a very good sense of the legal moment. He read the social context in which courts would be making decisions, and the impact that those conditions would have on the courts, with exquisite accuracy. His generalizations based on sparse prior case law may have bordered on being misleading, but he was right on target in suggesting that what he said had already happened would soon be happening to a much greater extent.

It is possible, we acknowledge, that even if Prosser's direct influence cannot be seen in citations to the treatise in the cases decided in the 1940s and 1950s, he had an indirect or at least undisclosed influence. The fame of Prosser's treatise, owed mostly to the material on the torts that involve liability for physical harm, may have given cover to the courts that were asked to rule on claims for IIED and invasion of privacy. Although they did not cite the treatise, the courts might well have consulted it, and its few pages about IIED and privacy may have given some courts considering the recognition of these torts comfort—indeed, in a sense unjustified comfort—that doing so would place them in the mainstream of tort law jurisprudence. And so we cannot rule out the possibility that the cases recognizing IIED and invasion of privacy proliferated partly by reason of this form of influence.

Mid-Twentieth-Century Flirtations with Unification

We have been speaking thus far of the "dignitary" torts, implying a potential common character, or unity, among them. We call the recognition of commonalities among different torts, and of the possibility that different torts will eventually be treated as functionally falling under the same umbrella, the idea of "unification." There is not much discussion about ideas related to unification in the recent tort literature. But there was a good deal of discussion for about thirty years in the middle of the twentieth century. Much of that discussion has now been forgotten—we might call it another example of lost history.

The notion that the forms of action had unduly restricted the development of tort liability in the twentieth century surfaced in mid-twentieth-century commentary about the common features of different forms of tort liability generally, and of the dignitary torts in particular. The most prominent torts scholars in that period, varied though they may have been in other respects, shared two related points of view. The first was that nineteenth-century legal formalism was inadequate to the needs of the twentieth century.[89] The second was that such formalism artificially limited tort liability, which required expansion.[90] Those scholars focused much of their attention on liability for accidental bodily injury.[91] Doctrinal limitations on liability for negligence, whether for bodily injury or for other forms of loss, contributed heavily to their dissatisfaction.[92]

By the mid-1960s some of those limitations on liability were being dismantled, and many torts scholars foresaw the same fate for others. They envisioned the development of a more expansive cause of action for negligence, and many thought that this would eventually evolve into strict liability for bodily injury and property damage.[93] This model of movement toward unification through what was happening in the field of negligence liability—and what some tort theorists believed would continue to happen—may be what scholars had in mind, in a vague and general way, when some of them also began to identify a series of different torts that had the common purpose of redressing emotional harm, and others identified torts that protected dignity. Their inchoate visions, which we describe below, are tantalizing evidence of the tort law future they were picturing.

Prosser's early treatment of the IIED and privacy torts suggest that he was interested in their common features, with a view to folding them into a generic action protecting something like the right of individual autonomy. Prosser declared, for example, that the "privacy" torts were essentially about "protection of the plaintiff's peace of mind against unreasonable disturbance."[94] As such, he predicted, "the great majority" of privacy torts seemed likely to be "absorbed" into "the new tort of intentional infliction of mental suffering once it receives recognition."[95]

Prosser's intuition that "privacy" cases might be best understood as a subcategory of cases allowing recovery for emotional harm was shared by a number of other American commentators in the 1930s and 1940s. As they became aware that the courts were tending to award recovery in two sorts of cases, those in which plaintiffs had suffered emotional harm without any accompanying physical injury and those in which plaintiffs had complained of being humiliated, degraded, or embarrassed without any consequent loss of reputation, commentators began to search for the common features linking those cases.

In 1938 Fowler Harper and Mary Coate McNeely attempted to approach emotional harm cases by identifying the "interests" at stake in them.[96] They began by noting that the common interest invaded in such cases was thought to be "the plaintiff's interest in peace of mind, emotional tranquility, or freedom from emotional disturbances," but to describe the cases in that fashion was conclusory, since it equated an "interest" with "its invasion," so a more precise analysis was necessary.[97]

Harper and McNeely then produced a catalogue of "interests" being protected in emotional harm cases.[98] Those interests included "bodily security," "courteous service and decent treatment from public utilities," "the body of the dead," "the memory of the dead," "the life of the unborn," and "domestic relations."[99] The awkward language used to describe some of those interests reflected the fact that they more accurately captured the factual settings in which courts had allowed recovery for emotional harm than doctrinal categories capable of being employed across a range of cases. They also defined the privacy torts so as to emphasize that at bottom they were connected to the maintenance of "emotional and mental tranquility."[100]

The most notable feature of Harper and McNeely's catalogue of "privacy" interests was their identification of an "interest in personal dignity and self-respect."[101] They described that interest as being "offended by insulting and abusive language, by proposals that offend the sense of decency and by the creation of situations which expose the person to ridicule or embarrassment."[102] The "dignity" cases they surveyed had two characteristics. One was the judicial employment of fictions, such as the existence of a property interest, an interest in reputation, or a technical physical touching, to allow recovery where the gist of the action clearly lay in the emotional distress triggered by the defendant's conduct.[103] The other was that virtually all of the cases Harper and McNeely cited involved incidents that occurred in public, and that fact contributed to the plaintiff's distress.[104] Included were cases in which plaintiffs were accused of shoplifting; ordered out of an amusement park, office, or theater; or wrongfully evicted from their homes.[105]

Prosser's and Harper and McNeely's work contained the most extended early treatments of the common features of, or the common interests protected by, actions for emotional harm, with a view toward formulating a generic tort. But there were others. In 1954, for instance, Harry Kalven referred to "emotional dignitary torts," and in 1959 the first edition of Kalven's and Charles Gregory's new torts casebook noted that "the law protects emotional tranquility and personal dignity from intentional invasion under many specific categories" of torts.[106]

We should emphasize that it was never very clear exactly what doctrinal structure Prosser and his mid-twentieth-century colleagues had in mind when they wrote about the commonalities among the dignitary torts. They were not naive enough to think that there could be complete unification of the various causes of action.[107] Exactly what they had in mind, or where they thought the law governing those torts was headed, they never indicated. Perhaps they were simply trying to identify dignity as a common value underlying those various torts, without fully realizing that dignity is a composite concept. Or perhaps, as we noted earlier, they were distracted or even misled by the unification they were contemporaneously seeing and hoping to see develop further in the field of negligence liability. Prosser, never a deep theorist, did not subsequently push the unification theme any further.

On the contrary, Prosser came to believe that the torts he had once thought of as variations on a generic action for "peace of mind" did not have as much in common as he had suspected.[108] Once it became apparent, after the emergence of more such cases, that "privacy" cases were not being absorbed into the category of intentional infliction of emotional distress cases; that the common elements ostensibly connecting those actions—that they sought to redress emotional injuries for conduct thought to be going beyond the bounds of ordinary civil conduct in intentionally disturbing "peace of mind"—were insufficiently precise to explain the several torts; and that the "privacy" torts appeared to be a collection of quite diverse actions, doctrinal clarity would be lost in the unification of intentional infliction of emotional distress and privacy cases.

Prosser's misgivings, however, were not always shared by contemporary scholars. In the next decade other prominent scholars took up the unification theme. They began to search for a more promising way to integrate "privacy" cases with others in which recovery was primarily being sought for emotional harm. In the early 1960s two such commentators launched their searches in reaction to Prosser's "Privacy" article. John Wade was dean of the Vanderbilt Law School, co-author (with Prosser) of the leading torts casebook of the time, and a member of the board of advisors of the *Restatement (Second) of Torts*.[109] Wade sought to revive Prosser's 1941 suggestion that privacy actions amounted to a subcategory of actions seeking recovery for "mental disturbance" and would eventually be absorbed in a generic action for damages based on emotional harm.[110] Wade went further: he attempted to integrate actions for defamation in that generic tort, hoping that by so doing some of the archaic, technical elements of defamation actions might be eliminated.[111]

Wade agreed with a court's statement that the interest protected in privacy cases was "peace of mind," and that in defamation cases the interest was "reputation," but felt that the two areas had enough in common to merit "a careful study" of their relationship.[112] Most of his analysis of privacy cases was designed to show that a large number of them, whether falling into Prosser's categories of disclosure, false light, or appropriation, were about a "false impression" being created of the plaintiff, whether or not that impression lowered the plaintiff's reputation and whether or not statements made about the plaintiff were true.[113]

Wade then suggested that if most privacy cases were "false impression" cases, the overlap between the torts of invasion of privacy and defamation was considerable.[114] This meant that "the great majority of defamation actions can now be brought for invasion of the right of privacy," and consequently, "many of the restrictions and limitations of libel and slander can be avoided."[115] It also meant that "as lawyers come to realize this, the action for the invasion of the right of privacy may come to supplant the action for defamation."[116]

Wade noted that the "anomalies and absurdities" of the common law of defamation had been "condemn[ed] . . . by judges and legal writers" over the years, and that efforts to reform defamation law through judicial decisions had been hampered by "the numerous detailed rules, which have resisted synthesis into broad principles or standards," while "legislative reform" had been "generally ineffective" because it required "a complete revision of the whole system" of defamation law, and legislatures were not willing "to undertake a statutory code covering the whole subject."[117]

Wade believed that "the penetration of the law of privacy into [the] field [of defamation] affords a splendid opportunity for reform of the traditional law regarding the actionability of language which harms an individual's peace of mind or his reputation."[118] The reform could "take the customary common law method of gradual judicial development."[119] "If the law of privacy then absorbs the law of defamation," Wade believed,

it will merely afford a complete "unfolding" of the idea or principle behind that law. Indeed, there is real reason to conclude that the principle behind the law of privacy is much broader than the idea of privacy itself, and that the whole law of privacy will become a part of the larger tort of intentional infliction of mental suffering. That tort would then absorb established torts like assault and defamation and invasion of the right of privacy and join them together with other innominate torts to constitute a single, integrated system of protecting plaintiff's peace of mind against acts of the defendant intended to disturb it.[120]

Two years after Wade's article appeared, Edward Bloustein of NYU Law School embarked on a similar search, seeking to ground a generic action for emotional harm on the protection of "dignity."[121] Bloustein argued that the actions Prosser had identified as protecting "privacy" were only concerned with that interest in a secondary sense: the core interest they protected was rooted in the individuality of private lives.[122] It was an interest in what Bloustein called "the individual's independence, dignity, and integrity."[123]

Bloustein attempted to show that none of the "interests" Prosser's formulation saw privacy actions as protecting were what Warren and Brandeis had associated with "the right of privacy."[124] Rather, another interest lay at the basis of the privacy action. He analyzed each of the privacy actions Prosser had catalogued in an effort to show that they were at bottom actions designed to vindicate and protect human dignity.[125] Bloustein concluded that "our Western culture defines individuality as including the right to be free from certain types of intrusions," and "this measure of personal isolation and personal control over the conditions of its abandonment is of the very essence of personal freedom and dignity."[126] Such intrusions "may be the occasion and cause of distress and embarrassment," but they were "wrongful because demeaning of individuality," whether or not "they cause emotional trauma."[127]

Bloustein next turned to public disclosure cases, concluding that Prosser's characterization of the interest in reputation supposedly being protected in those cases was not only "completely at odds with that of Warren and Brandeis" but "at odds with the cases."[128] Warren and Brandeis had maintained that the right to privacy was "radically different" from defamation because it existed not only "to prevent inaccurate portrayal of private life, but to prevent its being depicted at all."[129]

Bloustein also addressed the "name or likeness" cases, now commonly referred to as appropriation cases.[130] His discussion was largely directed at demonstrating that Prosser's characterization of such cases as invasions of a "proprietary" interest, akin to an interest in property, was mistaken.[131] Bloustein argued that these cases were at least partly about protecting against "assault[s] on individual personality and dignity."[132]

Bloustein had made a powerful argument that the four species of torts which Prosser had grouped under the rubric of privacy could be better understood as dignitary torts. His formulation served to explain why some of those torts, at first glance, did not seem to be protecting privacy at all, and why some appeared to have little in common with others. In addition, his analysis provided an explanation of the reason that Prosser, and then subsequently Wade, had contemplated the possibility that the privacy torts, together with defamation and perhaps other torts such as false imprisonment, assault, and nonphysical battery, might eventually be subsumed in a general action for intentional infliction of mental suffering, representing what Wade called "a single, integrated system of protecting . . . peace of mind."[133] And although Bloustein was not very specific about what the interest in "dignity" was actually composed of, the possibility that "peace of mind"—a combination of respect for the privacy, individuality, and feelings of human beings—flowed from the attribution of an intrinsic dignity in all persons seemed intuitively plausible. Thus, unpacking the "interest" in dignity seemed to be a promising way for commentators and courts to surmount some of the analytical confusion associated with the expansion of privacy actions in torts.

By the mid-1960s Prosser, Wade, Gregory, and Kalven were at the peak of their influence.[134] Bloustein was younger but a member of the faculty at a major law school.[135] Although he soon became president of Bennington College and then Rutgers University, from time to time he still published in law reviews.[136] Had those scholars continued to explore the commonalities among the torts redressing intangible loss, and especially the nature of the dignitary interests many of these torts protect, torts scholarship and tort law's doctrinal structure might have moved in a different direction. The question is why that did not happen.

The Diversity of Interests Protected

Part of the answer is that the interests the dignitary torts protect reflect a diversity of values. Prosser and contemporaries seem never to have clearly recognized the constraints to which this led, although Prosser (as we noted) began to have second thoughts about the issue when writing about privacy in the 1960s.

To reveal the challenge for unification that this phenomenon generates, it is necessary to tease out the different values connected to the concept of dignity. Doing so involves a considerable amount of interpretation on our part, both because the courts often have no need to address the precise interest that the tort under consideration protects and because the courts have had no reason at all to examine what the different actions grouped under the category of "dignitary torts" may or may not have in common.

Each of the dignitary torts protects a core interest although they some-times also protect secondary interests. But the different torts do not protect the same core interest. We have discerned three distinct core in-terests that the dignitary torts protect. At the core are protections against interferences with liberty and personal autonomy; protections against speech or conduct that embarrasses, humiliates, or shows blatant disrespect; and protections against communications that diminish the regard that others have for the plaintiff.

LIBERTY AND AUTONOMY

Certain features of a person's individuality are so central to being human that liberty and autonomy require they be off-limits to others without consent. At the heart of individual liberty and autonomy is control over one's own body. "It's my body" is a sufficient answer to the question why others may not touch you without your consent. Battery protects this interest: even a touching that causes no physical harm is actionable in battery if it "offends a reasonable sense of personal dignity."[137] Spitting on the face of the plaintiff, for example, is an offensive battery.[138] False imprisonment redresses a similar interest. Confining a person against his or her will interferes with personal autonomy.

In the modern world, the secrecy and solitude of one's intimate af-fairs also are essential to individual liberty and autonomy. The form of invasion of privacy often termed "intrusion" protects this interest. As a practical matter, the more intimate the space or setting, the more offensive an intrusion on it is likely to be. Although some cases have held that actually accessing the information obtained by the invasion is not required, clearly the core interest this tort protects is the right to keep others from witnessing, hearing, or viewing what is private and intimate.[139]

Finally, the interest in controlling use of one's name or likeness has an affinity with the interests in controlling one's body and intimate space. One's name and how one looks are an essential part of an individual's identity. Using part of that identity without consent infringes on the in-dividual's liberty and autonomy. The tort of commercial appropriation often protects only the economic interest associated with unauthorized use. But there are also appropriation cases in which the interest protected is the right not to have one's name or likeness involved in commerce at all, or only involved in a manner that is in keeping with one's conception of oneself.[140] These cases protect liberty and autonomy.

There is no doubt that, although the torts of battery, false imprisonment, intrusion, and appropriation primarily protect liberty and autonomy, those four torts sometimes simultaneously, though secondarily, protect other interests. For example, what often makes an offensive battery offensive even in the absence of physical harm is the defendant's intentional disregard of the plaintiff's right not to be touched. The disregard itself demeans the plaintiff, sending the message that the defendant does not regard him or her as worthy of bodily protection. Liability for battery protects against, or redresses, such disrespect. Similarly, an intrusion on private space may produce emotional distress or embarrassment by virtue of what has been witnessed by the intruder—for example, being seen naked by all but one's intimates is embarrassing for most people. Liability for intrusion protects against such embarrassment. And unauthorized use of one's name or likeness in certain circumstances may be embarrassing because of the inaccurate implication such use entails.

But those protections are secondary, and the torts are actionable whether or not those secondary interests are involved, as long as liberty and autonomy have been invaded. However, there is little if anything in the other dignitary torts—defamation, false light, IIED, or even public disclosure—that is directed as strongly at this interest in liberty and autonomy.

EMBARRASSMENT, HUMILIATION, AND DISRESPECT

Two of the other dignitary torts are directed primarily at protecting against embarrassment, humiliation, and disrespect. First, the form of invasion of privacy called public disclosure applies when matter concerning another person's private life is made public. Usually it is offensive to make the information public because it is embarrassing or humiliating.

Second, the tort of IIED is actionable because intentionally inflicting emotional distress on the plaintiff is most demeaning, contemptuous, or disrespectful when the defendant's conduct is extreme and outrageous. In a sense, the fact that this conduct is extreme and outrageous is what makes the conduct demeaning, contemptuous, or disrespectful.[141] IIED also often protects not only against disrespect but also against the embarrassment and humiliation that typically accompany it, although the tort is actionable without them—for example, when the distress a plaintiff suffers constitutes or results from fear or extreme irritation.[142]

In contrast, the other dignitary torts have much less to do with embarrassment, humiliation, and disrespect. Offensive battery and intrusion may sometimes involve these interests since an unconsented touching or an intrusion into intimate matters may produce such emotions. But those torts mainly protect the liberty and autonomy interests we described above. Defamation, false light, and commercial appropriation also are at most concerned only secondarily with embarrassment and humiliation. Those torts focus on the defendant's portrayal of the plaintiff and the resulting way in which others perceive the plaintiff. Embarrassment, humiliation, and disrespect may or may not be consequences of such a portrayal, but protecting against their occurrence is not the central object of the torts.

DIMINISHED REGARD OF OTHERS

Another important feature of one's individuality and therefore dignity in the broad sense turns on the regard of others. We are relational beings; our welfare depends heavily on the regard that others do or do not have for us. As the Supreme Court has said of defamation, "The individual's right to protection of his own good name 'reflects no more than our basic concept of the essential dignity and worth of every human being.'"[143] Defamation, false light, and commercial appropriation (in certain of the cases involving noneconomic loss) centrally protect this interest. The consequences of such interference may sometimes be embarrassment, humiliation, or disrespect, and damages awarded may consist of compensation for this kind of suffering. The principal indignity involved in those torts, however, is that a person has not been portrayed as he or she actually is; the wrong lies in the misrepresentation of something important about oneself.

This is not the core interest protected by the other torts—battery, false imprisonment, intrusion, disclosure, or IIED. Those torts are not concerned with inaccurate portrayal of or misrepresentation about the plaintiff. For intrusion and disclosure, the interest at stake is not accuracy at all but others gaining access to or publicizing something that is in existence and/or is in fact accurate. And for IIED, accuracy has little bearing one way or the other. Emotional distress can be intentionally created by

the assertion of something true, of something false, or by words or conduct that having nothing to do with what is true or false. And of course,
neither battery itself nor offensive battery are concerned in any way with
the regard that others have for the plaintiff.

Consequences of the Incomplete Coincidence of Interests

In describing the interests that the dignitary torts protect, we teased out
a number of different concepts that surface in that analysis: liberty, autonomy, respect, humiliation, embarrassment, the regard of others. It is
no stretch to describe all those terms and the concepts they represent
as involving dignity or infringement of dignity. Each has something to
do with the worth of the individual. In this sense the practice of referring to the torts in question as dignitary is accurate and unobjectionable,
and to some extent assists in understanding what they have in common.
Given this common thread among the torts, it is no surprise that so many
scholarly references to the "dignitary" torts seem to presuppose that what
makes a tort dignitary can go without saying.

Our analysis, however, reveals two difficulties that are entailed in attempting to go beyond this simple labeling. First, even setting aside exactly what constitutes dignity and an infringement on dignity, in at least
some instances the putative dignitary torts also are actionable to redress
non-dignitary interests. Thus, battery can cause physical harm; it may
also be offensive to be physically harmed by an intentional contact, but
obviously the principal concern in such cases is the harm rather than the
offense. Dignity is a secondary interest in most such cases. Defamation
may cause economic harm without infringing dignity, as when someone
is incorrectly said to have died or no longer to be practicing medicine.

In the privacy torts there is a similar division. Intrusion may infringe
dignity, but it may instead simply be objectionable for other reasons, as
when someone observes a business competitor's bank transaction. The
same is sometimes true of false light, and it is obviously true of commercial
appropriation, which is most often about something other than dignity. For
this reason, calling those torts dignitary is a partially inaccurate description. Sometimes this term just does not fit, even if sometimes it does.

Second, dignity is a complex concept, comprising a series of interests.
But not all the dignitary torts protect all those interests. And even when
the torts protect a combination of core and sometimes secondary interests,

they are often different combinations. Offensive battery, intrusion, and certain cases of commercial appropriation are centrally concerned with liberty and autonomy, whereas the other torts are not. Intrusion and IIED are centrally concerned with embarrassment, humiliation, or disrespect, whereas the other torts are not. And defamation, false light, and certain cases of commercial appropriation are centrally concerned with the regard of others for the plaintiff, whereas the other torts are not.

This incomplete coincidence of protected interests goes a long way toward explaining why there has been so little analysis or elaboration of what makes those causes of action dignitary torts. Although dignity is implicated in the torts, they protect different forms of dignity. Those different forms of dignitary protection underwrite the torts, not the more general concept of dignity. Because of the variety of interests involved, the concept of dignity cannot bear much operational weight or do much doctrinal work. Dignity is a general and complex concept from which it would be difficult to deduce rules that would decide particular cases. That is a large part of the explanation for the failure of the concept of dignity ever to be developed in the tort literature or case law addressing particular dignitary torts.

This has had three important consequences. First, often it is not necessary for the courts to make very extended or deep reference to the interests that a particular tort protects. For example, that battery and especially offensive battery at their core protect liberty and bodily autonomy usually can go virtually without saying. Similarly, public disclosure at its core protects the privacy of intimate or confidential information about oneself. Only when a fact situation poses issues at the periphery, rather than at the core, of those and the other dignitary torts is there occasion for a court to drill down into the granular details of the interest that a cause of action protects.[144] This phenomenon naturally impedes the development of self-conscious articulations of the nature of the interests that a particular tort protects.

Second, because different torts protect different core interests but secondarily sometimes protect interests at the core of other torts, there is a complicated and varied overlapping of the interests protected. The whole messy picture discourages efforts to tease out and identify what interests which torts protect. The mere potential for greater descriptive insight without any corresponding doctrinal or operative impact is therefore insufficient to tempt the courts to make the effort.

For those reasons, there has been virtually no examination or analysis of what makes the dignitary torts "dignitary," or of the particular interests that the different dignitary torts sometimes protect in common. A reflexive tendency to label them "dignitary" frequently manifests itself but without any analytical or theoretical follow-up. Our analysis has suggested that such follow-up would have revealed that the torts are related, and some of them closely related, but that not all are related in the same way.

This has led to a third consequence, which implicates the process by which common law tort actions emerge and develop in the United States. Although common law torts may protect multiple and overlapping interests, the theory governing the bringing of tort actions is that each tort is a discrete entity, with its own doctrinal requirements. In that respect actions in defamation, in one or another forms of privacy, and in IIED, although they might each be seen as efforts to redress a loss of "dignity," are treated as separate from one another. Courts and commentators have devoted a good deal of attention to demonstrating why an action based on a set of facts might fail if brought in defamation but succeed if brought in disclosure or in false-light privacy.[145] Their efforts reflect the fact that protecting "dignity" cannot easily be reduced to the vindication of a single interest, or seemingly to the vindication of any interest that lies unprotected in other torts. Thus, there is an inherent incompatibility between the American common law system and the development of any generic tort action designed to protect dignity. In short, we believe that all of these consequences of the incomplete coincidence of protected interests in the concept of dignity can be seen as providing reasons why the project of creating a unified, generic "dignity" tort action never got off the ground.

In addition, as we describe in detail in chapter 4, beginning in 1964 the Supreme Court began to place constitutional limits on the scope of liability under certain of the dignitary torts, most notably defamation. In light of those limits, the opportunities for protecting "dignity" interests have been reduced. It is possible, therefore, that as the dignity of Americans is increasingly violated because those who do so are constitutionally privileged, something like a deadening of the interests in dignity itself has resulted.[146] Constitutional privileges are not merely "balanced" against the interests ostensibly protected by dignitary torts; they serve to reduce the cultural and personal significance of those interests. If previously "unseemly" public portrayals of individuals are increasingly the norm, it becomes harder to ascertain what conduct a society treats as unseemly. Dignitary torts now may be harder to conceptualize, simply because constitutionalization has reduced the space for, and therefore the very meaning of, dignity.

Cultural and technological developments have of course both reflected and reinforced this phenomenon. Once presidential candidates have willingly answered questions about their underwear, and images of individuals in a variety of awkward, humorous, or salacious poses are commonly posted on social media, what counts as an "undignified" or "extreme and outrageous" portrayal becomes increasingly difficult to determine.[147] The importance of dignity itself comes into question, and the practical strength of the torts that protect dignitary invasions wanes as a result.

Conclusion: Broader Implications

It is no surprise that Prosser concluded that his early efforts to conceptualize a cause of action that unified invasion of privacy and infliction of emotional distress had been unsuccessful. He saw that the developing case law did not support him.[148] There was not even a unified cause of action for invasion of privacy, let alone one for interference with dignity.[149] Plaintiffs did not bring suit for invasion of privacy but for intrusion, disclosure, false light, or various forms of appropriation.

If there had instead been a unified cause of action for redress of an interference with one of the many different forms of dignitary invasion, one of two things would have happened. Either liability would have been imposed in some situations in which it would have been normatively unattractive, or the supposedly eliminated distinctions between the elements of the different dignitary causes of actions would have been smuggled back into the calculus, probably by way of application of the concept of a dignitary invasion to different fact situations. Little would have been accomplished substantively; old wine would simply have been poured into new bottles. To take that approach and create a unified cause of action for interference with dignity would have been to reject the common law approach. The American law of torts would have protected an abstract right to dignity but left the content of the right to be filled in over time, through the development of different rules governing the protection of different interests.

This is fundamentally because the character of the law governing the dignitary torts is not simply the path-dependent legacy of the *particular* forms of action that evolved into some of the modern dignitary torts but a reflection of the deep structure of the common law of torts itself. Given that under this structure, each tort is composed of its own separate elements, it is hard to imagine the state of affairs we have just described being otherwise. After all, the causes of action for IIED and invasion of privacy did not exist at all even late in the age of the forms of action.[150] Nonetheless, their development followed the approach of the old forms of action, with different elements being slowly identified, until each separate cause of action could be discerned from the case law.[151] IIED and invasion of privacy were simply new forms of action.[152]

In addition, one of the consequences of the common law process of developing all these causes of action has been to erect boundaries between them that have prevented cross-pollination across torts that protect the same kind of interest. Not only have these boundaries necessarily prevented unification; they have unnecessarily prevented inter-doctrinal enrichment. The forms of action may have long ago disappeared, but their legacy continues to influence the nature of common law reasoning in tort law. The courts simply have no occasion, for example, to observe or rely on the fact that offensive battery and intrusion on solitude each protect a liberty/autonomy interest, or that public disclosure and IIED often protect the same or a very similar interest in avoiding embarrassment or humiliation. The principles that develop in each tort to protect these interests therefore remain separate. There is no synergy among these separate torts, and no mutual influence. There certainly is no recognition that different torts protect a like interest, aside from the occasional use of the label "dignitary" to describe them.

The imposition of constitutional limits on the permissible scope of some but not all of the dignitary torts that we discussed earlier has been yet another obstacle to even partial conceptual unification or cross-pollination of them. The scope of offensive battery, false imprisonment, and intrusion on solitude are unaffected by any such constitutional considerations because they are not accomplished through speech or expression. Each of the other torts, however, is subject to at least some constitutional constraint. The resulting gulf between the elements of the torts that involve speech and those that do not has rendered unification or cross-pollination even more difficult and unlikely. The already-inevitable divisions between the torts have been reinforced by a constitutionally mandated set of separations. The next chapter takes up those constraints and separations. It shows how a different dimension of the history of American tort law, its partial constitutionalization, has influenced the development of tort liability.

4

The First Amendment and the Constitutionalization of Tort Liability

FOR THE first one hundred years of tort law's existence in the United States, there were no constitutional limits on the scope of tort liability. The U.S. Supreme Court expressly held, for example, that despite its guarantee of freedom of speech, the First Amendment placed no limits on liability for defamation, which can only be accomplished through speech of one form or another.[1]

Then, in 1964 all that began to change. The Supreme Court ruled that the First Amendment required limits on liability for defamation, in order to protect freedom of speech. Additional limits followed, both on liability for defamation and on a number of other forms of tort liability that involve speech. There can be no doubt that this constituted a break with the history of the First Amendment, which has since continued to extend its reach in unprecedented ways.[2] And there can be no doubt that in important respects it was also a break from the history of tort law.

Nonetheless, although the First Amendment now applies to certain forms of tortious speech to which it would not have applied in the past, we think that the concerns of the First Amendment and the traditional approach of tort liability to conduct involving speech are largely compatible. First Amendment–directed changes in tort law are generally consistent with much that had been occurring in the torts which are now subject to constitutional limits. For example, tort law has historically depended heavily on the distinctions between truth and falsity, and between facts and ideas, which have figured centrally in the First Amendment jurisprudence of the last half-century or so. Further, in affording privileges protecting against liability for fair comment and for matters of common interest, tort law historically has had its own version of constitutional law's breathing-space rationale for insulating even some forms of false speech.

It would not have been entirely surprising if, had the Court not injected First Amendment considerations into the law of defamation and some forms of privacy beginning in the 1960s, tort law would have become increasingly sensitive to concerns about civil rights and the free expression of ideas on its own. Tort law might have introduced some of the same protections against liability that at that point came to receive constitutional protection. The substance of tort liability for harms involving speech might well have ended up being similar to what the First Amendment has turned out to require.

We will never know whether this counter-history would have come to pass. There is a potential constitutional future, however, on which the history of tort law also has a bearing. Future application of constitutional protection to liability for fraud, other commercial torts, and tortious speech about matters of purely private concern, for example, would constitute a sharp break with both the traditional scope of tort liability and with the principles underlying the provision of First Amendment protection to defamation and the other forms of liability currently subject to constitutional constraint. Although the structure that is now in place is largely compatible with the historical trajectory of the torts that involve speech, extension of First Amendment limitations on the scope of tort liability much beyond where they now stand, we argue, would not be compatible with either the history of tort liability or First Amendment jurisprudence that we recount in this chapter. We propose to explain why this is the case, and why additional constitutionalization of tort actions with speech dimensions would be unsound.

The Rise and Expansion of First Amendment Coverage

The forms of speech to which the Supreme Court has extended First Amendment protection are impressively broad: symbolic conduct,[3] political campaign expenditures,[4] commercial advertising,[5] beer labels,[6] animal abuse videos,[7] video games with violent imagery,[8] the description of additional fees imposed on consumers paying merchants with credit cards,[9] and lying about receiving the Congressional Medal of Honor.[10] Although the established First Amendment restrictions on the permissible scope of tort liability are limited, the very existence of those restrictions suggests that torts involving speech potentially are subject to being brought within the coverage of the First Amendment. Partly as a consequence of recent First Amendment decisions by the Court, forms of tort liability that were once thought to have "nothing to do with the First

Amendment" have now been swept within the amendment's coverage by lower courts or made subject to calls for that coverage by commentators.[11] What makes this possible is that speech—and therefore potential First Amendment coverage—figures in virtually all endeavors, many of which are currently subject to legal regulation of one sort or another. As Justice Elena Kagan recently put it, these and similar possible developments pose the risk of "weaponizing the First Amendment."[12]

Our narrative of developments in late twentieth- and twenty-first-century First Amendment jurisprudence treats those developments as efforts to bring within the ambit of the First Amendment forms of speech previously regarded as *uncovered* by the First Amendment. This treatment is to be distinguished from accounts of those developments as efforts to increase the *level of protection* accorded to forms of speech deemed already to be within the scope of First Amendment coverage. In nearly all current constitutional casebooks the narrative of twentieth- and twenty-first-century changes in First Amendment jurisprudence emphasizes distinctions between "high" and "low" value speech, assuming that Court decisions have primarily been concerned with the level of protection accorded a particular form of speech rather than whether that form is covered by the First Amendment at all.[13] We think that description of the changes is, for the most part, historically inaccurate.

The comparatively late arrival of a robust First Amendment jurisprudence in America—as late as 1919 the Supreme Court had not squarely held that the First Amendment invalidated any restrictions on speech other than "prior restraints" (government censorship of expressions before they had been published)—can be attributed to two factors, one doctrinal and the other cultural. The doctrinal factor was the absence of any application of the provisions of the First Amendment against the states. Since virtually all of the restrictions on expressive activities in the late nineteenth and early twentieth centuries came at the state level, as the states invoked their police powers to promote the safety or morals of their citizens against "subversive" or "offensive" expressions, there were no acknowledged constitutional restraints on those restrictions.

The Court's First Amendment jurisprudence only became more robust when provisions of that amendment began to be applied against the states between 1925 and the 1940s, and free speech challenges were accordingly launched against state statutes criminalizing "subversive advocacy," most commonly in the form of collectivist ideological statements. Beginning in the 1940s cultural pressure to tighten the standards for convictions in subversive advocacy cases began to be reflected in Court decisions that altered those standards from expressions merely having a "tendency" to produce evils that the state had a right to prevent to expressions posing a "clear and present danger" to the existence of the state.[14] And as the tests for subversive advocacy convictions were made more stringent, other sorts of expressive activities engaged in by persons protesting governmental policies emerged, such as picketing in labor disputes, protest marches by member of the civil rights movement, and "sit-ins" at racially segregated restaurants. Those cases were to place pressure on the distinction between "speech" and "conduct" in free speech jurisprudence, and eventually that distinction was abandoned and expressive activities such as wearing clothing displaying political messages were swept into the category of protected "speech."

Eventually the Court articulated a very speech-protective test for subversive advocacy cases, one that gave numerous speakers considerable freedom to make provocative comments about public officials and on public issues that stopped short of direct advocacy of imminent illegal action. And in the second half of the twentieth century, the Court's free speech decisions expanded to focus on forms of expression that hitherto had not been given *any* protection, such as symbolic conduct, campaign finance, commercial speech, defamation, invasion of privacy, and intentional infliction of emotional distress (IIED). The Court's expansion of covered speech amounted to a formidable structure of protection for forms of speech that would otherwise result in a criminal conviction, be subject to regulation, or risk the imposition of civil liability for any harm it caused.

The Initial Twentieth-Century Decisions

The earliest twentieth-century First Amendment decisions permitted the suppression of any speech that had a "tendency" to produce "substantive evils that [the state] had a right to prevent."[15] That standard left much speech bereft of First Amendment protection. Then there were categories of speech that were wholly unprotected. The baseline against which to assess the scope of First Amendment expansion in the mid-twentieth century is the Supreme Court's 1942 decision in *Chaplinsky v. New Hampshire*.[16] *Chaplinsky* contained an extensive discussion and enumeration of "certain . . . classes of speech, the prevention and punishment of which have never been thought to raise any Constitutional problem." Those included "the lewd and obscene, the profane, the libelous, and the insulting or 'fighting' words—those which by their very utterance inflict injury or tend to incite an immediate breach of the peace."[17] The Court observed that the classes of speech excluded from coverage were "no essential part of any exposition of ideas," and "any benefit which is derived from them is clearly outweighed by the social interest in order and morality."[18]

Then, within little more than a decade, the Supreme Court began an expansion of First Amendment protection for speech already regarded as within the amendment's coverage, where government sought to regulate expressions that contained ideas or information allegedly posing a threat to the security of the state. In a series of cases from 1957 through 1969,[19] the Court made it progressively more difficult for Congress, the states, and municipalities to suppress such expressions, culminating in a standard that in subversive advocacy cases "a State [could not] forbid or proscribe advocacy of the use of force or of law violation except where such advocacy is directed to inciting or producing imminent lawless action and is likely to incite or produce such action."[20] This doctrinal evolution garnered considerable attention.[21]

The Court almost never acknowledged, when it was tightening the standards for convictions in subversive advocacy cases or sweeping new expressive activities into the protected category of "speech," that it was making dramatic doctrinal changes. In the Court's opinion in *Brandenburg v. Ohio*, for example, where it formulated a very demanding constitutional standard of proof for subversive advocacy cases, it simply stated that although a 1927 decision, *Whitney v. California*, had held that "without more, 'advocating violent means to effect political and economic change involves such danger to the security of the State that the State may outlaw it,'" *Whitney* had been "thoroughly discredited by later decisions."[22] It only cited one "later decision" in support of that statement, and all that decision had said about *Whitney* was that its employment of the "bad tendency" test for subversive advocacy had been supplanted by a "clear and present danger" test.[23]

The *Brandenburg* opinion then declared that "these later decisions have fashioned the principle that the constitutional guarantees of free speech and free press do not permit a State to forbid or prosecute advocacy of the use of force or of law violation, except where such advocacy is directed to inciting or producing imminent lawless action and is likely to incite or produce such action."[24] No subversive advocacy decision of the Court after *Whitney* had "fashioned" that "principle." The most that could be said of the decisions between *Whitney* and *Brandenburg* is that in some the Court had distinguished between the advocacy of "abstract doctrine" and that of "concrete action."[25] The requirements of "direct" advocacy of "imminent lawless action . . . likely to incite or produce such action" were all supplied by *Brandenburg* itself, and they represented a considerable tightening of the Court's "clear and present danger" standard. None of that was acknowledged in *Brandenburg*. The opinion represents a striking example of a court's cloaking the extent and significance of change accomplished in its decisions.

The tightening of the requirements to criminalize subversive advocacy was, however, not the only, or arguably the most notable, feature of the Court's free speech jurisprudence in the late twentieth century. By the 1970s nearly all of the examples listed in *Chaplinsky* as illustrations of "uncovered" speech playing "no essential part of any exposition of ideas"—"lewd and profane" speech, libelous speech, "insulting or 'fighting' words," "true threats,"[26] "words that provoked a hostile audience reaction,"[27] as well as commercial advertising[28]—had been swept within the First Amendment's coverage.

Symbolic Conduct

In this same period, the Court also struggled to identify the distinction, for First Amendment purposes, between speech and conduct. That struggle was the product of a new context in which speech issues appeared. Beginning in the 1960s, participants in the civil rights movement began organizing protests against racial segregation that took the form of picketing of various businesses, sit-ins in segregated restaurants, and marches in public places in which the marchers held up signs, chanted messages, and congregated in particular spaces.[29] The Court was faced with the question whether, in those situations, expression that took the form of symbolic communicative conduct, rather than actual "speech," could be excluded from the First Amendment's coverage.[30]

The distinction between speech and expressive or symbolic conduct was prominently attacked in 1968 and was inconsistent with the Court's earlier recognition that some forms of expressive conduct amounted to "speech."[31] Subsequently, the Court treated the public burning of a draft card,[32] the wearing of black armbands in a public school,[33] and the unauthorized wearing of a military uniform in a public skit demonstrating opposition to the war in Vietnam[34] as activities engendering some measure of First Amendment protection. And in a 1969 case in which the appellant was convicted for burning the American flag on a public street as a political protest, the Court overruled the conviction because the flag-burning was accompanied by contemptuous comments about the flag.[35]

The culmination of this tendency on the part of the Court to sweep forms of expression that arguably combined "speech" and "conduct" into the ambit of the First Amendment came in the 1971 decision in *Cohen v. California*.[36] Cohen had worn a jacket displaying the words "Fuck the Draft" in the corridor of the Los Angeles County Courthouse. Cohen's message was self-evidently "lewd" and "profane," in the language of *Chaplinsky*, although under the Court's existing definition of obscenity it lacked sufficient erotic content to be "obscene."[37] It was also arguably "fighting words" and words "inciting a hostile audience reaction" because it communicated a message of opposition to and potential resistance to the U.S. government's process for conscripting eligible men into military service. Therefore, applying the language of *Chaplinsky* to Cohen's communication, which the state sought to criminalize as "offensive conduct," there seemed to be no First Amendment issues implicated in Cohen's conviction.[38]

But there were. The majority opinion in *Cohen* took pains to show that under the First Amendment a state could not make non-obscene, "offensive" speech the basis of a criminal conviction. Since Cohen could not have been convicted merely for displaying a message of opposition to the draft, he was being convicted for the words that he used in communicating that message. The argument for state censorship of "offensive" words seemed "inherently boundless": how could one distinguish the word that was sought to be criminalized in *Cohen* "from any other offensive word"?[39]

After *Cohen* it was plain that one category of speech *Chaplinsky* had excluded from First Amendment coverage—"lewd" and "profane" expressions—was no longer outside the ambit of the First Amendment. And the scope of another category—"fighting words" and words provoking a hostile audience reaction—had been narrowed in scope. But the most significant feature of *Cohen*, for our purposes, is that its inroads into the Court's traditional exclusions of categories of speech from the First Amendment's ambit came in a case in which the expression sought to be criminalized was not a traditional form of speech. It was a message neither spoken in public nor written for publication but worn on an article of clothing.[40] This not only continued the process of sweeping a variety of expressive activities into the First Amendment's ambit but also laid the conceptual groundwork for the contention that tortious conduct that is accomplished through speech should be included in that group of protected activities.

MONEY AS SPEECH: CAMPAIGN FINANCE

The Court next turned to a category its recent decisions had made more salient. As we have seen, when speech and conduct were combined in an activity, regulation of the speech elements posed issues that came potentially within the First Amendment's coverage. Consequently, it turned out that even spending money could be the subject of First Amendment protection.

The Federal Elections Act of 1971 established dollar limits on campaign contributions and expenditures in federal elections.[41] *Buckley v. Valeo* was a challenge to the constitutionality of major provisions of the Act.[42] The opinion in *Buckley* treated giving to or spending money on political campaigns as more like "pure speech" than symbolic communicative conduct. Although the Court acknowledged that "some forms of communication made possible by the giving and spending of money involve speech alone, some involve conduct primarily, and some a combination of the two," it added that "this Court has never suggested that the dependence of a communication on the expenditure of money operates itself to introduce a nonspeech element or to reduce the exacting scrutiny required by the First Amendment."[43] It maintained that giving money to and spending money on political campaigns directly implicated the freedoms of political speech and association, since they signaled which candidates and their ideas contributors wanted to associate themselves with, and how those candidates wanted to get their messages across to the electorate.[44]

The *Buckley* decision upheld restrictions on campaign contributions but invalidated limitations on campaign expenditures. Not a single justice in *Buckley* suggested that because sometimes giving money to political candidates and spending money on political campaigns involved activities that were not "pure speech," they were outside the coverage of the First Amendment. At one point in the opinion, in response to the argument that a "governmental interest in equalizing the relative ability of individuals and groups to influence the outcome of elections" served to justify the Act's limitations on expenditures, the Court declared that "the concept that government may restrict the speech of some elements in our society in order to enhance the relative voice of others" was "wholly foreign to the First Amendment," whose "protection against governmental abridgement of free expression cannot properly be made to depend upon a person's financial ability to engage in public discussion."[45]

That was a signal that future efforts to regulate the financing of campaigns would bear a heavy constitutional burden. And in *Citizens United v. Federal Election Commission*,[46] the Court majority asserted that the "antidistortion" rationale for regulating corporate campaign contributions was inconsistent with the *Buckley* proposition that restricting the speech of some elements in society to enhance the relative value of others was wholly foreign to the First Amendment.[47]

The significance of *Buckley* and *Citizens United* for tort law is that those decisions represent the inclusion in First Amendment coverage of yet another category of speech that previously had been thought to fall completely outside of First Amendment protection. If even monetary expenditures on certain forms of speech fall within coverage, then the prospect that tortious speech might be protected becomes all the more conceivable.

COMMERCIAL SPEECH

In a number of cases decided in the period of the Court's early coverage decisions, commercial speech was treated as wholly outside the First Amendment's ambit of protection.[48] Those decisions, when compared with another decision invalidating the application of a city ordinance prohibiting door-to-door distribution of leaflets announcing a religious meeting because the leaflets contained no commercial advertising,[49] suggested that the Court at that point was employing a somewhat opaque definition of "commercial speech," possibly including any instance in which ideas were communicated primarily for profit. Nonetheless, the notion that prohibitions or regulations on "commercial speech," which the Court eventually defined as proposing a commercial transaction, might raise First Amendment issues had begun to creep into the Court's cases in the same time period.[50]

In *Virginia State Board of Pharmacy v. Virginia Citizens Consumer Council,*[51] the Court identified as relevant the interest of prospective consumers and users of commercial products in receiving ideas and information about the state of such products. As Justice Harry Blackmun's opinion put it, "Freedom of speech presupposes a willing speaker," and where "a speaker exists . . . the protection afforded is to the communication, to its source and to its recipients both. . . . If there is a right to advertise, there is a reciprocal right to receive the advertising."[52] It went on to say that "as to the particular consumer's interest in the free flow of commercial information, that interest may be as keen, if not keener by far, than his interest in the day's most urgent political debate."[53] In the case of information about the prices of prescription drugs, the subject matter of the prohibition challenged in *Virginia Pharmacy,* the Court noted that "when drug prices vary as they do, information about who is charging what . . . could mean the alleviation of physical pain or the enjoyment of basic necessities" for some consumers.[54] It followed that "speech which does 'no more than propose a commercial transaction'" was not "so far removed from 'any exposition of ideas'" as to "lack . . . all protection" under the First Amendment.[55] Given the strength of the interest of consumers in receiving information about commercial products and that of advertisers in communicating that information, "no line between publicly 'interesting' or 'important' commercial advertising and the opposite kind could ever be drawn."[56]

At this point, even "classic" commercial speech had been brought within the First Amendment's coverage. But, it turned out, not all such classic commercial speech. Five years after *Virginia Pharmacy,* in *Central Hudson Gas & Electric Corp. v. Pub. Serv. Comm'n of New York,* a case challenging the constitutionality of a statute banning an electric utility from advertising to promote the use of electricity, the Court noted that the classic commercial speech that was protected was *factually accurate* speech. First Amendment protection was afforded to commercial speech, the Court said, only if it is "not misleading," and further indicated that it had not approved a ban on commercial speech in recent years "unless the expression itself was flawed in some way, either because it was deceptive or related to unlawful activity."[57]

TORT LIABILITY

One additional category of speech received extended First Amendment protection during the period when the series of expansions we have described was occurring. In less than twenty-five years, a series of Supreme Court decisions transformed the law governing tort actions involving communication about matters that were of "public concern" or "newsworthy." Those were the torts of defamation, invasion of privacy through the publication of true but private facts or by portraying the plaintiff in a false light, and intentional infliction of emotional distress (IIED).

Some years earlier, *Chaplinsky* had characterized libel and slander as outside the scope of any First Amendment protection. In addition, as far as we can determine, until the late 1960s there had never even been a reference in a Supreme Court opinion to the constitutional status of the torts of invasion of privacy and IIED, which we showed in chapter 3 were creatures of the twentieth-century expansion of tort liability. The strong implication was that the speech associated with those torts also fell wholly outside of First Amendment protection. Before the end of the century, all that had changed.

COMMON LAW LIABILITY FOR DEFAMATION

The tort of defamation, as we saw in chapter 3, had long existed in English and American common law. Defamation is the making of a false statement to a third party ("publication") that injures the defamed individual's reputation. By the middle of the twentieth century its elements, some of them technical, had long been established.[58]

There were two halves of defamation, one strongly protective of reputation at the expense of freedom of expression and the other, counterbalancing half ensuring that there was freedom to speak in situations where speech was valued. To understand how the tort of defamation actually worked, and the extent to which it protected speech through its common doctrinal structure, it is necessary to appreciate both halves.

The first half of defamation provided that there was no requirement that the defendant intend to harm the plaintiff, have been negligent, or even have known that the statement made about the plaintiff was false. Even typographical errors could be a basis for recovery, and republication of defamatory statements made by a third party could result in liability by the republishing party. Certain categories of false statements were actionable even without proof of any out-of-pocket losses by plaintiffs. Nor was the falsity of a defamatory statement an element of the plaintiff's prima facie case; rather, statements damaging to a plaintiff's reputation were treated as presumptively false. In short, there was strict liability, damages were often presumed, and the burden was not on the plaintiff to prove that a defamatory statement was false.

Under the second half of defamation, however, there were counterbalances that rendered the picture more complicated and actually provided a good deal more protection of speech than black-letter summaries of the elements of defamation imply. First, the truth of the defamatory statement, though it had to be proved by the defendant, was an absolute defense to liability. In most states there could be no liability in defamation for making true statements about an individual, even if the motive for doing so was a malicious desire to cause the plaintiff harm. Second, defamation was actionable only for making a false statement of *fact*. There could be no liability for expressing an *opinion* or an *idea*, unless the opinion or idea presupposed a defamatory matter of fact. Third, there was a series of what were called "privileges" that functioned as defenses to an otherwise valid suit.

As Prosser would describe the state of defamation law in 1955, there was an absolute privilege against liability for statements made in legislative, administrative, or judicial proceedings.[59] And there were two important "conditional" privileges. One was a "common interest" privilege that applied to defamatory statements made between parties who had a common legitimate interest in communication about the subject matter of the statement. Examples included most legitimate business communications—employee evaluations, letters of recommendation, and credit reports—but also extended to communications within religious, professional, social, and philanthropic organizations, and statements made among members of a family about matters of concern, such as potential suitors.[60]

There was also a "fair comment" privilege for statements made about matters of public interest, including reports to proper authorities and discussions of public affairs.[61] The majority of the courts had held that this privilege extended only to the expression of opinions, not to statements of fact.[62] But there was a distinct minority position that applied the privilege to statements of fact as well.[63] Under this position, false statements made about public officials or matters of public concern were privileged.

What made the common interest and fair comment privileges conditional rather than absolute was that they protected the maker of a defamatory statement from liability unless the statement had been made with knowledge that it was false or with reckless disregard for the truth or falsity of the statement.[64] This would later be called "actual malice" by the Supreme Court, but it was not given that term at common law. Terminology aside, the standard protected anyone who had an honest belief in the truth of what he said about matters of public interest or concern that were the subject of the common interest and fair comment privileges. The privilege could only be defeated by something like the state of mind (*scienter*) required to commit fraud. For practical purposes, there was a sense in which a defamatory statement to which other privileges applied was actionable only if it amounted to fraud or misrepresentation.

In sum, the common law of defamation gave considerable protection to speech. There was never liability for true statements, no matter how badly they damaged someone's reputation. There was never liability for expressing an opinion or an idea unless it implied facts that were false. There was never liability for making even false statements about matters of common interest unless the maker of the statement knew they were false or had no idea whether they were true or false. And in a minority of jurisdictions there was never liability for making false statements about matters of public interest or concern unless the maker of the statement knew they were false or had no idea whether they were true or false.

By the 1960s the majority rule governing fair comment had come to be perceived as posing a problem from the standpoint of freedom of speech. A majority of states still applied the privilege to opinions but not to statement of facts about public issues. The political and cultural changes that began to occur in the 1960s might well have propelled more common law courts—perhaps even a majority—to redress this deficiency in the privilege, by extending it to statements of fact about matters of public concern. The result would have been a common law barrier to liability for defamation closely analogous to what the Supreme Court subsequently constructed on constitutional grounds. But the Supreme Court's intervention cut off the possibility of common law change in that direction.

A NEW "CONSTITUTIONAL PRIVILEGE"

The suit in *New York Times v. Sullivan*[65] involved an advertisement taken out by the "Committee to Defend Dr. Martin Luther King and the

Struggle for Freedom in the South." L. B. Sullivan, commissioner of public affairs in Montgomery, brought a libel action in the Alabama courts against the New York Times Company and some of the individuals whose names were listed as endorsing the ad. Sullivan, whose responsibilities as commissioner for public affairs included supervision of the police, maintained that some inaccurate references in the ad to "the police," "Southern violators," and "They" could have been understood to refer to him.[66] Sullivan demanded damages in the amount of $500,000, and a jury awarded him the full amount.

The Alabama courts applied the common law rules governing defamation, including the strict liability standard and the presumption of damages that still applied in that tort. Those courts therefore ruled in favor of Sullivan on a whole series of issues that favored plaintiffs such as Sullivan at the expense of the speech rights of defendants such as the *Times*.[67] The case then was appealed to the Supreme Court.

New York Times v. Sullivan came to the Court in 1964, in the midst of the same sorts of civil rights demonstrations in the South that had fostered the Court's symbolic speech cases, contributing to the early stirrings of First Amendment expansion. It was not difficult for the justices to grasp the potential of libel suits to have a "chilling effect" on speech: the *New York Times* case was an ideal vehicle for bringing that feature of defamation law to the forefront.

In an opinion written by Justice William Brennan, the Court set aside the strict liability standard and ruled the award of punitive damages impermissible in Sullivan's suit, on First Amendment grounds. The Court held that, at least when public officials were plaintiffs in defamation suits, they were required to demonstrate that not only were statements about them false and damaging to their reputations but also that the defendant had made the statements with knowledge of their falsity, or with reckless disregard of whether the statements were true or false. It called this *scienter* standard "actual malice." Punitive damages remained available to public official plaintiffs but only when actual malice had been shown. And actual malice had to be shown by "clear and convincing" evidence, not merely a preponderance of evidence.[68]

Brennan's opinion advanced two rationales for conditioning defamation actions against public officials on a showing of actual malice. One was that there was "a profound national commitment to the principle that debate on public issues should be uninhibited, robust, and wide open, and that it may well include vehement, caustic, and sometimes unpleasantly sharp attacks on government and public officials."[69] Belief in that principle was linked to the proposition that the First Amendment was designed to further criticism of the government and those representing it. Commentators recognized that *New York Times v. Sullivan* represented the Court's adoption of Alexander Meiklejohn's "self-governance" theory of the First Amendment.[70]

The other rationale involved the treatment of "factual error." Brennan maintained, citing two previous Court decisions, that constitutional protection for statements did not necessarily turn on whether they were factually accurate. "Erroneous statement is inevitable in free debate," he declared, and "it must be protected if the freedoms of expression are to have the 'breathing space' that they 'need to survive.'"[71] Even false statements of fact that adversely affected the reputations of others were not actionable, where public officials were concerned, absent a showing of malice. A "breathing space" for inaccuracies was sometimes necessary in order to ensure that the freedom to comment on public affairs or on the conduct of public officials was "uninhibited, robust, and wide open." And the *New York Times* ruling implied, without expressly saying so, that imposing the burden of proving the truth of a statement on defendants, instead of requiring plaintiffs to prove falsity in "public official" defamation cases, was incompatible with the First Amendment.[72]

The implications of the decision for defamation law were momentous. A large portion of a category once wholly excluded from First Amendment protection—false statements of fact lowering the reputations of individuals—had been brought within the amendment's coverage, at least where "public officials" were concerned. Only false statements made with "actual malice" were excluded. *New York Times v. Sullivan* thus suggested that many additional defamation suits might raise free speech issues.

That suggestion proved accurate. Between 1964 and 1985 the Court extended First Amendment protection to defamation actions in which defendants were various classes of "public figures," ranging from persons who had achieved "such pervasive fame or notoriety" that they became public figures "for all purposes and all contexts," to persons who "voluntarily inject[ed themselves]" or were "drawn into" particular "public controvers[ies]," to "involuntary public figures" who "become public figures through no purposeful action of their own."[73] In all such "public figure" cases the *New York Times*'s "actual malice" standard had to be met in order to negate a defendant's First Amendment protection.

Although it requires a bit of detail to demonstrate, the Court's expansion of coverage from public officials to public figures was a paradigm example of cloaking the degree to which this extension went beyond the rationale the Court had originally given for applying the First Amendment to defamation suits by public officials. In 1967 the Court decided *Curtis Publishing Co. v. Butts* and *Associated Press v. Walker.*[74] The plaintiffs in the cases were not public officials: Wally Butts, the University of Georgia's football coach, had his salary paid by a private alumni organization, and Edwin Walker, a former U.S. Army general, had led college students in an attack on federal marshals enforcing a desegregation order at the University of Mississippi.

A plurality of the Court declared that the *New York Times* privilege in defamation cases extended to "public figures" as well as "public officials." The central rationale for injecting a free speech privilege into the common law of defamation had been the freedom of citizens to criticize their government and participate in public affairs. Since neither Butts nor Walker were public officials, it was hard to see how false and damaging comments made about them constituted criticism of the government. On the other hand it was plain, by the 1960s, that a class of visible persons—"celebrities"—had emerged in entertainment, sports, and business circles whose careers and lives were of comparable interest to the media and to the public generally as holders of public offices.

Chief Justice Earl Warren's plurality opinion in *Butts* and *Walker* represented the sole effort on the part of the Court to analogize "public figure" to "public official" status. Warren noted the post–World War II blurring of the lines between "the governmental and private sectors," so that not only had more power become consolidated in private enterprises but those institutions often worked closely with government, helping it to set and execute policy. He also noted that "public figures," by virtue of their visibility and prominence, had greater opportunities to counter erroneous allegations made about them in the media and other outlets. Finally, he claimed that "our citizenry has a legitimate and substantial interest in the conduct" of "public figures," apparently because of their celebrity status. Consequently, people should be as free to "engage in uninhibited debate" about their lives and careers as they were to comment on public officials.[75]

Warren, however, obscured the significant doctrinal change that *Butts* and *Walker* had made in the constitutionalization of defamation law by cloaking the new rule regarding public figures in the inapposite rationale that applied to public figures. He had shifted the rationale for a constitutional privilege to make false and damaging statements about certain defamation plaintiffs from "self-governance," as embodied in a breathing space to make inaccurate statements about persons holding public office, to something like "substantial public interest." Public officials represented government, so criticism of them was a version of self-governance. Visible private citizens were simply that: persons whose activities or occupations brought them into the public eye. It was hard to know why a speaker's substantial interest in the conduct of a celebrity should, as a constitutional matter, give the speaker a privilege to make false and damaging statements about the celebrity so long as they did not meet the standard of constitutional malice.

Yet Warren's opinion in *Butts* and *Walker* proceeded as if, as he put it, "differentiation between 'public figures' and 'public officials' and adoption of separate standards of proof for each has no basis in law, logic, or First Amendment policy."[76] What Warren had actually done in his opinion, rather than showing the legal or logical doctrinal connections between the *New York Times* and the *Butts* and *Walker* cases, was to emphasize a dimension of social policy that he took to be vital, the fact that many private celebrities, in post–World War II America, had become even more interesting to the citizenry at large than holders of public office. Warren seemed to believe that the enhanced public interest in celebrities required giving the public greater "breathing space" to make false and damaging comments about them. He gave the impression that the *Butts* and *Walker* decisions were merely logical extensions of the *New York Times* decision, a kind of doctrinal reorganization of constitutional privileges in defamation law. That was an example of judicial cloaking because the decisions did not follow from the rationale the Court had given in *New York Times*.

MATTERS OF PUBLIC CONCERN AND THE STATUS OF OPINIONS

At the same time that it was elaborating the scope of First Amendment protection afforded to speech about public officials and public figures, the Court turned to actions by private figures about matters of public concern. In *Gertz v. Robert Welch, Inc.* it held that in such cases the First Amendment also constrained the scope of constitutionally permissible liability but only by precluding strict liability.[77] The First Amendment required that in such cases the plaintiff prove at least that the defendant had been negligent with respect to the falsity of a defamatory statement. Further, "presumed" damages, a regular feature of defamation suits at common law where a plaintiff could recover damages from showing a lowering of reputation without any proof of out-of-pocket loss, were no longer available without proof of "actual malice" as defined in *New York Times v. Sullivan.*

Justice Lewis Powell began his opinion for the Court in *Gertz* by saying,

> We begin with the common ground. Under the First Amendment *there is no such thing as a false idea*. . . . But there is no constitutional protection for false statements of fact. Neither the intentional lie nor the careless error materially advances society's interest in "uninhibited, robust, and wide open" debate on public issues.
>
> Although the erroneous statement of fact is not worthy of constitutional protection, it is nevertheless inevitable in free debate. . . . The First Amendment requires that we protect some falsehood in order to protect speech that matters.[78]

Powell very likely intended to mean that, although false statements of fact had no value in themselves, the First Amendment required some protection even for factual "falsehoods" that were "inevitable in free debate." That suggestion seemed consistent with Brennan's *New York Times* opinion, which, before announcing the principle that debate on public matters needed to be "uninhibited, robust, and wide open," had cited previous decisions suggesting that some "inaccuracies" in debates on public issues were inevitable and should not be made a basis for constraining debate on such issues.[79]

Then, in 1990 the Court decided *Milkovich v. Lorain Journal Co.*,[80] a case in which a high school wrestling coach brought a defamation action against an Ohio newspaper. The newspaper had published a column about a hearing that was investigating allegations the coach had incited a brawl at a wrestling match. A headline to the column read, "Maple [the high school in question] Beat the Law with the 'Big Lie,'" and the columnist stated that "anyone who attended the [match] . . . knows in his heart that [the coach] lied at the hearing after . . . having given his solemn oath that he would tell the truth."[81] The Court used the occasion to review the question whether the First Amendment should be understood as granting protection for "opinion," even where a statement arguably phrased as an opinion ("anyone who attended the [match] . . . knows in his heart that [the coach] lied") contained a suggestion that the speaker was possessed of underlying defamatory facts. A majority concluded no, and although two dissenters disagreed that the statement about the coach could reasonably be understood as stating or implying underlying defamatory facts, they agreed that there was no independent First Amendment privilege for "opinion."[82] The *Milkovich* case has thus come to stand for the proposition that a defendant cannot deflect a claim that he or she made a false statement of fact about another merely by declaring that the statement was couched as an opinion.

Despite the extensions of the *New York Times* ruling over the next two decades, there were limits to the constitutionalization of defamation law. It was limited to statements about public figures and matters of public concern. When the subject matter of the defamation involved a private citizen on a matter "not of public concern," no First Amendment protection applied. It was therefore possible for plaintiffs in "private/private" suits to recover presumed and even punitive damages without a showing that the defendant had been negligent in issuing a false and defamatory statement, as the Court apparently held in a case where the solvency of a corporation had been negligently reported to a limited group of investors in a confidential report by a credit agency.[83] In cases involving public plaintiffs or matters of public concern, however, defamation law had been fully constitutionalized. And as a practical matter, this meant that the First Amendment limited the liability of virtually all traditional media defendants because most of what they published was a matter of public concern.

These developments between 1964 and 1990 were undoubtedly revolutionary from the standpoint of constitutional law. Never before had constitutional issues been seen as being implicated in defamation law; after *New York Times* the Court had transformed that body of law. But if one considers the changes instituted by *New York Times v. Sullivan* and its progeny alongside existing doctrines in the common law of defamation, the core doctrinal structure of defamation law and the post–*New York Times* development can be seen as having more in common than might first appear. At common law the conditional privileges for matters of common interest and fair comment had given protection against liability for damage to reputation caused by false defamatory statements in order to encourage the making of true statements. The undoubted policy behind those privileges was to help ensure that honest people were not inhibited from engaging in the forms of communication that were necessary to the ordinary business of life by the fear of liability for having made a statement honestly believed to be true that turned out to be false.

Although, to the best of our knowledge, no one ever described this underlying common law policy as affording what the Supreme Court in *New York Times v. Sullivan* would call giving "breathing space" to speech, that is exactly what the policy was. The common law was affording breathing space for true speech by refraining from imposing liability for harm to reputation caused by some forms of false speech. The purpose of those common law privileges was to avoid chilling true speech.

EXTENSION OF THE CONSTITUTIONAL PRIVILEGE
TO INVASION OF PRIVACY AND IIED

Once defamation actions involving public figures and issues of public concern were treated as within First Amendment coverage, other torts with communicative dimensions became candidates for comparable treatment. One form of invasion of privacy, public disclosure of true private information, was actionable at common law if a disclosure would be "highly offensive to a reasonable person" and the matter disclosed was not of "legitimate concern to the public."[84] In a number of cases involving the public disclosure tort, the Supreme Court found that the defendants had First Amendment protection. The cases emanated, for example, from the inclusion in a newspaper story of the name of a rape victim[85] and the disclosure, on a radio broadcast, of an incriminating telephone conversation illegally wiretapped.[86] Public disclosure in such situations was not subject to liability at all when the facts disclosed were in public records.[87] When this was not the case, the courts balanced the interests in seclusion, dignity, and autonomy against the public's right to know, holding that the test was whether the private information revealed was "newsworthy."[88]

The Supreme Court obviously was going further in protecting speech than the common law courts in such cases had done. The imposition of liability in common law true disclosure cases had reflected common law courts' application of the requirement that the facts of a disclosure be "of legitimate concern to the public" to be privileged. In contrast, the Supreme

Court's test was that the disclosure not be "newsworthy" in order to fall outside of First Amendment protection. But the two requirements are analogous and serve roughly the same function—providing that disclosure of wholly private matters remains subject to liability, while ensuring that there would be no liability where a disclosure involves information connected to the public's right to know about matters of public concern. The Supreme Court simply weighed "newsworthiness" more heavily than some courts in common law cases had done. The overall purpose and interest-reconciling structure of both the common law and the new constitutional privilege were closely analogous.

Two of the three other privacy torts also were made subject to the First Amendment, leaving only "intrusion on seclusion" outside its coverage. False light was actionable at common law when the defendant publicized matter that placed the plaintiff in a false light which would be highly offensive to a reasonable person.[89] Probably the same common law privileges that were available in actions for defamation would have been available in false light, although we have not found any cases addressing the issue. Addition of a constitutional privilege to false light liability was therefore no more of a break with the past than it was in defamation. In a case involving a magazine article on a family's being held hostage by escaped convicts,[90] the Court held that the false light form of the tort was subject to the same constitutional privilege as in defamation cases.[91]

Misappropriation of the plaintiff's name or likeness also turned out occasionally to implicate First Amendment concerns. The filming and broadcast, on a local television station, of the "entire act" of a man shot from a cannon at a county fair[92] and the "creative" use of characters resembling real people in comic book science fiction[93] were both treated as raising First Amendment issues, although no privilege was accorded in the former case, apparently because the plaintiff's "entire act," which lasted less than two minutes, was filmed and broadcast without his permission.[94] In cases involving the commercial use of one's name or likeness, the issue of the First Amendment's protection for artistic "appropriations" was resolved through a rule that protected "transformative" uses.[95] Those new constitutional limits had no express analogues in common law appropriation doctrine, but had there not been constitutional intervention, we suspect that over time they would have been handled similarly by the common law, probably by interpretation of what it meant, or did not mean, to engage in an "appropriation."

One additional tort was constitutionalized in a similar fashion in the decades following *New York Times v. Sullivan*. In 1988 the Court ruled that a parody of the prominent evangelist minister Jerry Falwell in *Hustler* magazine, although it qualified as sufficiently "extreme and outrageous" to meet the Virginia standard for intentional infliction of emotional distress, was protected under the *New York Times* line of cases because it amounted to satiric comments about a public figure.[96] And in 2011 the Court extended that ruling to statements that might have been expected to cause severe distress but were nonetheless constitutionally protected speech about matters of public concern.[97] The latter case involved signs displayed in the vicinity of a funeral for a soldier killed in Iraq that condemned "Fag Troops," asserted that "Priests Rape Boys," and contained the message "Thank God for Dead Soldiers." In both cases the Court found the expressive conduct to be protected under the First Amendment because it was directed at a public figure or associated with a matter of public concern.

Unlike what had been the case for defamation and public disclosure, there certainly was nothing in common law IIED jurisprudence up to this point reflecting analogous kinds of limitations on liability. Unlike the privileges that had applied in common law defamation and that the Supreme Court had fashioned to apply to defamation for First Amendment purposes, there was no evident breathing-space rationale underlying the constitutional limitations on liability for IIED. Rather, there was a more straightforward application of free speech values in public figure and public issue contexts to this form of liability. The free speech values simply trumped the interests that IIED protected, rather than their being some form of compromise between free speech concerns and those interests. This represented much more of a break with the common law past than the decisions that had partially constitutionalized defamation, public disclosure, false light, and appropriation.

The Current Status of First Amendment Coverages

There have been no significant Supreme Court decisions regarding the application of the First Amendment to tort liability in over three decades. Nonetheless, there can be little doubt that the scope of First Amendment coverage is as broad or broader than ever. Three decisions during the last decade and a half, in which the Supreme Court applied and reflected on its First Amendment jurisprudence, confirm that the principal inquiry in

cases perceived as raising First Amendment issues is whether a particular form of speech is within or outside coverage of the amendment, and
the forms of speech in the former category are growing.

Thus, in *United States v. Stevens*[98] the Court struck down a statute
criminalizing depictions of animal cruelty, as applied to certain videos showing graphic illustrations of animals being crushed to death. In
Brown v. Entertainment Merchants,[99] the Court held that a California
statute prohibiting the sale or rental to persons under eighteen of "violent
video games" violated the First Amendment.[100] And in *United States v.
Alvarez,*[101] the Court held that the federal Stolen Valor Act, which made
it a crime to falsely claim the award of military decorations or honors and
added a penalty if the Congressional Medal of Honor was involved, did
not pass constitutional muster.

In each case the principal opinion for the Court gave illustrations of
categories of speech that were not covered by the First Amendment. The
most exhaustive of those lists came in *Alvarez:* "advocacy intended, and
likely, to incite imminent lawless action; defamation not subject to *New
York Times* or *Gertz;* speech integral to criminal conduct; so-called 'fighting words'; child pornography; fraud; true threats; and speech presenting
some grave and imminent threat the government has power to prevent."[102] The Court described the categories as "limited areas" where the
First Amendment "has 'permitted restrictions on the content of speech,'"
and "categories of expression where content-based regulation is permissible."[103] In *Stevens* the Court added that, although it was not concluding
that the list of uncovered categories of speech had been exhausted, any
creation of further categories of speech not covered by the First Amendment would need to rest on a showing that a category had "historically
been treated as unprotected."[104] The plurality opinion in *Alvarez* followed
that formulation.[105]

Setting aside the descriptive awkwardness of those efforts to identify
cases outside the coverage of the First Amendment, the substantive message is clear: there are only limited categories of speech that *do not* fall
within the coverage of the First Amendment. The next question, therefore, is what the First Amendment may have in store for the forms of tort
liability that it has not yet affected.

Tort Law and the Future First Amendment

We have now explained how the expanding scope of the First Amendment led to the addition of categories of covered speech and to the consequent placement of constitutional limits on liability for torts that sometimes or always involve speech or expression: defamation, invasion of privacy, and intentional infliction of emotional distress. Those are not the only torts, however, that may involve speech or expression. There are a number of other torts in which the tortious activity emanates from speech or communicative conduct that, in our view, do not implicate First Amendment concerns. These include fraud, negligent misrepresentation, product disparagement, the duty to warn in products liability, intentional interference with contract, and intentional interference with prospective economic advantage.

We organize our analysis by reference to the three dimensions of assessment that have figured in the Supreme Court decisions we have discussed: the distinctions between facts and ideas, between matters of public and private concern, and between true and false statements of fact. Each of the speech torts mentioned above has thus far fallen outside the coverage of the First Amendment for good and sufficient reasons. None of them implicates any of the concerns that those distinctions reflect. For this reason, tort law's past, and what we predict will be the First Amendment's future, will in our view remain continuous and compatible.

IDEAS VERSUS FACTS

It is clear from the Supreme Court's reasoning that a primary consideration in First Amendment jurisprudence involves the distinction between the expression of ideas, which tend to receive First Amendment protection, and statements of fact, which receive less or no protection. In the context in which it was made, Justice Powell's statement in *Gertz* that, under the Constitution, there is no such thing as a false idea may be overbroad, but at the least it means that the First Amendment precludes imposing liability for the expression of an idea when falsity is an element of the tort in question.[106] Because none of the torts that currently are uncovered by the First Amendment involves the expression of an "idea" in this constitutional sense of the term, First Amendment concerns do not extend to any of them.

There is no canonical definition of what counts as an "idea" for First Amendment purposes, but the kinds of statements that have been treated as a basis for imposing liability under the torts we are considering do not fall into any reasonable definition of an idea. Admittedly, the fact-idea distinction is not as sharp as Powell's language in *Gertz* suggested. Sometimes there is no bright line between "false ideas," which are invariably protected, and false statements of fact, which are unprotected or (under *New York Times* or *Gertz*, for example) only partially protected. Although ideas cannot always fully be disentangled from underlying facts associated with them, when those facts are false, ideas associated with them become tainted with that falsity and the reasons for treating them as protected First Amendment speech drop out of the picture. In tort law, when the assertion of what seems to be an idea is made a basis for tort liability, it is because the idea was predicated on false facts. And none of the speech torts we are considering here imposes liability for expressing a pure idea.

Warnings can be understood as expressions of fact—in each instance, a warning states facts about risks posed to the intended recipient of the warning. It is true that warnings are not only communications about empirical facts. Rather, they reflect opinions about which risks do and do not exist, which risks are not already known by intended recipients, which risks are significant, and which risks are insignificant enough to be omitted from a warning. These are not ideas, however, but opinions that, in the *Milkovich* sense, implicitly rely on a factual premise.[107] Similarly, when a warning fails to disclose risks associated with a product that are serious enough that they reasonably should have been communicated, the nondisclosure is either a false or misleading statement of fact or a false or misleading statement of an opinion ("users need not concern themselves with any risks of the product that are not disclosed") based on a false factual premise.

For essentially the same reasons as for product warnings, fraud, negligent misrepresentation, and product disparagement do not involve actionable assertions of ideas. Both fraud and negligent misrepresentation are actionable only on the basis of a (false) statement of fact. Even advice negligently given through misrepresentations by lawyers and accountants, and the assessments given by such nonprofessionals as soil testers and title searchers, rely on underlying facts. A lawyer advising a client is typically giving advice that is premised on underlying facts, in which instance the advice is tainted if the facts are false and the advice actionable if "unreasonable." Similarly, to the extent that a statement disparaging a product is superficially something other than a pure statement of fact, it is an opinion that presupposes a fact about the product in question, or it does not constitute a disparagement at all.[108]

Finally, although in theory statements constituting intentional interference with contract or prospective economic advantage could be ideas, in practice that is extraordinarily unlikely. Statements that accomplish actionable interferences are designed to persuade a particular recipient to engage or not to engage in a business transaction. As efforts at persuasion, such statements offer reasons for breaching contracts or taking other actions. The reasons typically constitute opinions premised on asserted facts, such as the reason that the listener or hearer would be economically better off breaching or taking other action.[109]

It is true that, in principle, anything might be offered as a reason in such cases for doing what the defendant suggests, including reasons based on a genuine idea rather than an opinion premised on a fact. "Breach your contract with Exxon because Exxon's promotion of fossil fuels is destroying the planet" might or might not be a "genuine idea." But, as a practical matter, it will rarely have a persuasive effect, and therefore will rarely be the basis for one of the interference actions.

In short, the distinction between facts and ideas, whatever its role in determining the constitutional protections that are available in defamation, privacy, and IIED, plays only a minimal role in connection with other torts with speech dimensions because those torts virtually never involve the imposition of liability for the expression of ideas.

THE PUBLIC-PRIVATE DISTINCTION

It is a fair generalization from the Supreme Court decisions that expression about matters of purely private concern rarely if ever warrants First Amendment protection. A defamatory statement is completely unprotected, for example, when it is made about a "private citizen" plaintiff on a subject deemed not a matter of public concern. The maker of the statement receives no First Amendment "breathing space" protection. We have also noted that the Court's decision in *Dun & Bradstreet* made it clear that First Amendment coverage does not extend to defamation suits between private parties when the alleged defamatory statement does not involve a matter of public concern. Similarly, in *Snyder v. Phelps*, the Supreme Court appeared to limit the First Amendment protection provided to statements alleged to constitute intentional infliction of emotional distress to matters of public concern.[110] And First Amendment protection is afforded against liability for public disclosure of true private facts only when they are "newsworthy."[111]

The Court has not made a blanket statement that First Amendment protections are inapplicable to *any* tort suit involving a matter of private concern only, but that is certainly a reasonable inference to draw from the case law. The Court's statement in *Virginia Pharmacy* that it would not distinguish between publicly interesting or important advertising and the "opposite kind," should be read, we think, as limited to publicly disseminated and widely available statements.[112] In effect, the Court was holding that such communications are necessarily matters of public concern, or subject to the same constitutional treatment as such matters, for much the same reasons.

It follows that virtually all of the torts of interference with contract and with prospective economic advantage would fall outside of First Amendment protection. The statements at issue in actions alleging those forms of tortious conduct almost always are private communications, between private parties, about matters involving their businesses or professions. Only rarely do such actions involve matters of public concern. It is possible to imagine reasons of "public concern" for such interferences, but such cases are rare (we mention a few below). Moreover, the actions do not require falsity; indeed, in most of the settings in which they appear the plaintiff is not complaining about the misleading character of the defendant's action, only that it existed.

The same is true of most cases involving nonproduct warnings as well. Disclosure of material medical information in order to obtain informed consent from a patient involves a matter of private concern, as do virtually all warnings provided, or that should have been provided, to licensees, a category consisting mainly of the social guests of the owners or renters of private property. And the subject matter of most actions for fraud and negligent misrepresentation is limited to matters of private concern that also would eliminate them from protection.

Finally, the elements of fraud and product disparagement fall squarely into the exception for any breathing space protection that they might otherwise warrant. Fraud consists of a statement of fact made with knowledge that the statement is false, or in reckless disregard of the truth or falsity of the statement. Product disparagement is also not actionable unless the defendant satisfied this same *scienter* standard—a false statement about another's product must be made with knowledge that the statement is false or in reckless disregard of its truth or falsity.[113]

No decision of the Supreme Court has held that the First Amendment places limits on the scope of tort liability for statements made with this sort of constitutional malice. Indeed, the holding of *New York Times* is that the breathing-space rationale for protecting false statements about public officials from defamation liability runs out when a statement is made with this form of malice. There is no reason to think that fraud or product disparagement actions are subject to even greater constitutional protection than defamation. Consequently, although they involve communication, the torts of fraud and product disparagement should always be understood to fall outside the scope of First Amendment protection because liability is never imposed for those wrongs under conditions that could trigger this protection. The torts are unprotected *per se.*

The Truth-Falsity Distinction

Falsity has a much lower constitutional value than truth. The protection that *New York Times* and *Gertz* extends to false statements of fact exists only for prophylactic and instrumental reasons. The decisions provide protection (in varying degrees) against tort liability for certain false statements of fact in order to provide "breathing space" for speech that does have constitutional value. This is speech pertaining to matters of public concern or speech that is "newsworthy."

For this reason, false or misleading commercial speech receives no constitutional protection. *Virginia Pharmacy* made it clear that there is no automatic exemption of commercial speech from First Amendment coverage. But that decision applied to the regulation of commercial advertising. It has been understood in subsequent cases, and especially in *Central Hudson*, not to mandate First Amendment protection of false or misleading commercial speech. For this reason, product warnings would clearly fall outside the reach of First Amendment protection. Warnings result in liability only if they are not "adequate," either because they are false statements of fact or misleading inferences about the product's risks. And of course, most fraud, negligent misrepresentation, and product disparagement cases also involve false commercial speech and therefore would fall outside of constitutional protection for that reason as well.

The distinction between unprotected false statements of fact and other forms of speech highlights a fundamental dynamic that implicitly is reflected in both tort law and free speech jurisprudence. Protecting some speech presupposes that other forms of speech which remain outside protection may be regulated, inhibited, or suppressed through the imposition of tort liability without raising First Amendment concerns. The consequence is a signal about what forms of speech are culturally valued and what forms of speech are not. Not including most false statements of fact within a tort law privilege or the coverage of the First Amendment can thus be understood as an implicit recognition that such statements have a lower cultural value than some other forms of speech within the amendment's coverage.

It follows that the more additional forms of tortious speech and speech-related conduct are brought within the coverage of the First Amendment, the more difficult it may be to determine what forms of speech are truly valued in American culture. If First Amendment protections were extended to nearly all forms of speech—including the torts involving speech that are not now covered by the First Amendment—speech arguably would cease to become culturally special; it might even tend to become the equivalent of noise. The more categories of speech that are swept within the coverage of the First Amendment, the less those categories may be seen as vitally important. This dilution effect thus can influence perceptions regarding not only protected but also unprotected forms of speech.

Consider the claim that statements made about an individual or an event are "fake news." A straightforward way to understand that claim is that the statements are factually inaccurate, being invented by someone with an interest in falsely reporting the matter. But the claim may be more commonly understood, in contemporary American culture, as operating at a deeper level. It may be understood as suggesting that all "facts" are capable of being constructed by those who report them; they have little objective reality in the face of the "spin" that accompanies them. The idea of "fake news" suggests that manufacturing such "news" is comparatively easy because "true news" is elusive. Factually objective reality is so easily capable of being transformed and distorted in its reporting, the argument goes, that it is sometimes impossible to know what the "truth" is. If that is the case, a person distressed at the reporting of information about him or her can simply label the information "fake," and because of the perceived great capacity of individuals reporting factual information to distort it for their own purposes, thereby undermine its authenticity.

If American culture reached an epistemological state in which truth was widely perceived to be the equivalent of constructed truth, the idea of objective factual reality might well be deemed elusive, and the truth-falsity distinction might have far less salience, both culturally and constitutionally. We think that the very persistence of the truth-falsity distinction in tort law and in First Amendment jurisprudence, however, suggests we have not reached that point. Were we to do so, both tort law and First Amendment jurisprudence might become incoherent.

Doctrinal incoherence in a legal field is reached when the field's core distinctions have become unintelligible. If the First Amendment to the Constitution is designed to protect government from abridging "freedom of speech," we need to know what "speech" is protected. If protected speech extends to any sort of utterance, true or false, public or private, benign or malign, meaningful or nonsensical, the term "protected speech" would cease to have any meaning. This is why, we believe, the truth-falsity and public-private distinctions in First Amendment and tort law jurisprudence matter and will continue to matter. Those distinctions help us understand what speech we value and devalue. As such they can serve as useful bases for excluding, or partially excluding, torts with speech dimensions from the pressures of the First Amendment.

Defamation, invasion of privacy, IIED, and a few very narrow categories of other torts with speech dimensions are subject to First Amendment protection and therefore clearly are not outside the amendment's coverage, though they once were. But the protection applied to those torts has limits—it does not apply, depending on the circumstances, when a statement at issue is false and made with malice or negligence, or when a false statement is commercial speech, or when a false statement involves a matter of purely private concern. And in our view that is where matters should, and in all probability will, remain, despite the pressures generated by the First Amendment among other things, because of the potential dilution effect on "speech value" that would be created were more torts brought within the First Amendment's coverage.

WHAT REMAINS: THE VERY LIMITED EXCEPTIONS

What is left for potential First Amendment protection, then, are slivers of liability under some torts with communicative dimensions that do not automatically fall outside of protection for the reasons we have already discussed, or that also implicate breathing-space concerns.

First Amendment protection may legitimately be afforded, for example, to interferences with prospective advantage (and perhaps contract as well) that occur because of matters of public concern. Those rare cases merit First Amendment protection under current doctrine. In *Missouri v. National Organization for Women, Inc.*, for example, the state of Missouri sued an organization that discouraged groups from holding conventions in that state because it had not ratified the Equal Rights Amendment.[114] The court held, on common law grounds, that this "interference" was not an improper interference. And in *NAACP v. Claiborne Hardware Co.*, a civil rights organization encouraged a boycott of white merchants,[115] but the Supreme Court held that the boycott constituted constitutionally protected activity. The communications in both settings deserve First Amendment protection because they involve statements—apparently true statements—that pertained to matters of public concern.[116]

Conclusion

How can we explain the important extent to which the expanded coverage of the First Amendment only modestly affected the doctrinal structure of common law principles and privileges that had developed in tort cases with speech dimensions? In addition, how can we be confident that, despite the expansive momentum of First Amendment decisions, many other tort actions in which speech can be seen as an element of tortious activity will not be brought within the First Amendment's coverage?

The First Amendment certainly has affected tort liability in important ways. Defamatory speech was one of the early prominent examples of a category of speech once excluded from the First Amendment's coverage being swept within it. And once that occurred, some other tort actions with speech dimensions followed: most forms of privacy and intentional infliction of emotional distress. We believe that the general impression of commentators is that the partial constitutionalization of tort law has been a massive late twentieth-century constitutional development.

But we are suggesting otherwise and have emphasized two reasons. The first is that if we look carefully at the doctrinal structure of the torts that have been partially constitutionalized, and especially at the elements, privileges, and defenses in defamation, the various forms of privacy, and intentional infliction of emotional distress, their cumulative effect was always to create "breathing space" for speech and expressive conduct that would otherwise have been actionable. At first glance the common law of defamation, privacy, and IIED may appear tilted in favor of plaintiffs, with doctrinal rules seemingly giving assiduous attention to interests in reputation and various types of privacy, as well as the interest in being free from persistent harassment or publicly unpleasant conduct. A closer look reminds us that attention to the common law elements of those torts, with their emphasis on false and damaging statements of fact, "offensive" disclosures of true information, the painting of individuals in a "false light," the absence of "transformative" commercial appropriations of names or likenesses, and "extreme and outrageous" conduct on the part of defendants in IIED cases, suggests that the interjection of constitutional privileges into the torts may not have been as revolutionary as assumed.

The second reason is that many torts with speech dimensions have remained outside the coverage of the First Amendment. We have advanced arguments as to why this is and should remain the case. Our point here is that despite the partial constitutionalization of some torts with speech dimensions, the mere presence of an expressive component in activity thought of as potentially tortious does not necessarily mean that First Amendment concerns are implicated. Some torts involve speech but not protected speech, even under generous definitions of the categories of speech eligible for constitutional protection. For those reasons the First Amendment's inroads into tort law since *New York Times v. Sullivan* have not been as substantial as may first appear. We are confident that, comparing the doctrinal frameworks of the torts that began to be constitutionalized in the 1960s with the changes in the elements of those torts that process of constitutionalization effectuated, and bearing in mind the many torts that remain outside the coverage of the First Amendment, the overall relationship between tort law and the First Amendment is both understandable and unsurprising.

5

Torts without Names, New Torts, and the Future of Liability for Intangible Harm

THROUGHOUT THIS book we have been discussing the relationship between the past and the present of tort law. Much of this discussion has concerned the establishment of new torts and new forms of liability that are now features of the mainstream of tort law. In this chapter we shift focus by considering the relationship of tort law's past to its twenty-first-century future. Specifically, we are interested in two forms of harm for which tort law currently provides limited or no redress.

The first form of harm results from what has been called "sexualized misconduct." Some sexual wrongdoing is already actionable in tort, often under torts we have discussed in previous chapters. In contrast, we want to consider harassing and offensive sexualized behavior that is not currently actionable in tort and does not violate employment discrimination laws. We have chosen to focus on this form of harm because it has recently become so much more prominent as a result of the #MeToo movement. We are sensitive to the fact that we could instead, or in addition, focus on what might be called "racialized misconduct," which is equally important and harmful and certainly also has been highlighted, to say the least, by the Black Lives Matter movement. Our hope is that our analysis of the former will help begin to shed light on how tort law addressing the intangible harms involving racialized misconduct might also develop.

The second form of harm is cyber-related harm, which is unrelated to the first (other than when it also involves sexualized misconduct) except for the fact that neither involves directly caused physical harm. For this reason, we can think of both these harms as "intangible," although by doing so we do not mean to imply that these forms of harm have less moral or metaphysical importance than so-called tangible harm.

Our analysis begins by considering an episode that did not culminate in the creation of a new tort or the establishment of a new form of liability. Rather, the episode is the story of the failure, and virtual disappearance, of a putative new tort. Although it is a story of failure, the episode is still a part of tort law's past that can tell us a lot about change, and about the development of tort liability.

The putative new tort from the past that we are discussing had a name, but only barely. It was called "prima facie tort." We have spoken previously about a number of different torts without saying anything about the source of their names. Since the name of a tort almost always describes the wrong that the tort addresses, the source of that name generally seems obvious enough. But prima facie tort was different. Its name did not describe the wrong it was designed to redress because it could not do that. This feature of prima facie tort made it historically unique. The names of the torts "invasion of privacy," "intentional infliction of emotional distress (IIED)," and even "negligence" were descriptions of the core content of those different causes of action. The same is true of all the other torts. A tort without a name, or with a name like "prima facie tort," is very nearly a contradiction in terms because it does not describe itself. But torts do not always get names immediately upon birth. Typically, it takes some time to recognize what they are because they are in search of an identity or have a vaguely defined content. As we have seen in earlier chapters, this was at first true for IIED and the privacy torts, the last new intentional torts to be adopted, about a century ago.

Interestingly, new torts sounding in negligence have largely camouflaged this process, through the combined force of doctrinal structure and misdirected emphasis. The principle that there is no liability in negligence without the existence of a predicate duty means that new negligence torts often are created by recognizing a new duty not to negligently risk causing a particular form of loss.[1] When this happens it often appears, incorrectly, that an artificial restriction on liability for negligence has been removed, not that a new form of liability—and certainly not a new tort—has been created. This has been true, for example, of liability for negligently inflicted emotional loss and of a landlord's liability for failure to maintain adequate security for its tenants.[2] But for practical purposes, those were unrecognized new torts.

Because not a single, expressly named new tort has been adopted in nearly a century, it might appear that the process by which new tort liabilities are created has become static or even moribund. In our judgment, this conclusion may soon prove to be dramatically incorrect. If harms involving tangible physical forces—railroads, cars, durable products, drugs, and chemical wastes—were the most frequent subjects of twentieth-century tort litigation, harms involving intangible forces and intangible harms may be at the cutting edge of the law of torts in the twenty-first century.[3]

For this reason, the law of torts of the future may be the farthest thing from static or moribund. The present age may be about to witness the same degree of cultural pressure, with corresponding turmoil and expansion of liability for intangible forces and the intangible harms they cause, that we experienced in the nineteenth and twentieth centuries regarding physical harm. For example, varieties of sexual and sexualized misconduct recently have garnered much more attention and concern than in the past. Each of those forms of wrongful conduct generates mainly intangible loss rather than physical harm. In addition, because of inadequate data security, cyber hacking now commonly results in both economic loss and invasions of the privacy of those whose credit accounts or digitized personal information have been hacked.

The form taken by any new tort liabilities arising out of those wrongs will be important to the development and predictability of the liabilities, and to their impact on wrongful conduct. We have emphasized throughout this book that the dominant form new tort liabilities have taken has been through the establishment of new, particularized torts. An alternative but much less known form of liability, however, competed with the named-tort approach during this same period, and to some extent still competes with it. This is the application of what we call a "residual category" of liability.

The idea of a residual category of tort liability first surfaced more than a hundred years ago when Oliver Wendell Holmes, Jr., partly described, and partly proposed, that there be tort liability for "intentional infliction of temporal damage."[4] In addition to Holmes, this contention had eminent supporters—Frederick Pollock, Francis Bohlen, and William Prosser, among others. Cases decided in the following decades imposed liability on grounds that appeared to reflect this residual category, which came to be principally illustrated in the concept of what eventually was termed "prima facie tort." Prima facie tort continues to be asserted sporadically as a potential basis for the imposition of liability in lawsuits. Yet this general, residual category of liability was never established as a robust alternative to the adoption of particular, named torts and currently occupies a marginal doctrinal status.

This chapter explores the reasons Holmes and some other eminent scholars were wrong in their conceptualization of prima facie tort as a residual category of tort liability, and why that residual category never developed. We then undertake to demonstrate why we think the residual category of liability approach will not be adopted for the most salient forms of intangible harm on the current scene—harms that inevitably will be candidates for tort liability in the years to come. The torts of the future, we think, will take the same form as the torts of the past and present. We identify the aspects of several types of intangible loss that we think may well become actionable through the adoption of new torts or the expansion of existing torts, as well as the aspects of loss that will continue not to be actionable.

We conclude by arguing that, despite the fact that invasions of intangible rights or interests may be more common in the future, and may increasingly be perceived as wrongs that reflect widespread social concerns, the invasions should not be, and are unlikely to be, redressed through the application of a residual category of liability for the intentional infliction of intangible harm. Rather, the inevitability of history will again manifest itself. If new torts associated with intangible forces and harms are adopted, they will be discrete, concrete, and contained. In short, any potential new tort liability that is created to deal with those harms will take the form of expansion of existing torts, or the establishment of new torts with particularized elements, defined limitations, and eventually their own names.

The Invention of Prima Facie Tort and the Early Cases

No one, to our knowledge, has ever contended that there is, or should be, residual liability in tort for "wrongful infliction of harm." That would be a residual category of tort liability as broad as possible. The principal actual example of a putative residual category of liability in tort involves a narrower, but still comparatively broad, form of liability. This cause of action started out as "intentional infliction of temporal damage," which meant something like inflicting "tangible" harm. Holmes seems to have been the first, or one of the first, to use the term "temporal" in referring to tort liability, but he did not define what he meant by it.[5] It is possible that he meant "tangible" damage, such as injury to persons or property, as opposed to intangible damage such as emotional harm. An alternative definition is "capable of being compensated with money," which to the modern ear sounds virtually unlimited, and therefore may not be what he had in mind.

The notion of liability for the intentional infliction of temporal damage soon evolved into what was called "prima facie tort." The rise of prima facie tort, and its subsequent failure to mature and develop, is the best example we have of putative residual liability in tort—of a broad form of presumptive tort liability, without a meaningful name—in actual operation. The story of prima facie tort therefore has considerable historical and practical significance, even though prima facie tort itself has only a tiny place in contemporary tort law.

This story demonstrates that there is an important distinction between the potential for new forms of tort liability to be adopted and the existence of a residual *category* of tort liability. The former potential always exists, but that potential is not realized through the invocation of the latter. This is the paradox of residual tort liability. No form of liability supposedly falling within that category actually stays there once it is recognized. Residual tort liability is, at most, merely a conceptual placeholder. To demonstrate this, we canvass in some detail the history of prima facie tort, explaining how it first existed without bearing that name, was then recognized and named in a few states, yet later proved to have little traction.

Setting the Conceptual Stage: Holmes and Pollock

In the 1870s Holmes in the United States and Pollock in England both began doing legal scholarship. Holmes and Pollock were contemporaries who had first met in England in 1874 and would correspond with one another until 1932.[6] Holmes contributed legal essays and digests of cases to the *American Law Review,* of which he became co-editor in 1872, and in 1881 he published a series of lectures as *The Common Law.*[7] Pollock's *Principles of the Law of Contract* appeared in 1876, and in 1881 he published the first edition of his *The Law of Torts.*[8] As we saw in chapter 2, both Holmes and Pollock were particularly interested in deriving and articulating general principles of liability around which common law subjects could be organized.

Holmes argued in *The Common Law* that standards of tort liability should be objective rather than subjective, and that there was a sharp distinction between acts that offended morality and acts that were legally culpable.[9] His intuition seems to have been that malicious motives were irrelevant if one kept within the law. Holmes's initial inclination was thus to subsume "malice" in "intent" and to treat the existence of intent as an objective inquiry.[10]

A few years later, Pollock stated his position on the same issue a bit differently:

> There is no express authority that I know of for stating as a general proposition of English law that it is wrong to do willful harm to one's neighbor without lawful justification or excuse. . . . Thus in the Anglo-Saxon and other early Germanic laws . . . only that harm which falls within one of the specified categories of wrong-doing entitles the person aggrieved to a legal remedy. . . .
>
> Such is not the modern way of regarding legal duties or remedies. . . . The three main heads of duty with which the law of torts is concerned—namely to abstain from willful injury, to respect the property of others, and to use due diligence to avoid causing harm to others—are all alike of a comprehensive nature.[11]

In the meantime, Holmes's thinking had evolved toward Pollock's, and he modified the position on "malice" he had taken in *The Common Law*. In an article in the *Harvard Law Review* in 1894, Holmes maintained that "the intentional infliction of temporal damage, or the doing of an act manifestly likely to inflict such damage and inflicting it, is actionable if done without just cause."[12] He appeared to think that this reflected an existing common law principle. We doubt very much that he thought he was proposing a new tort or even a new basis for imposing liability.

THE RISE OF THE PUTATIVE CAUSE OF ACTION

Holmes's formulation suggested that causing "malicious" economic injury (for example, to a competitor) was prima facie tortious. But in Holmes's view, this seemingly residual category of potential liability did not automatically result in liability for intentional economic damage inflicted on another. That depended on whether the conduct in question had a justification. This is evident in the cases in which Holmes applied this principle after his *Harvard Law Review* article appeared. The most important was *Vegelahn v. Guntner*,[13] in which workers went on strike for shorter working hours and higher pay, organizing a picket line outside Frederick Vegelahn's factory and seeking to encourage persons to boycott Vegelahn's business or to discourage others from doing business with or working for Vegelahn. The Massachusetts Supreme Judicial Court entirely prohibited both the picketing and the boycott.[14]

In his dissent in *Vegelahn*, Holmes treated the case as demonstrating that the "intentional infliction of temporal damage" was "warranted" by the "law" when it was "justified." In "numberless instances," Holmes wrote, an actor could intentionally do harm to another if the basis for inflicting that harm was justifiable. Whether the harm was justifiable turned on "considerations of policy and social advantage."[15] Holmes thought that in the context of labor disputes, efforts on the part of workers to secure better wages and working conditions justified strikes, boycotts, and picketing in pursuit of those aims, so long as they were peaceful. In short, Holmes had announced the proposition that the intentional infliction of temporal damage was tortious unless justifiable, and in *Vegelahn* had analyzed justifiability to limit the scope of liability.

Holmes was alone in dissent in *Vegelahn*.[16] But despite focusing on the justification for "intentional infliction of temporal damage," rather than the mere fact that acts had been done intentionally or had caused harm, he still acknowledged the possibility that a number of such inflictions might end up being actionable. Similar opinions, applying similar logic and doctrinal structure, followed, often with Holmes dissenting but sometimes in the majority, depending on what counted as sufficient "justification."[17]

After Holmes was appointed to the U.S. Supreme Court in 1902, he was afforded another opportunity to articulate the elements of the form of residual liability in tort he had been identifying. The case, *Aikens v. Wisconsin*,[18] did not come to the Court as a common law decision but as a challenge to the constitutionality of a Wisconsin statute prohibiting the combination of two or more persons from willfully or maliciously interfering with another in trade or business.[19] Since the defendants had admitted they had malicious motives in making the agreement, and the Wisconsin court had stopped short of concluding that the statute could fairly be applied to non-malicious "willful" acts as well as malicious acts, the case reduced itself to whether a legislature could constitutionally punish malicious acts that damaged others.

This led Holmes to assert that the acts of the defendants would have been actionable at common law. In that assertion, Holmes provided his clearest statement of the elements of that action. "It has been thought by other courts as well as the Supreme Court of Wisconsin," he maintained, "that such a combination, followed by damage, would be actionable even at common law. It has been considered that, *prima facie*, the intentional infliction of temporal damage is a cause of action, which . . . requires a justification if the defendant is to escape."[20] In addition, because "malicious mischief is a familiar and proper subject for legislative repression," he was prepared to conclude that "it would be impossible to hold that the liberty to combine to inflict such mischief . . . was among the rights that the Fourteenth Amendment was intended to preserve."[21]

Finally, Holmes suggested that when what he called "disinterested malevolence" could be shown as a basis for the intentional infliction of temporal damage, it could serve to take such actions "out of the justification by the motive with which they were made."[22] Although Holmes did not make explicit whether, if "disinterested malevolence" was paired with some other appropriate motive, such as furthering competition in business or securing leverage in labor negotiations, a tort action could be maintained, he nonetheless said that the statute in *Aikens* should be limited to "combinations of a kind for which no justification could be offered."[23]

In light of the progression of those decisions, at this point it would have been plausible to conclude that there was an emerging residual category of liability for "intentional infliction of temporal damage," and that "disinterested malevolence" would be a key to determining when there was liability and when there was a justification that insulated a potential defendant from liability. Certainly the broad language that Holmes used would have supported that conclusion.

But given the actual facts of the cases in which this kind of broad language had been used, a different conclusion would also have been possible. All of the cases we have discussed involved labor disputes. In each of those disputes, multiple parties, or an organization composed of multiple parties, were the defendants, and the common characteristic of the alleged wrongful conduct was that the defendants had acted in concert. The crux of the alleged wrong was the exercise of collective power to affect market competition. In the cases we discussed above and in his writing, Holmes took the position that this kind of conduct was not actionable when it was not violent. The point, however, is that whether or not the conduct was actionable in a given case, use of this particular species of market leverage by labor was often considered wrongful in the *laissez-faire* world of the late nineteenth century, and that was what the cases were all about. Once we understand labor disputes to be the subject matter of those cases, then the proposition that when liability in the cases was imposed it was for the "intentional infliction of temporal damage" ends up being considerably broader than is necessary to explain what was going on.

Nonetheless, after the labor cases faded into the background, those cases, and the doctrinal explanation that had been given for them, were invoked by some courts in another set of cases in business settings that did not involve contests between labor and management. But not all courts took this route. Rather, other courts began to recognize that many of the cases involved or could be explained by reference to a narrower basis of liability. This would come to be called "intentional interference with prospective economic advantage." We therefore turn next to those two lines of cases.

Two Different Lines of Doctrinal Development

After courts had begun to recognize, at that point exclusively in business settings, that recovery for the unjustified "intentional infliction of temporal damage" was possible, the stage was set for two different lines of cases to emerge. In some settings the tort of interference with prospective economic advantage emerged and thrived. But over time, that tort proved to be more limited than had once been thought, and for that reason its contours turned out to be quite different from the putative cause of action for intentional infliction of temporal harm. At the same time, the notion that there was also a residual category of liability for intentional interference with temporal advantage was separately maintained in a few jurisdictions but only developed sporadically. Where this basis for the imposition of liability was recognized, it came to be called "prima facie tort."

INTERFERENCE WITH PROSPECTIVE ECONOMIC ADVANTAGE

The foundations of the tort of interference with prospective economic advantage were laid in *Temperton v. Russell,* an English decision of 1893 in which the court held, by analogy to the existing tort of inducing breach of contract, that inducing someone not to enter into a contract could also be actionable under some circumstances.[24] The facts in that case were similar to those in the U.S. labor dispute cases invoking Holmes's rationale. But the rationale for the imposition of liability for interfering with prospective economic advantage, and the situations to which the tort might apply, seemed narrower.

American courts soon picked up the theme. Sometimes the courts were not entirely clear which cause of action was involved. In the celebrated case of *Tuttle v. Buck,*[25] for example, a wealthy banker opened up a barber shop, allegedly for the sole purpose of driving an existing barber out of business. In the barber's suit against the banker, the Minnesota Supreme Court allowed the case to proceed. The court said that the proposition that malicious motives could not render an otherwise lawful action unlawful was flawed. What was "lawful" was based on grounds of policy, and sometimes "the purpose for which a man is using his own property may . . . determine his rights."[26] Where the *sole* purpose of operating a business was to drive a competitor out of business rather than to make a profit, that conduct was unlawful. The court cited Pollock's treatise and suggested that the basis of liability, if it were imposed, would be for intentional infliction of temporal damage, without justification. Other cases followed.[27]

By 1941 the cause of action for which *Tuttle v. Buck* had provided a remedy had acquired the name "interference with prospective economic advantage." Prosser sought to describe the case law, as of 1941, in a section of his treatise expressly entitled "Interference with Prospective Economic Advantage." As he put it, "Since a large part of what is most valuable in modern life depends on 'probable expectancies' . . . the courts must do more to discover, define, and protect them from undue interference. . . . For the most part the 'expectancies' thus protected have been those of future contractual relations. . . . The tort began with 'malice,' and it has remained a matter of at least intent to interfere."[28] After this the case law accumulated further, and in 1979 the *Restatement (Second) of Torts* referred to the tort as "Intentional Interference with Prospective Contractual

Relations," providing that there was liability when an actor "intentionally and improperly" engaged in this form of interference.[29]

As time went on, however, the courts recognized that, as in *Tuttle v. Buck,* whether the defendant had mixed motives often rendered decisions difficult. For decades, as the *Restatement (Third)* recently put it, the courts "sometimes hedged on the extent to which the defendant's motives" were relevant, focusing instead on the means the defendant had used to interfere with the plaintiff's prospects.[30] Consequently, the *Restatement* concluded, the defendant's motive has now fallen completely out of the picture, and there is liability, regardless of motive, only if the defendant "committed an independent and intentional legal wrong," though not necessarily a tortious one.[31] Probably the most prominent recent case to make that clear was decided by the Supreme Court of California in 1995.[32]

Prima Facie Tort

In contrast, the subsequent development of liability for intentional infliction of temporal damage based on prima facie tort was considerably more limited. A prominent precursor here was *Beardsley v. Kilmer,*[33] in which the defendant was the manufacturer of a patent medicine known as "Swamp Root" that he and his father sold in Binghamton, New York. The plaintiff, owner of a local newspaper, published a series of articles about the medicine, which suggested that it had few medicinal properties. The defendant, after unsuccessful efforts to get the plaintiff to cease writing about his product, opened a rival newspaper, which eventually had the effect of attracting subscribers, employees, and advertisers from the plaintiff's newspaper and causing it to close.[34] The New York Court of Appeals acknowledged that "lawful" actions undertaken solely out of "malicious" motives could be deemed unjustifiable and actionable.[35]

In *Beardsley,* however, the defendant apparently had some experience in the newspaper industry before starting a competing paper and continued to operate his paper after the plaintiff had closed his. That suggested to the Court of Appeals that his motives were mixed, and in its view this defeated recovery. "The genesis which will make a lawful act unlawful," the court announced, "must be a malicious one unmixed with any other and exclusively directed to injury and damage of another."[36]

In retrospect, the facts in *Beardsley* seem highly similar to those in *Tuttle v. Buck.* Both can be understood to involve interferences with business opportunities. But *Tuttle v. Buck* became a seminal case in the development of interference with prospect economic advantage, whereas *Beardsley* was a precursor of prima facie tort.[37]

There also were a few cases not described, or at least not easily described, as intentional interference with prospective advantage. This was because they involved loss that did not arise out of interference with a business opportunity. Those cases might well have been examples of a residual, unnamed category of tort liability, but there were so few of them that identifying them as members of a "category" would have been strained. In essence, they were outliers.

For example, in one case a defendant utility company sought to undermine the influence of the plaintiff, a prominent physician, regarding a forthcoming bond issue. To do this, the defendant attempted to induce the physician to perform an illegal abortion.[38] Although the plaintiff sought damages measured by the injury to his reputation and damage to his business, the purpose of the defendant was to influence the election, not to interfere with the plaintiff's prospective economic advantage.[39] The court nonetheless ruled that the case could properly be submitted to a jury.[40]

Cases of this sort also appeared in the New York courts, and occasionally something like purely "disinterested malevolence" (to use Holmes's term) in a nonbusiness context was found to have existed. In *Al Raschid v. News Syndicate Co.*,[41] the defendant newspaper gave false information to immigration authorities that caused the plaintiff to be arrested and deported, despite his being a native-born American citizen. He sued for malicious prosecution, but that case was dismissed because the information was disclosed in a deportation hearing, which was not a judicial proceeding, and the defendant had not instituted any action against the plaintiff.[42] After the dismissal at the trial court, the plaintiff appealed to the New York Court of Appeals, which held that although the malicious prosecution claim was properly dismissed, the plaintiff might maintain an action for the intentional infliction of temporal damage without justification, citing *Tuttle, Beardsley,* and Pollock's treatise. The court noted that the plaintiff had not alleged the proper elements to make out a cause of action but gave him ten days to replead.[43] Nothing further was ever reported.

Al Raschid was a rare, tenable example of the as-yet-unnamed residual category of prima facie tort. It did not involve concerted action in the labor context, nor could it be characterized as intentional interference with prospective economic advantage. But there were not many such cases. Prior to 1946 the New York Court of Appeals had not referred to prima facie tort by name, and most of the cases in which it had suggested there might be an action for the unjustified, intentional infliction of temporal damage were ones in which other causes of action also were alleged. But in a 1946 case the Court of Appeals used the phrase "prima facie tort."

In *Advance Music Co. v. American Tobacco Co.*,[44] the plaintiff had published musical compositions in the form of sheet music, which it then sold to jobbers and dealers in the music industry. The defendant compiled a weekly list of the nine or ten "most popular" current songs in the nation, in the ostensible order of their popularity, allegedly based on an extensive and accurate survey it conducted. The plaintiff alleged that the defendant's surveys repeatedly failed to include its compositions in lists of popular songs or listed them in an "improper order of popularity." The ratings of popular songs, Advance Music charged, were simply "the choice or result of caprice or other considerations foreign to a selection" based on accuracy. The defendants had acted "wantonly and without good faith" in failing to include Advance Music songs in its lists.[45]

The plaintiff had suffered economic loss, but not through the defendant's having intentionally interfered with any particular prospective contractual advantage of the plaintiff. The court held that New York courts had adopted Holmes's view that "*prima facie*, the intentional infliction of temporal damage is a cause of action which requires a justification if the defendant is to escape," and that the plaintiff "alleges such a prima facie tort and, therefore, is sufficient in law on its face."[46]

Subsequent New York decisions, however, imposed three limitations on this action.[47] First, the infliction of harm had to be based *solely* on "malice," described by Holmes in *Aikens* as "disinterested malevolence." "Mixed motives" for a defendant's conduct, such as appeared in *Beardsley* and arguably in *Tuttle*, were insufficient. Second, prima facie tort actions could only be brought where no other tort action was available to a plaintiff. Since many cases existed in which intentional infliction of temporal damage in a business context might give rise to an action for intentional inference with contractual relations or intentional interference with prospective advantage, this limited prima facie tort to cases in which the elements of those torts could somehow not be satisfied. Finally, damages in prima facie tort were limited to "special" damages, which typically meant out-of-pocket losses and did not include emotional harm.

That limitation tended to exclude from the category of prima facie tort any actions in which the defendant appeared to have intentionally and gratuitously sought to injure the plaintiff, but the damage the plaintiff suffered only was reputational and therefore not "special."[48]

Despite those limitations on the cause of action, however, in 1979 the *Restatement (Second) of Torts* virtually duplicated Holmes's broad description of intentional infliction of temporal damage in *Aikens*.[49] "One who intentionally causes injury to another," the provision read, "is subject to liability to the other for that injury, if his conduct is generally culpable and not justifiable under the circumstances." The provision added that "this liability may be imposed although the actor's conduct does not come within a traditional category of tort liability." Nowhere was there mention of the three limitations New York courts had placed on the prima facie tort. The provision (§ 870) did add a requirement that the conduct be "generally culpable," but folded that requirement into unjustifiability, treating the intentional infliction of damage without a justification as culpable conduct.[50]

Adopted in 1977, a time when most observers thought that tort law's recent expansion would actively continue, § 870 laid out a potential basis for the development of a broad category of residual liability in tort. Like a number of other liability-expanding provisions that have been adopted in *Restatements* with little case law to support them, it might have been prophetic.[51] At this point, therefore, the idea that a residual category of tort liability existed had been widely noted, if not necessarily widely accepted. Over the next few decades, however, cases would demonstrate that, practically speaking, there was no such residual category.

THE MODERN PERIOD

It turned out that both Holmes and those responsible for § 870 were wrong. Prima facie tort has been adopted in only a few jurisdictions. And the even more broadly stated, arguably "residual" cause of action adopted by § 870 has garnered little support. Rather, most of the types of conduct that might have constituted intentional infliction of temporal damage without justification fell within the classic categories of other intentional torts, such as assault, battery, intentional damage to property, false imprisonment, trespass, or malicious prosecution, or the later-appearing business torts of interference with contract or interference with prospective advantage. Each of those torts includes its own "justifications" for conduct that would otherwise be actionable in the form of distinctive defenses and privileges.

Holmes and Pollock seem never to have envisioned this alternative route to the development of previously unrecognized forms of tort liability. They were so focused on conceptualizing a unified theory of tort liability that what mattered most to them was identifying a residual category of liability not exhausted by the existing torts. What Holmes would have said about the subsequent emergence of new named torts, such as intrusion on seclusion, public disclosure of true private facts, and intentional infliction of emotional distress, is unclear. All of those are intentional torts, though none involves "temporal" damage.

Outside of New York, there are perhaps several dozen reported cases in which the courts have contemplated prima facie tort without directly rejecting it. There are only three other states, however, in which it can plausibly be said that prima facie tort has been squarely adopted: Missouri,[52] New Mexico,[53] and Ohio.[54] Even in those states, the cause of action sometimes is not favored.[55] One commentator has suggested that there are a few other states in which adoption is arguably implied.[56] But cases in which the prima facie tort allegation actually bears weight are rare. And even in New York, where there have been over a thousand reported cases mentioning prima facie tort, it has had the same fate. The cause of action is applicable in only a tiny percentage of those cases.[57]

In the few jurisdictions where it has been adopted, allegations that fall within prima facie tort are narrow. They are made primarily in business contexts where a defendant's conduct inflicted pecuniary damage on a rival and was arguably unjustified but could not be made the basis of one of the classic tort categories because of technical limitations on them. In fact, as we have seen, New York, the leading late twentieth-century jurisdiction that nominally had adopted prima facie tort, limited the action to instances in which recovery in a classic intentional tort was unavailable.

Moreover, it has been the rare case in which some form of justification is completely unavailable. In cases that arise out of business dealings, the motives of securing a profit, obtaining a competitive advantage in the marketplace, or furthering one's interest in labor relations are readily discernible and serve as barriers to findings of disinterested malevolence. Even a showing that a defendant whose competition with another business forced that business to close, but the defendant failed to operate a profitable enterprise, as in the *Beardsley* case, would not

necessarily result in such a finding: a defendant might simply have er-
roneously assessed the profitability of his or her undertaking. The combination of there being few factual situations in which intentional injury
causing damage is not actionable under any other tort, and in which there
was no justification for the defendant's conduct, has meant that very few
standalone actions of prima facie tort have been brought, and even fewer
have been successful.[58] These involve such conduct as improperly stop-
ping payment on a check,[59] wrongfully seeking collection on a note,[60] and
humiliating an employee where the facts did not constitute intentional
infliction of emotional distress.[61]

All this is confirmed by the ongoing projects in the *Restatement (Third)
of Torts* series. There is no mention of prima facie tort or § 870 at all in
Restatement (Third) of Torts: Liability for Economic Harm, except for a
passage in the Reporters' introduction indicating that § 870 has not been
carried forward.[62] And *Restatement (Third) of Torts: Intentional Torts to
Persons* relegates mention of prima facie tort and § 870 to a Reporters'
note, indicating that only a few jurisdictions have recognized either cause
of action.[63]

The upshot of our examination of the cases in New York and elsewhere, then, is this: cases in which the weight-bearing basis of liability, or
even of potential liability, is prima facie tort are extremely rare. We doubt
that in the entire history of the tort there are more than a dozen reported
cases nationwide in which the actual imposition of liability on the basis
of prima facie tort, and prima facie tort alone, has been upheld on appeal.

The Lessons of the Story

The story of prima facie tort may seem to be sobering for those who
favor the creation of new torts. This putative tort had highly respected
supporters, and it seemed to fill a gap in the protections provided by tort
liability. Yet the tort never thrived and has all but disappeared from view.
In our opinion, however, the reason is not that new torts cannot or will
not be created in the future. Rather, prima facie tort had a number of
characteristics that rendered it unlikely to grow into an accepted and acceptable cause of action. It is those characteristics that should be kept in
mind in thinking about the possible creation of new torts.[64]

First, prima facie tort was vague and general. Unlike every other tort
we have discussed in this book, its name did not describe the wrong, or

wrongs, that it redressed. This may seem like a trivial and petty criticism, but we mean it to be more than a statement about the putative tort's public image. Without a particular wrong at its core, the tort had no identity. Holmes had come closer, but not close enough, in suggesting that there could be liability for "intentional infliction of temporal damage." But the problem was that the notion of "temporal damage" was almost as vague as "prima facie tort."

Second, one of the principal wrongs that prima facie tort would have addressed, intentional interference with prospective economic loss, could be named and was quickly split off from what became prima facie tort. With the most viable component of the tort removed, what remained was considerably less clear.

Third, as a residual category, there simply were few cases that fell into prima facie tort rather than into one of the established, named torts. Without a critical mass of cases, there was very little opportunity for a jurisprudence of prima facie tort to develop. Courts were much less likely to spend time developing a jurisprudence regarding a cause of action that they would rarely encounter. The game was not worth the candle.

Finally, there was neither external pressure for the creation of liability in the situations addressed exclusively by prima facie tort, nor analogous case law precedents that would have permitted the courts favoring the imposition of liability to cloak the extent of their innovation by relying on such precedents. The absence of pressure was a function of the fact that the number of instances in which courts needed to consider recovery in prima facie tort, because no other tort actions were available, had been small, and even in those instances recovery was not always possible, as where mixed motives on the part of a defendant existed.

In short, there were simply not a lot of situations in which the "intentional infliction of temporal damage" could not be redressed through one of the existing named torts, and because there were few such situations, pressure for relief from a "wrong" that was not otherwise actionable in tort was minimal. Without such pressure, courts felt few imperatives to expand the scope of prima facie tort, with the result that standalone prima facie tort cases were doctrinal outliers. And without more such cases on the books to serve as precedents, the creation of standalone prima facie tort liability would have seemed too openly innovative for most courts.

Although those observations pertain specifically to prima facie tort, they also have some general significance regarding the conditions that are necessary for the creation of other new torts. New torts need to be responding to external pressures which suggest that there are novel "wrongs" emerging in society for which tort law should provide redress, and the wrongs need to be sufficiently recurrent, and sufficiently cognizable as tort actions, to generate an ongoing mass of cases. When that happens a new tort may emerge, but it is very likely that the new tort will have recurring features that help define its elements and give it a name. That is what happened when intentional interference with prospective advantage cases emerged out of the residual category of prima facie tort. Those cases were sufficiently numerous, and had sufficiently specific and recurrent common elements, to stand on their own. They were cases in an economic setting in which defendants intentionally sought to thwart the business prospects of plaintiffs, but by interfering with their future business success rather than with their existing contractual relations. Once that relatively large space in which the "intentional infliction of temporal damage" occurred was carved out of prima facie tort, much of the identity of prima facie tort was lost.

We have more to say in our conclusion about the conditions in which new torts have been able to come into being, and the conditions in which they were not able to emerge, in the history of tort law. It is no surprise, we contend, that when new torts come into being they look very much like the old tort law forms of action in modern versions. In the meantime, however, the lessons we have derived from the story of prima facie tort are relevant to the future of liability for intangible harm, so we turn to that topic.

The Future of Liability for Intangible Harm

There can be no question that we have entered a postindustrial era in which information, rather than things themselves, is playing and will continue to play an increasingly important role in our economy and in our social lives. New forms of harm—either caused by intangible forces, involving intangible loss, or both—are emerging and will undoubtedly be more prevalent as the information age proceeds.[65]

Predicting the exact nature of the intangible harms that have not yet occurred or even been imagined would, of course, be a fruitless venture. Even just a few years ago almost no one would have predicted that misuse of Facebook data would have influenced the 2016 election for president of the United States, that a series of prominent men holding powerful media positions would lose their jobs as a result of their sexual misconduct, or that an international pandemic would shut down the economies of most of the world. We will not attempt to envision a future than may be stranger than fiction.

Nonetheless, we are struck by certain parallels between the last period of great turmoil in tort law and what may well be about to occur. As we indicated in in the introduction, between about 1960 and 1985, the physical harms of the late industrial age generated new tort liabilities—and corresponding increases in compensation paid to victims—to meet them. Liabilities associated with products, drugs, and chemicals escalated. We may well be at the beginning of an analogous period in our history.

Harms caused by sexual misconduct have long been understood to occur regularly, and both statutory and common law liabilities have long been available to redress some harms involving sexual misconduct. But it has become obvious in the last few years that those harms have been even more widespread than some people had previously recognized, and that legal regimes that might be used to compensate for such harms and also to deter them from occurring—such as tort and employment discrimination law—have in many respects failed at that task.[66] Catherine MacKinnon made this point decades ago, but it remains true today.[67]

Similarly, in the past few decades, the cyber revolution has spawned forms of activity, and of wrongdoing, that simply did not exist in the past. The same kind of pressure to afford the victims of wrongdoing compensation for the harms they suffer that led to the explosion of liability for physical forces and physical harm more than fifty years ago may now be starting to develop in the context of the intangible forces and intangible harms of the digital world.

What form may tort liability for these kinds of intangible harms take? We focus on three kinds of intangible harms that have already occurred, and that can be expected to occur with considerably more frequency or to be the subject of greater scrutiny in the future: sexualized misconduct that does not involve or pose the threat of imminent bodily contact, consumer credit losses resulting from digital hacking, and the publication of medical or other private information obtained from confidential websites.

We have singled out those harms for discussion for obvious reasons. The #MeToo movement has generated a large amount of publicity for wrongful or inappropriate sexualized behavior, primarily directed at females by males, that (as we explain below) does not come within the definitions of assault, battery, or statutory sexual harassment. In addition, the hacking of credit accounts has become a nearly ubiquitous phenomenon, and typically consumers are protected against losses through arrangements with the banks that issue credit cards or otherwise support accounts.[68] Massive data breaches of large enterprises, including hospitals and universities, also have resulted in large amounts of private information being compromised.[69] Some social websites also have inadvertently released to third parties the information supplied by their subscribers—information that was intended to be limited to a circumscribed group of other subscribers.[70]

Those intangible harms are, no doubt, the proverbial tip of the iceberg. For example, Danielle Keats Citron has shown the myriad of ways that sexual privacy can be invaded over the internet, through sextortion, nonconsensual pornography, and fake sex photos, among other things. The problem for the (almost always female) victims of these wrongs is not the unavailability of a tort remedy in principle but the anonymity of the online wrongdoers. Citron argues that it is the cyber platforms that enable this wrongdoing—Facebook, Instagram, and so on—that should face liability.[71] In addition, the unexpected sharing of digital data by one source with another—think of Google's sharing of consumer shopping data with other vendors, under terms of use that arguably "authorize" Google to do so—also may eventually lead to tort litigation.[72] And the casual quip that "a smartphone is a surveillance device which also permits communication" directs our attention to the possibility of future suits over unauthorized surveillance of personal devices. Our analyses of the three kinds of harms on which we do focus are primarily intended to serve as illustrations of the manner in which courts in the future may go about addressing new types of tort claims involving intangible losses.

One of the insights that we glean from our earlier analysis is that residual categories of liability are abstractions, maintained only before the imposition of liability under particular circumstances becomes a live possibility. Nothing stays for long in the residual category. For this reason, in our view there will never be a residual category of tort liability for sexual misconduct. The question will be whether forms of what has been called "sexualized" misconduct that do not currently fall within the confines of one or more of the existing torts will continue not to be actionable in the future, or instead will result in the expansion of an existing tort or the creation of a new tort or torts that would permit the imposition of liability for intangible harm not actionable at present.[73] Similarly, we doubt very much that there will ever be a residual category of liability consisting of something like "invasion of data privacy."[74] This would be a novel move, and as Anita Bernstein has argued, there is a "paradox" that inclines courts to shy away from novelty. The more important a change is, the more reluctant are the courts to draw attention to it. This is one of the dynamics that leads to what we have repeatedly called "cloaking." For this reason, if any of these new forms of liability is established, it will either be assimilated to an existing, possibly expanded tort, or a new but contained and limited tort will be created.

Intentional and Negligent Sexualized Misconduct

The much-heightened scrutiny of sexual misconduct that has occurred over the last several years will undoubtedly trigger liabilities that fall into a number of already-existing common law and statutory categories: the common law torts of assault, battery, and IIED, and statutory liability for creation of a hostile work environment, among others. Another form of misconduct, however, falls outside those categories in many instances. In order to distinguish this misconduct from conduct that is actionable under existing forms of liability—but not to diminish in any way the significance of either form of misconduct—we adopt a term that is not yet in common use but that has been used elsewhere, and call the currently not actionable forms of behavior "sexualized" (rather than "sexual") misconduct.[75]

THE NATURE OF THE WRONG

This form of misconduct is not easy to define with precision because it takes many forms. To speak in the vernacular, this is offensive, sometimes frightening conduct, usually by males, that has sexual connotations or overtones. Often the conduct is verbal only, consisting of references to another person's appearance or attractiveness, or that person's relationship with someone else. It may also consist of requests for social interaction that are clearly not welcomed but continue to occur.

The courts would have to create a new tort for this kind of conduct when the harm that it causes is not actionable, as it usually is not. From a normative standpoint, the conduct probably qualifies. Admittedly, it is the kind of conduct at which many people in the past merely rolled their eyes or complained about to their friends and then ignored. But new and higher standards have resulted in such conduct being perceived as more objectionable, to a much larger percentage of the population, than it was in the past. Already tortious conduct uncovered by the #MeToo movement has rendered this currently non-tortious conduct more salient, and more widely understood to be improper, than previously. The external pressure necessary to support the imposition for liability for this conduct certainly is present in a way that it was not even a few years ago.

On the other hand, tort law has refrained over a long period from imposing liability for similarly objectionable but non-sexualized, misconduct. The tort of IIED, for example, requires that conduct intended to cause emotional distress be "extreme and outrageous," partly on the ground that everyone must learn to live with a certain amount of offensive conduct from others, and that the expensive machinery of tort law should not be invoked until the conduct is more than merely offensive.[76] Much of the objectionable sexualized misconduct that we have in mind is offensive, but arguably it is not always necessarily "extreme and outrageous." Moreover, there is a difference between unintentional or unconscious microaggressions and conduct that a person intends to cause serious discomfort to another or knows will do so. That distinction would have to be drawn in a way that makes it operational across a range of cases.

In our view, however, the damages that could be awarded for engaging in sexualized misconduct could be modeled on what happens in cases where IIED is actionable. And it is possible that the ordinary practical obstacles to bringing suit for sexualized misconduct could be overcome. Most lawyers would not take such cases on a contingent-fee basis because the amount of damages likely to be awarded would often be small. We can picture some plaintiffs nonetheless being willing to pay lawyers an hourly fee to sue on their behalf even when the prospect of recovering more than $5,000, for example, would be small. There might not be many such suits, but it might not take very many to send potential violators a strong message.

Challenges to Workability

But there would be other challenges. First, it would be difficult to articulate discrete and limited standards governing liability. We saw that this weakness was part of what doomed prima facie tort. "I know it when I see it" would be inadequate as a test, not only because that standard is vague but because the question would also have to be whether the defendant knew "it" when he did "it." For this reason, sexualized misconduct that received an explicit negative reaction and then was repeated by the defendant might have to be required. If this were the case, the tort would effectively be for a pattern of sexualized misconduct, except when no reasonable person could think that the first act was acceptable, in which case a single instance would be actionable.

An important (though nonexclusive) source for rendering the new liability standard discrete might be the rules governing what constitutes a "hostile work environment" under Title VII of the federal Civil Rights Act.[77] Sexual harassment in the workplace has taken various forms that would often be equally objectionable in non-workplace settings: leering at a woman and offering her money to engage in sexual intercourse,[78] repeatedly asking a woman to "do something nice for me,"[79] making demeaning sexual inquiries,[80] and making sexual references to parts of the plaintiff's body.[81] The making of sexual jokes, negative remarks about people of a particular gender or sexual orientation, displaying sexual material or pictures, inappropriate emails or other forms of communication, scapegoating, and name-calling, for example, could also easily qualify.[82] Some such conduct might be more objectionable in the workplace than outside of it, depending, among other things, on how free the victim was to avoid the individual who engaged or attempted to engage in objectionable conduct. But the Title VII analogy is a good starting point for making the standard of liability concrete.

Second, there would be a risk that the threat of liability for sexualized misconduct might have a chilling effect on tolerable social interaction. It may be even less desirable for the law to risk promoting sexually "sanitized" social interactions than promoting sexual sanitization of the workplace.[83] And because sexualized misconduct would not be tortious in the absence of a defendant's knowledge that it was offensive or his intent that it be offensive, insurance against this form of liability would be either unavailable or against public policy, on the ground that it created excessive moral hazard.[84] The anticipated self-insured costs of defense even in cases that were not successful could be significant for defendants.[85]

The consequence might be that, for all but the most egregious and judgment-proof individuals, refraining from engaging in conduct that plausibly could be alleged, even unsuccessfully, to constitute sexualized misconduct would be the wisest course for most people. We might even move slightly more toward the kinds of more formal and "proper" interactions between men and women that characterized upper-class relationships in the nineteenth century. For many women, that might be preferable to what they have been forced to tolerate over the course of their lives. But in the parlance of tort theory, in an effort to obtain desirable safety-level effects, the threat of liability might generate arguably suboptimal activity-level effects.[86]

Sources of relief outside any new tort admittedly would sometimes be available. Employers have some liability for creating or knowingly tolerating a hostile work environment. Even in instances in which there would be no such liability, adverse publicity recently has produced firings and suspensions of prominent individuals who might be defendants if a new form of tort were created, for example. Antiharassment statutes are available in some jurisdictions to enjoin the more egregious forms of misconduct (sexualized or not) that involve physical proximity, phone calling, or other vexatious communications.[87]

But much of the misconduct we have in mind does not readily fit into existing categories of common law tort liability or statutory antidiscrimination law. Imagine the sort of encounter, now commonly recounted by participants in the #MeToo movement, in which a male occupying some sort of authoritative position in an industry or a corporate enterprise—a movie producer or a senior executive—invites a junior female in that industry or enterprise who is not his employee—an aspiring actress or a colleague from another company—to his residence, purportedly to discuss a role in a forthcoming film or to offer career advice. In the process the male engages in sexualized behavior toward the female—sitting uncomfortably close to her, making remarks about her appearance, or calling attention to his own physical characteristics—that stops short of an assault or intentional infliction of emotional distress but that in a formal workplace setting involving an employee might qualify as sexual harassment. Tort law, as presently constituted, provides no remedy for that sort of behavior in that setting, and Title VII does not apply.

In the past a warning visit to the culprit from the police, or from a member of the victim's family, might have been available to some victims of sexualized misconduct and might have been effective. This kind of self-help still may occur sporadically. Courts know about those other possible sources of relief, although they also know that relief of those sorts is likely only to be sporadically available, and only to some victims. And of course the courts know that, even when those sources of relief prevent future offensive conduct, they do nothing to compensate victims for the losses they have already experienced.

In view of this analysis, we are uncertain about the future of potential tort liability for harm caused by sexualized misconduct. The courts might decide, reluctantly, to refrain from entering the field and refuse to recognize liability for conduct that falls outside the confines of the existing torts. Or the courts might begin, as they did with negligent infliction of emotional distress, by permitting the imposition of liability in a core set of especially appealing cases, without initially articulating the limits and standards governing other conduct lying further from the core, but eventually doing so as more new cases were brought.

Which path is taken may well depend on how developments in our culture evolve beyond where they are at present. The #MeToo movement marks the beginning of a new cultural moment, not the end of one. The one thing our analysis leads us to be confident about is that, if liability is imposed, it will not take long for the courts to recognize that it is not a reflection of a residual category of liability but the introduction of a new tort.

Negligent Release of Hacked Consumer Credit Information

There are almost weekly reports of the hacking of consumer credit and other data maintained by businesses with whom consumers deal. In most instances the consumers whose information is obtained are protected by contract against direct losses resulting from fraudulent charges made on their accounts.[88] However, by contract, the banks issuing credit cards that are used by hackers or their successors to make fraudulent charges on credit card accounts must pay those charges.[89] In addition, consumers whose information is wrongfully obtained may suffer other losses caused by the misuse of the information, the most salient of which is identity theft. We discuss below both the banks' and the consumers' potential causes of action for their losses.

The Issuing Banks' Losses

To date the principal issue in banks' negligence suits against merchants and others whose data reservoirs have been hacked has been whether the "economic loss rule" applies. This is the general rule that there is no liability in negligence for pure economic loss, and the particular application of this rule to instances in which the parties have contracted, or had the potential to contract, regarding liability for such losses.[90]

Legal scholarship about those suits has identified a number of considerations that might bear on their treatment.[91] The important point for us is that the merchants' failure to protect consumers' data is highly blameworthy, but the principal wrong is to the consumers whose data they failed to protect, not to the issuing banks. There does not seem to be much external pressure to afford the banks a right of recovery in this situation. Most people do not consider whether banks might have such a right, and if they did, they would likely think that the banks have no one to blame but themselves for their losses, since they could have protected themselves by contract. The banks are strategically placed to enter into contractual arrangements with merchants, and possibly even with consumers, limiting their exposure to consumer losses suffered when merchant data reservoirs are hacked but, for whatever reasons, do not seem to have done so.[92] As a consequence, we do not anticipate the expansion of existing forms of tort liability, or the creation of a new tort, to address the issuing banks' losses in this situation.

Consumer Losses

The situation of banks issuing credit cards is obviously not the same as that of consumers whose data is hacked. Although consumers are protected against direct losses on their stolen credit card accounts, they are vulnerable to other misuses of their stolen data. In principle, consumers' potential claims against the negligent merchants who stored now-hacked data might be subject to the economic loss rule. Consumers may or may not be in privity of contract with those merchants, but if they are, contracts between the two could address potential economic losses resulting from the merchants' negligence.[93]

On the other hand, contracts between consumers and merchants are boilerplate contracts whose terms arguably should have less binding force than those between the merchants and issuing banks. From a normative standpoint, the merchants' wrongdoing is often serious. Consumer data has been entrusted to those merchants; they know or should know that there is a substantial risk that their customers will suffer losses beyond their existing credit accounts if the security of their data is not maintained; and they know that there is a significant threat that hackers will attempt to obtain the data. A failure to exercise reasonable care to protect the data under those circumstances is highly blameworthy. Interestingly, however, there does not seem to be much pressure to afford a remedy for such negligence. In our experience, most people who are notified that their data has been hacked appear to be satisfied, once they have been reimbursed for any authorized use of credit cards, if they are given a free year or two of membership in a credit and identity protection service by the merchant in question.

In addition, there are considerations that may adversely affect efforts to establish a new tort governing liability for this type of harm. First, developing standards to define what constitutes reasonable care in the maintenance and protection of consumer data could be a challenge. Some of the highly publicized data breaches in recent years seem particularly egregious and sloppy but not all will be.[94] And there will possibly be vexing causation questions, since hackers may well be capable of overcoming even reasonable efforts at protecting consumer data, in which instances a merchant's negligence may not necessarily be a cause of the breach.

Second, consumers' damages from identity theft resulting from data breaches may lie at the margin of what it is practical to determine. One of the reasons for the economic loss rule is the difficulty of tracing the economic effects of negligent behavior.[95] Consumers' immediate losses from data breach—for example, the cost of establishing new accounts and of disputing charges made on a new, fraudulently obtained credit card—may be possible to determine, but the ripple effects of other disruptions suffered by the party in question may be harder to trace. This difficulty may be aggravated when the consequences of identity theft are not recognized or manifested until a considerable period after the theft actually occurs.

Consumers may suffer other losses, however, upon learning that their data, and therefore their identities, may have been compromised. They may worry about what may occur in the future, for example, if their identity is not merely stolen in bulk with the identities of others but actually compromised. The analogy to fear of future bodily injury is suggestive but not dispositive. Except under unusual circumstances, fear of experiencing bodily injury or disease in the future is not compensable in tort until some tangible injury has occurred.[96] This makes sense on several grounds, not the least of which is concern for avoiding multiple lawsuits, the first for fear of injury and the second for actual injury if it later materializes.[97] Data theft may seem closer to constituting an actual loss—perhaps analogous to the theft of property—than to being exposed to the pure risk of suffering harm in the future, but we think the same difficulties with recovery for emotional harm before any tangible harm occurs are presented when someone becomes anxious about the future release of private information that might compromise his or her identity.

Finally, as a practical matter, both the financial and emotional losses of most victims are likely to be comparatively small, but the sum total of such losses suffered by hundreds of thousands of victims (or more) may be enormous. One of the other justifications for the economic loss rule is that liability for pure economic loss would impose catastrophic liability of this sort on a single party, whereas the absence of liability spreads a series of comparatively small losses among a large number of victims who can insure against or mitigate their losses more effectively.[98]

In light of all these considerations, we suspect there will be no tort liability for what might be termed the "ordinary" financial and emotional losses associated with credit data breaches and resulting identity thefts. Rather, we think that tort liability for those losses will be limited to those who suffer unusual emotional loss, beyond what the reasonable person would be expected to suffer, or demonstrable out-of-pocket financial loss, analogous to special damages that must sometimes be proved in order to recover for loss caused by defamation.[99] A plaintiff will have to have suffered losses different in kind or magnitude from what other victims suffered in order to have a right to recover for them.

Negligent Release of Confidential Personal Information

Massive amounts of medical and other confidential information are now maintained in digital form. Much of this information is insecure and vulnerable to breaches of confidentiality. To give just two examples, the health insurer Anthem[100] and the marital dating site Ashley Madison were both hacked,[101] and the identities of some of the individuals registered on the former were released.[102] Here the principal, and often exclusive, harm to the individuals in question is the invasion, or potential invasion, of their privacy, with its attendant consequences, including possible or actual identity theft.

Such harms fall within the potential gravitational pull of two of the interests protected by the existing privacy torts, intrusion on seclusion and public disclosure of true private facts. Because of the unavailability of the parties who conducted a cyberattack, however, efforts to impose liability for losses caused by cyberattacks will have to focus on the parties who "enabled" the attack, through the alleged failure to exercise reasonable care to prevent the attack.[103] There is ample precedent for imposing such liability, depending on the circumstances. We predict that this will not pose a significant obstacle.

On the other hand, the interests at stake vary. First, as we indicate below, we doubt that there will be liability for enabling an intrusion on seclusion itself. Second, liability for enabling the release of private or confidential information might well be assimilated into the existing cause of action for public disclosure, in the sense that the new liability will be for invasion of the same interest that is already protected by this tort. But this tort currently requires the defendant to intend to invade the plaintiff's privacy. The new tort will be actionable even in the absence of intent on the part of the defendant, by analogy to other enabling torts, as long as the defendant has been negligent in failing to protect the plaintiff's privacy.

Data Breach Itself

The first type of harm involved in breaches of this sort is the invasion itself. The possible analogy between this kind of invasion of private data, and intrusion on seclusion through such means as eavesdropping or visual spying, as we discussed in chapter 3, is evident. In each instance, a party without the right to do so gains access to something highly private or confidential. Intrusion on seclusion is actionable even in the absence of a showing that an individual witnessed what was secluded. Recording an intimate conversation, for example, would be actionable even without proof that anyone listened to the recording.[104] Clearly the core of the wrong in the invasion of private data, however, is not the fact of intrusion itself but the combination of intrusion and the fact that someone listened to or saw what was intruded upon. The core of the wrong lies in something private being accessed.

Consequently, the mere negligent enabling of hacking of private or confidential information lies outside the core of the interest that the tort of intrusion on seclusion protects. Conventional intrusions on seclusion usually involve a single or only a few victims.[105] Even without proof that the tortfeasor actually listened to or witnessed what was intruded upon, there is often a substantial possibility, perhaps even a *de facto* presumption, that this occurred. Moreover, often at least part of the outrage victims reasonably feel upon learning of an intrusion is that a particular, identified individual may have actually witnessed them in a private or intimate setting. That is emphatically not what occurs with mass digital intrusions in which a wrongdoer gains access to medical or other private information about tens or hundreds of thousands of individuals. Victims have no reason to imagine that anyone, let alone a particular individual, actually has gained personal knowledge of the information in question merely by virtue of successful hacking. On the contrary, victims' legitimate concern is not about the fact of hacking alone but that the hacking will lead to disclosure of the information to third parties.

In this situation, we think that the courts would neither impose liability for negligently enabling intrusion on seclusion nor create a new tort to govern liability for such an intrusion. The emotional harm that victims suffer from merely knowing that their private information is no longer safely maintained is real but likely in most cases to be minimal and difficult to quantify; this harm is not easily quantified.[106]

Public Disclosure

In contrast to the mismatch between hacking and intrusion on seclusion, the actual release of improperly obtained confidential digital information resembles the harm that is addressed by the tort of public disclosure of true private facts. Negligently enabling such disclosure might well be actionable. Much, and arguably all, of an individual's medical information is sufficiently personal, even if its release does not reveal anything embarrassing, to satisfy the element of this underlying tort requiring that the disclosure be "highly offensive" to the reasonable person.

Moreover, the damages that result from such disclosure will be of the same order as those that plaintiffs suffer in more conventional cases of public disclosure—embarrassment, anxiety, and the like. Although damages for such losses may be difficult to quantify, tort law has already determined that they are sufficiently cognizable to warrant being awarded.

However, the courts will have to surmount a different, substantial barrier to adopting liability for the release of this form of information. Currently there is no liability in negligence for public disclosure of true private facts.[107] The tort requires an intent to disclose. Although there may be occasions on which a defendant deliberately publicizes private information that it maintains in digital form, much more frequently the disclosure will result from invasion by an unknown hacker, and the defendant ordinarily will be an entity whose alleged negligence in not maintaining adequate data security merely enabled the hacking. On the other hand, what was enabled would be serious, intentional wrongdoing.

Adopting a tort of negligent failure to protect against public disclosure of true private facts would no doubt be a major expansion of liability. Some courts will refuse to take such action. But if the disclosure of private information from hacking becomes common and widespread, and there is no statutory or regulatory regime rigorously deterring negligent failure to provide adequate data security by imposing severe penalties for violations, then eventually some courts will expressly or impliedly recognize this under some circumstances.[108] There has been enough attention paid to data security breaches, and enough public concern about them, that the failure to maintain adequate cyber security is a matter of increasing social salience. Negligent failure to do so is widely regarded as blameworthy and will be regarded as especially blameworthy in cases involving embarrassing or other confidential facts.

The kinds of disclosures that have occurred thus far involve such facts as medical data on tens of thousands of individuals. The liability faced by an allegedly negligent defendant under such circumstances would be catastrophic in magnitude. As we noted earlier, this prospect is one of the considerations that underlies the economic loss rule. Imposing liability focuses an enormous cost on a single party, whereas denying liability spreads a large number of small losses among victims who have the potential to buy health, disability, property, and business interruption insurance against them.[109] In contrast to economic losses incurred by victims of data breaches, however, emotional losses from public disclosure of confidential information will be much more difficult for potential victims to insure against. There is no prospect that such insurance will become available any time soon, and we doubt that such insurance will ever be feasible. There has never even been a separate market for first-party insurance against pain and suffering associated with physical injury, for example, despite the fact that such loss is likely to be more easily quantified than embarrassment associated with disclosure of private information.

Taking all these considerations into account, we predict that, in contrast to what we suggested would be considerable judicial reluctance to recognize broad liability for economic loss resulting from data breaches, a limited cause of action for negligently enabling public disclosure of confidential digital information will be recognized. We think that, at least initially, successful actions will be restricted to cases in which comparatively small groups of victims have suffered distinctive and severe forms of harm. The small size of the victim group would serve as a counterweight to the fear of imposing potentially unlimited liability. That has been the model in the analogous area of misrepresentation of the financial condition of a business.[110]

Thus, health insurers, and others who maintain individuals' medical data, as well as dating or similar websites as to which the mere fact of participation is confidential, will simply have to recognize the enormous potential liability they face if they do not maintain reasonable security against hacking. They may find it in their interest to purchase substantial amounts of insurance against such liability, in the same manner that major corporations now purchase hundreds of millions of dollars' worth of insurance against liability for bodily injury and property damage.[111]

For companies such as Anthem and other leading health insurers, this is a feasible approach. We suspect that the major consequence for smaller companies that experience a data breach resulting in widespread public disclosure, however—Ashley Madison, for example—will be bankruptcy and only limited compensation, if any, for the victims of such disclosures. That is a prospect of which users of confidential social websites should be aware.

A major, and unpredictable, factor affecting the potential emergence of torts providing redress for the intangible injuries we have discussed above will be the cultural setting of those injuries. The pervasiveness of the injuries, the seriousness with which they are viewed by the general public, and the magnitude of losses they cause will play a role in generating pressure for legal relief. Once that pressure reaches a certain point, the question will become not whether to provide that relief but how the terms of the relief can be squared with practical considerations that invariably affect tort liability, such as how easily losses from injuries can be quantified; whether, if certain categories of intangible losses are deemed legally compensable, the extent of those losses can be contained; and whether mechanisms for spreading and shifting those losses exist so as to prevent crushing liability for them. Those considerations have come into play every time the tort system has recognized a new form of liability or a significant extension of an existing form. But before such considerations come into play, there needs to be substantial enough external pressure to convert an emerging feature of contemporary life into a "problem" to which it is thought tort law should respond. We are not currently in a position to determine which of the forms of intangible loss we have sketched above will evolve from being a feature of contemporary life to being a problem addressed by tort law. But we can predict that pressure emanating from society at large will serve to determine those future outcomes.

Conclusion

We began this chapter asking how torts come into being. We then showed that the notion that there is a residual *category* of tort liability has not been borne out in practice. New torts are not illustrations of the existence of an unnamed residual category of tort liability, for the simple reason that satisfaction of the preconditions for new torts results in the torts being named.

The paradox of residual tort liability is that every time a new tort is named and comes into being, it can no longer be understood as residual, even if it once were conceived in that fashion. But it is not difficult to understand why the concept of a residual category of tort liability might seem theoretically attractive. There is something counterintuitive about the notion that tort law is simply an aggregation of different causes of action. It is obvious that as tort law has evolved in the United States, something like the progressive extension of tort liability to diverse new situations has accompanied that evolution. To see that extension of tort liability as only taking place within existing tort actions does not seem quite accurate, and to characterize "tort law" as being limited to the aggregate of existing tort causes of actions at any point in time seems a cramped, conclusory view.

The concept of a sphere of residual tort liability existing in a space outside existing tort causes of action seems theoretically attractive, we believe, because there will always be occasional wrongs that fall outside existing causes of action but seem to call for legal redress. As the examples of potential tort liability for intangible harm we discussed illustrate, tort law is never static because new events and social attitudes toward them generate new perceptions of social wrongs for which some form of relief should be afforded, and tort law becomes a candidate to provide that relief. And since when tort law ends up providing some of the relief, the basis for that relief amounts to the naming of a new tort, it does not seem theoretically implausible to think of the relief as emanating from a sphere of residual tort liability. But in fact it does not.

Should some relief for harm from intangible forces, and harms largely of an intangible nature, end up being accorded by tort law, the new torts created to redress that harm will not serve to demonstrate the existence of an unnamed, residual category of tort law. Once the new torts are created, they will be named, and their naming will serve to strip them of any residual identity they may have had. In the end, the future of tortious relief for intangible harm, if it is to take any concrete form, will be in the form of new torts with names.

CONCLUSION

WE HAVE sought throughout this book to demonstrate that the construction of change in tort law occurs in a variety of ways and that continuity commonly accompanies change in tort law. We have also analyzed the different ways in which this occurs. The types of change we have chronicled have varied: legislative change of the witness rule that, along with other factors, was a prerequisite to the development of modern tort liability; change in the conceptual structure of tort law after abolition of the forms of action; substantive change in the law governing the dignitary torts, at both the common law and constitutional levels; the halting rise and eventual fall of prima facie tort; and possible future change in tort liability for intangible injury involving sexualized misconduct and cyber wrongdoing. In each instance, though in different ways, the change in question built on, was influenced by, reinterpreted, or filtered the past.

The notion that there has been more continuity with the past in the history of American life than has generally been recognized is a familiar theme in American history.[1] The manner and extent to which tort law maintains continuity in the face of change, however, have not been sufficiently recognized in tort law scholarship. The vast majority of tort law scholarship over the last century has been about change. This is understandable since the incidence of tort liability expanded enormously during this period, and there was important doctrinal change associated with increased tort liability as well. This focus on change, however, has underemphasized how much the judicial construction of change in tort law has been characterized by the effort to maintain continuity with the past.

In this chapter we draw together our observations about four general themes. These consist of the different forms of continuity—substantive and structural—that are associated with changes in tort law; the mix of internal and external influences on such changes; the role played by "lost history" and "counter-history" in our analysis; and the contrast between judicial decisions, which are most often responsible for both continuity and change in tort law, and legislative changes. The lesson of these observations is that history so substantially affects the construction of change in tort law as to amount to a fundamental feature of tort law itself. Without that feature, tort law as we know it would not be recognizable.

Substantive Continuity: Tort Law in Doctrinal Context

We have argued and demonstrated at length that much change in tort law takes a distinctive form. Tort law filters change through existing doctrinal frameworks that are internal features of the field, regularly using those frameworks to cloak the degree to which established doctrines are being modified or even abandoned.

THE DISTINCTIVE INTERACTION OF CHANGE AND CONTINUITY WITH EXISTING LEGAL DOCTRINE

When ideas or events in society raise arguably "new" issues for tort law, a "new" issue almost always fits somewhere in an existing doctrinal framework, either directly or by analogy. There is rarely such a thing as an entirely "novel" tort law issue. When an issue implicates concrete problems and choices in a way that it did not in the past, the courts nonetheless consider the issue against the backdrop of established doctrine. Even when the entertainment and resolution of the issue seems to require a modification, or an abandonment, of established doctrinal rules and principles, it is considered with those rules and principles in mind, and the resolution of the issue occurs in the language of those rules and principles. Thus, regardless of the novelty or urgency of an issue that surfaces because of developments in the larger culture, it is not simply taken to require a reconsideration of existing doctrine without being situated within that doctrine. Rather, if reconsideration is to take place, it is understood in the context of existing tort law rules and principles.

In establishing the new torts of intentional infliction of emotional distress and the various forms of invasion of privacy, for example, the courts made reference to and analogized the wrongs they were addressing to wrongs that were the subject of previous decisions which appeared to involve similar values. To some extent those references were attempts at cloaking in existing principles the degree of innovation they were accomplishing, but they were also efforts to identify the points of continuity between the past and the future. In short, change in the substantive orientation of tort law is never simply a reflexive response to changes in the external context that influences the field. Instead, it is constructed change, invariably filtered and sometimes the product of cloaking change with the structures of the past.

Harmonizing Precedent with Change

The construction of change in tort law and other common law fields takes a distinctive form because of the nature of judicial decision-making and the practices that have evolved in response to principles governing the proper role of the courts. Courts almost never invent new legal principles, at least not openly. The primary way in which judges communicate that their decisions are not simply the product of idiosyncratic personal preferences is by invoking established doctrinal rules and principles in support of those decisions.

The most important source of those rules and principles is the accumulation of prior judicial decisions thought applicable to the cases being decided—precedents. Precedents are taken to bear weight in the decision of current cases because, cumulatively, they establish doctrinal rules and principles, and because they represent the aggregated decisions of prior courts. This generates a built-in continuity to common law decision-making. The result is substantive continuity; there is a presumption that established legal doctrines and rules will be perpetuated in the decision of new cases, or if they are not, reasons for their modification of abandonment will be identified in the opinions accompanying new decisions. That is how the common law changes, even while maintaining continuity with the past.

Structural Continuity: Tort Law and the Modern "Forms of Action"

We have repeatedly encountered and identified a second form of continuity—in the very structure of tort law causes of action. The procedural heritage of common law fields—their origins in the writ system of pleading and the forms of action, which had distinctive requirements for bringing an action successfully into court—has had an effect on the kinds of legal disputes that a common law field, and especially tort law, can entertain.

In our focus on tort law, we regularly contrasted legal actions that have been recognized as "torts," meaning that they stem from injuries for which the legal system can provide redress, with other putative or potential actions which, although they can be shown to have caused "injury" to other persons, are not redressable through tort law. Initially courts and commentators referred to such actions, when they were deemed not redressable, as actions that were *damnum absque injuria,* injuries without remedies in tort. We have emphasized how difficult it has been for "novel" forms of injury to be identified as "new torts": when such injuries have emerged, the courts have typically either treated them as not compensable through tort law or folded them into existing tort actions, only occasionally recognizing new torts with separate elements, just as each form of action had its own particular elements.

In short, the number of tort actions has remained largely constant and relatively limited in number over the course of the history of American tort law. That feature of the common law of torts is not accidental. It is largely a product of structural continuity. Three illustrations of the continuing influence of the forms of action on the structure of tort law have been the persistent organization of casebooks and treatises to leave space for "miscellaneous" categories of tort actions that were products of the writ system, even after that system had been abolished; the failure of mid-twentieth-century commentators to reorganize some tort actions protecting various invasions of "dignity" or mental distress around a generic action for protection of "peace of mind"; and the difficulty "new torts" have in coming into being unless they can be shown to have discrete and limited elements that are not duplicated in existing torts, an echo of the discreteness required for successful tort actions under the forms of action.

In our view, two factors are responsible for modern tort law's replication of the structure—though obviously neither the substance nor the hyper-technicality—of the old forms of action. The first factor is that the actual and potential subjects of liability—various kinds of putatively wrongful conduct—have differing *normative weights.* Some kinds of conduct are perceived as more blameworthy than others and therefore have more appeal as targets of tort liability. The second factor is that the wrongs that are subject to tort liability must satisfy a number of practical and jurisprudential considerations, for which we use the term "justiciability."

Our contention is that doctrinal developments in tort law that are the distinctive product of the interaction of external developments and existing common law frameworks are affected by the factors of normative

weight and justiciability. The result is that something like natural selection singles out as good candidates for tort liability the causes of
action with elements satisfying those factors. Other potential causes
of action are either never considered, or are considered and rejected
or discarded, because they lack normative weight or present practical or
jurisprudential difficulties. Some causes of action, including new torts,
emerge and survive because their discrete and limited elements maxi-
mize normative weight and justiciability, while others do not. The consequence is a series of separate torts whose structure resembles the forms of
action that are their common law ancestors, in that they embody requisite
elements that have those maximizing characteristics. As has happened
for centuries, bright lines are drawn to separate actionable wrongs from
wrongs that do not qualify as torts.

NORMATIVE WEIGHT

At various times, widespread perceptions surface that certain kinds of
conduct are causing harms to others and that the conduct and resulting harms are socially troublesome enough to amount to "wrongs."
One example of this phenomenon we analyzed in detail was the emergence, about a century ago, of causes of action in tort for "pure"—that is,
standalone—emotional distress.

It was not as if people had not been subjected to emotional harm from
the negligent or intentional conduct of others prior to the decades in
which recovery in tort for that harm came to be permitted. The records
of nineteenth-century state courts are filled with cases in which plaintiffs sought, and were denied, recovery for standalone emotional harm in
situations where most modern observers would conclude that they had
been subjected to severe emotional distress by a defendant's conduct. The
denial of recovery in tort for pure emotional distress frequently took place
in cases where women were plaintiffs and was based on stereotyped attitudes about the nature of women's emotions. But the denial of recovery
for emotional harm also rested on a broader assumption, that misfortune,
suffering, and other negative features of life affected people on a regular
basis: "hurt feelings" produced by such phenomena were endemic. With
emotional distress so common a dimension of human experience, and
the continuum of emotional responses perceived to be so broad, it was
difficult for the courts to know what particular emotional reactions were
deserving of legal redress. As a result, until late in the nineteenth century,

identifying the causing of emotional harm as a "wrong" for which tort law should provide a remedy was not considered feasible.

This barrier to recovery was then surmounted because genuine emotional harm began to be taken more seriously by society at large instead of being dismissed as frivolous, idiosyncratic, or simply a necessary condition of individuals having contact with one another. As we argued in chapter 3, this was partly because the professionalization of specialists in mental health made emotional harm diagnosable and treatable. They could identify genuine emotional distress and distinguish it from idiosyncratic or feigned distress. In addition, the costs of diagnosing and treating emotional harm could be quantified and compensated through the payment of tort damages. Cumulatively, this social recognition of the normative weight of genuine emotional loss resulted in tort liability emerging as a basis for the redress of some conduct producing purely emotional harm.

The elements of any new tort also tend to reflect normative weight by focusing on what appears most "wrongful" about the conduct in question. Courts ensured that the principal new torts established in the twentieth century satisfied this condition by making only the most blameworthy forms of the conduct they addressed subject to liability. Thus, intentional infliction of emotional distress (IIED) is actionable only if the defendant's conduct in causing distress was "extreme and outrageous."[2] Analogous requirements apply in the torts involving invasion of privacy. Intrusion on seclusion is actionable only if the intrusion is intentional and would be "highly offensive" to a reasonable person.[3] Public disclosure of true private facts is actionable only if the matter publicized would be both "highly offensive" to a reasonable person and not "of legitimate concern" to the public.

What counts as having normative weight is heavily a matter of social perception, however, and therefore heavily determined by what the courts perceive to be normatively weighty. The white male judges of the early twentieth century could probably picture their wives and daughters traveling on railroads and being subjected to harassing or offensive treatment. They were much less likely to identify with the victims of racial bias or racist wrongdoing. The best remedy for this kind of deficiency in tort law, which after all is law made by judges, is to influence who wears judicial robes. As the judicial bench became more diverse, the wrongs recognized as having sufficient normative weight to support the imposition of tort liability became more diverse as well.

Another aspect of normative weight turns on the extent to which the wrongdoing in question can or cannot be fitted into an already-existing tort. The greater the fit, the smaller the residuum of wrongs that will go unredressed if a new tort is not created. Conversely, the less the fit, the larger the category of unredressed wrongdoing and the more likely the courts are to create a new tort. For example, intrusions on seclusion often did not involve physical trespass because they occurred through sight or hearing rather than physical presence, and public disclosure of true facts did not involve defamation because falsity of the defamatory statement is an element of that tort.[4] Establishment of those new causes of action redressed a major category of wrongful conduct that trespass and defamation could not capture.[5]

The point here is simply that the adoption of new torts may initially be driven by attitudes in the world outside the legal system about the normative weight—the perceived "wrongfulness" of the conduct—to which putative new torts are addressed. But then the emergence of new torts to provide redress for such conduct, as in the cases of liability for pure emotional distress and for invasion of privacy, has been subsequentially driven largely by doctrinal considerations internal to the tort system.

JUSTICIABILITY

A number of jurisprudential and practical considerations converge in the notion of justiciability. These include the availability of analogous precedent, the discreteness of the cause of action, the cognizability and adequacy of damages, and the number of potential suits. Along with normative weight, the justiciability of a particular potential cause of action in tort enhances the chance that it will be recognized as a new tort or identified as a previously unarticulated version of an existing tort. By sharply distinguishing actionable from nonactionable wrongs, those components of justiciability also make it more likely that the structure of any tort that is recognized will resemble the structure of the old forms of action. Thus, the justiciability prerequisite promotes structural continuity.

THE AVAILABILITY OF ANALOGOUS PRECEDENT

For the various reasons we have been discussing, courts are naturally in-clined to situate issues within existing doctrinal frameworks, largely but not entirely because of stare decisis. Continuity arises in part out of link-ing current decisions, even if they are innovative and constitute an expan-sion of liability, to the principles expressed or implied in prior precedents. We saw this occur, for example, in the early IIED decisions, in which the courts were able to cite cases resting on a common carrier's breach of its contract with a passenger as a basis for imposing liability, rather than openly imposing tort liability. Eventually, there were cases in which no contract was breached and tort liability was imposed nevertheless be-cause the courts were able to cite the principle thought to underly the earlier decisions, notwithstanding their having sounded in contract.

When analogous precedent is available in this fashion, the courts are more likely to be innovative because the availability of precedent facili-tates cloaking the actual basis for decision in the language of precedent, thereby serving to understate the extent to which innovation actually has occurred. The very fact that the courts tend to analogize innovative decisions to past precedents, which themselves already tend to reflect the structure of the forms of action, has a self-fulfilling quality that also maintains the structural continuity of tort law. The present and future tend to look structurally like the past because that is the path to which precedent and practice are directed.

DISCRETENESS

We believe that discreteness and self-containment are necessary elements of actions not only in tort law but in common law fields generally, and that those features are part of the heritage of the forms of action and the writ system. It would have been conceptually and theoretically possible for civil injuries not arising out of contract—torts—to have been orga-nized generically, with offenses against "human dignity," or "the person," or "property" being identified as giving rise to legal redress, leaving it to the courts to determine which offenses qualified in individual cases. That was in some sense the approach that the European civil law system took when codification occurred in the nineteenth century. The Napoleonic Code contains a very general provision imposing liability for "fault," leav-ing application to the courts.[6] And the German Civil Code contains three slightly more detailed general provisions.[7] The courts then filled in the details as the decades passed.

Not only did that not take place under the common law forms of action; in addition, their focus on procedural requirements resulted in tort actions not being described as general "wrongs" but as redressing specific types of injuries containing discrete elements. Moreover, the elements of actions established by the writ system—the requirement, for example, that actions brought under the writ of trespass be "direct" injuries produced by "force"—were exhaustive. If a prospective litigant could not meet the requirements of a form of action, he or she was altogether barred from bringing an action unless the circumstances of an injury could be shown to meet the requirements of some other form of action. The system thus functioned to place a number of activities that caused injury in the category of *damnum absque injuria*.

But the forms of action arguably did more than that. They placed emphasis on the specific elements of tort actions. Accordingly, very early on various kinds of "direct" injuries brought on by "force"—assault, battery, false imprisonment—were defined by their elements and separated from one another. Assaults were not batteries, although the same conduct by a defendant might result in both, and false imprisonments were distinct from each of the others. Torts did not overlap with one another. That was not only apparent in the "older" intentional torts but in the newer ones. The elements of defamation were not the same as those of invasion of privacy or of IIED.

The implicit requirement that tort actions characteristically be discrete and self-contained remains very important, and we predict will continue to do so with respect to putative "new torts" for intangible losses, such as those we identified in chapter 5. It is not enough for a putative new tort to be resonant with social norms, as with sexualized misconduct. A cognizable legal wrong must also have elements that allow it to be folded into an existing tort or elements that could result in its becoming a standalone new tort. Having those elements means more than having normative weight. It means having characteristics that separate the new tort from preexisting torts and are sufficiently discrete, concrete, and self-contained to apply squarely to a core set of fact situations.

All that is arguably a legacy of the forms of action. The elements of new torts and of expanded liabilities tend to be discrete, concrete, and contained, just as the forms of action were. A potential tort that would be open-ended tends to be unappealing to the courts because of the difficulties they anticipate it would later pose for them. The threat that there will not be a core set of routine facts to which a new doctrine can be easily applied, but instead a series of lawsuits in which the courts are called on in each case to define the scope of and fashion limits on liability, discourage creation of a new tort. On the other hand, if the scope of a potential new tort can be delineated to a reasonable extent in the early stages of its development, the prospect of recognizing it is far less threatening.

The elements of the two core privacy torts discussed in chapter 3, intrusion on seclusion and public disclosure of true facts, satisfied this requirement by specifying that the invasions in question must be "highly offensive" to the reasonable person.[8] This was so obviously limited to a discrete and contained (as well as normatively weighty) category of invasions that there was little prospect of its generating a series of suits posing challenges involving doctrinal formation and open-ended boundaries. In addition, whether an invasion was "highly offensive" posed a mixed question of fact and law, which meant that in many instances it would not be necessary for the courts to define in great detail the cases that fell into that category. Rather, if reasonable people could disagree about that question, answering it became the province of the jury, subject only to fairly general instructions.

The same was true of IIED, in which the defining and limiting criterion of liability was that the infliction be "extreme and outrageous." The lynchpin of this cause of action also posed a mixed question of fact and law that would be subject to application by juries on a case-by-case basis rather than requiring detailed standard development by the courts as a matter of law.[9] In short, the discreteness imperative played an important role in IIED becoming recognized as a new tort.

COGNIZABLE AND SUBSTANTIAL DAMAGES

A third feature of justiciability is that the damages that are awarded for commission of a tort must be cognizable and substantial. Tangible losses tend to be more quantifiable, and therefore more cognizable, than intangible losses. This is one of the many reasons that liability for bodily injury and property damage has traditionally been more robust than liability for intangible harm. Neither the privacy torts nor IIED had easily cognizable damages because the harm suffered by the plaintiff was almost always exclusively emotional.[10] For this reason, the courts had been reluctant, up to the point at which those torts were finally recognized, to countenance awards for pure emotional loss. A cause of action for negligent infliction of emotional distress, for example, still has been recognized in only very limited circumstances.[11]

We suspect that it was not merely increased comfort with awards of damages for pure emotional loss that led to the courts' acceptance of causes of action that involved this form of loss in privacy and IIED cases. Rather, the high degree of normative weight required by the elements of invasions of privacy and IIED to be actionable meant that awards for compensatory damages actually functioned something like punitive damages. Under such circumstances, the courts could overlook the difficulties associated with quantifying the amount of emotional loss the plaintiff had suffered, because they did not think of the awards as being completely geared to the amount of loss the plaintiff had suffered as they would have been in cases involving less blameworthy behavior by the defendant.

A number of contemporary proposals for new torts contemplate awarding damages that would fail the cognizability test pretty badly. For example, the damages available for the proposed tort of suppression of protected speech would compensate for "frustration, humiliation, feelings of powerlessness," and "the denial of a fundamental aspect of citizenship."[12] Similarly, a number of courts have refused to recognize a tort of spoliation of evidence because of the uncertainties associated with damages that may have resulted from spoliation.[13] The marginal cognizability of damages in many spoliation cases also seems related to the difficulty of proving a causal connection between spoliation and loss, since the harm often involves impairment of the ability of the plaintiff to have succeeded in a lawsuit, a quintessentially speculative question.[14] Unsurprisingly, many of the cases in which spoliation claims survive motions for summary judgment adopt an approach to causation whose proof is less problematic.[15]

In addition to being cognizable, the damages to be awarded in a new or expanded tort must promise to have considerable magnitude for two reasons. First, other things being equal, the greater the amount of damages involved, the greater the normative weight of the wrong involved. It is obviously more blameworthy to risk a lot of harm than to risk a small amount.

Second, the U.S. system of compensating plaintiffs' attorneys reinforces the adequacy prerequisite. Most attorneys representing plaintiffs in tort actions take the cases on a contingent-fee basis. If the plaintiff recovers damages, either through judgment or settlement, then the plaintiff's counsel is paid a previously agreed-upon percentage of the recovery. If the plaintiff recovers nothing, however, the plaintiff's counsel is paid nothing. Cases that promise only vindication, or nominal damages that merely signify indignation over the defendant's behavior, are less likely to be brought.

As a consequence, plaintiffs' attorneys make risk-reward calculations in deciding which cases to take. A case with a low probability of success must promise a significant payoff in the event that it is successful or it is not a good "bet" for an attorney considering whether to take it. Any case that would require establishing a new cause of action will necessarily involve an investment by the plaintiff's attorney that is substantially in excess of the investment required in a case falling within an established tort. Addressing legal issues of first impression at trial and on appeal is costly. A defendant who is a likely repeat-player in litigation if a new tort is established, or a liability insurer that will face repeated claims for coverage arising from that tort is involved, will oppose recovery even more strongly, and the investment of time and money required by the plaintiff's attorney will increase accordingly.

The upshot of these considerations is that cases that do not involve significant potential damages are much less likely to materialize in lawsuits than cases that have the prospect of a significant payoff in damages. This means not only that any individual case must present such a prospect but also that there be some prospect that there will be other cases in the future if a new tort is established, so that an attorney in the first case can amortize his or her substantial investment in establishing a new tort over a set of future cases, which will cost less per case to litigate than the first case. To put it another way, the greater the probability that the front-end cost of establishing a new tort can in effect be recovered in future cases, the greater the likelihood that the effort to establish a new tort will be undertaken. And only if such efforts are undertaken, sometimes repeatedly, can the courts rule about whether to recognize the putative new tort.

The cognizability and substantiality considerations thus have both a logical and a practical connection to structural continuity. Logically, cognizable and substantial damages are correlated with normative weight, and with discrete and limited elements. A broad, vague tort would produce some cases that did not satisfy those criteria. And as a practical matter, the tendency of plaintiffs' lawyers to bring cases that promise a positive return on their investment means they will characterize their claims as involving as little innovation as is possible. That will mean analogizing their claims to what has happened in the past. And what has happened in the past, as we know, is that causes of action that are structurally similar to the forms of action are the ones that have thrived.

A SUFFICIENT NUMBER OF CASES

The same considerations apply to the difference between claims that are likely to be numerous and those that will be rare. The former are much more likely to be analogous to claims that have been recognized in the past. The nearly infinite variety of life throws up any number of examples of objectionable conduct that might otherwise qualify as tortious. But the occasional one-off or rare kind of wrongdoing is unlikely to generate a lawsuit, or if it does, unlikely to prompt the courts seriously to contemplate recognizing the conduct as tortious. First, without a critical mass of cases, the courts simply will not have the opportunity to construct change—to articulate and develop the standards that govern a potential new tort. Faced with allegations that may well seem to be one of a kind, the courts will be presented with a motion to dismiss on the ground that the complaint fails to state a cause of action. When they conclude not only that the allegations do not fall into an existing form of tort liability but also that they are unlikely to be repeated very often, the courts will be disinclined to permit a suit to proceed. They are likely to shy away from recognizing the kind of claim that they predict will end after just a first step. Even if a court did recognize a cause-of-action, the absence of subsequent cases involving similar allegations would mean that the initial recognition had led nowhere, making it an isolated, unclassified instance of something indeterminate. This prospect will discourage permitting the imposition of liability in such cases.

In addition, a case that the courts perceive as being unique or extremely unusual will not be understood to reflect a form of wrongful conduct that requires what Oliver Wendell Holmes, Jr., called the "cumbrous and expensive machinery" of government to be called into action.[16] Actions in tort are typically perceived as addressing recurring patterns of misconduct that, precisely because they recur, warrant legal intervention. One-off wrongs simply do not qualify on this score. Although the perceived uniqueness of a form of wrongful conduct is an index of the low social salience that we have already identified as being a barrier to the development of a new tort, it is a highly practical consideration as well: very unusual wrongs are unlikely to be embraced by the tort system precisely because their uniqueness suggests they are unlikely to recur across a range of cases. And wrongs that are not unusual are likely structurally to resemble the wrongs redressed by torts that have the same structure as the old forms of action. It takes a set of cases before they can even be understood to satisfy the requirement that they be discrete and contained.

Internalist and Externalist Legal History

Our approach has associated the judicial construction of change in tort law with the interaction of potential changes in the field with established doctrinal frameworks and practices that foster continuity. Although the approach is thus informed by both "internalist" and "externalist" perspectives, our main focus has been on internal features of common law decision-making. The obvious and necessary reason for this focus is that both continuity and change in tort law occur and are reflected in tort law's doctrinal structure. By this focus we do not mean to suggest that external pressure for substantive change in tort law is retarded by internal features. But substantive change, we have argued, is invariably *filtered* by those features, even when external developments result in established common law rules and doctrines being substantially modified or abandoned.

Cloaking and Filtering Revisited

We have identified a number of different instances in which courts, while engaging in substantial modification of doctrine, articulated what they were doing in terms that we described as cloaking. There is admittedly a sense in which this phrase could connote disingenuous concealment. At a simplistic level, that is what cloaking is. But that is the case only for the legally unsophisticated reader of judicial opinions. Any sophisticated lawyer can read opinions that engage in this process, consult the sources of authority cited in the opinions, and understand that the precedents relied on by the courts are not directly on point nor closely analogous to the facts and issues being decided, or do not stand for the precise propositions the court asserts they stand for.

In such situations, it really would not be accurate to say that cloaking is disingenuous, or that it is concealment, or that it is misleading. Rather, it is a form of judicial reasoning that reflects respect for the past and honors the norms of continuity and the appropriate judicial role that are so important in common law decision-making. Cloaking is in that sense a legal convention about how to construct, explain, and justify change. The convention is not, and should not be, heavily subject to sincerity considerations, any more than other conventions, like standing to show respect for a judge in a courtroom, require complete sincerity in order to be wholly successful and appropriate. Rather, cloaking is simply one manifestation of the numerous ways in which history is an inevitable dimension of changes in tort law.

Virtually all historians, and most members of the general public, undoubtedly believe that history is a process of qualitative change in which the present never precisely resembles the past and the future never precisely duplicates the present. What serves as external pressure for legal change in our analysis might be thought of as distinctive only in that it is a special version of that pressure, directed at the American legal system in general and at judicial common law decisions in particular. External pressure exists in many other forms, ranging from protest rallies through changing consumer tastes to political campaigns. Most people think that such pressure is an ongoing "sign of the times," and we agree: we are simply focusing on the ways in which it has been accommodated in judicial decisions about tort law.

But our claim that the accumulated residue of prior judicial decisions "inevitably" affects the ways in which new cases in a common law field are decided may seem less intuitively obvious. This is because the claim runs counter to a strong version of the externalist perspective on legal history, which posits that legal decisions, including judicial decisions, simply mirror developments in the larger culture, and that there is nothing "autonomous" about legal decision-making. We are not only opposing that view; we are maintaining that external pressure for change in established common law doctrines is almost always filtered through received doctrinal frameworks. In that sense, notwithstanding how novel a legal issue clamoring for resolution because of external pressure may be thought to be, cases raising that issue will never truly be cases of "first impression," because the issue will invariably be situated in some doctrinal framework. And in that sense judicially constructed change in tort law, and we think in other common subjects as well, tends to take the distinctive form that we have been emphasizing.

What we have called judicial filtering is thus inevitable, although cloaking occurs only selectively. Many, perhaps most, judicial decisions are comparatively straightforward applications of existing common law rules and doctrines to new cases in which they are deemed apposite. But when the application of existing doctrine to new cases where it is perceived as applicable is straightforward and largely incontestable, those cases are not often litigated, or if they are, rarely reach appellate courts, whose major emphasis is on fashioning general propositions that are applicable to a range of cases. When, in contrast, external pressure invites a reconsideration and potential modification of existing doctrine, cloaking frequently occurs.

Patterns of Interaction

The interactions between external forces and internal, doctrinal frameworks that we have explored occurred in three different patterns. In the first pattern, external developments overwhelm established doctrines of practices. The most vivid example of this pattern was the abandonment of the prohibition on party testimony we described in chapter 1. In that episode, a longstanding set of assumptions about the epistemology of the civil trial (that the primary function of a trial was less a search for truth than a confirmation of what were thought of as indelible spiritual and social features of the world) was gradually abandoned, as modern epistemological attitudes began to surface. Suddenly, beginning in the 1850s in both England and America, the prohibition was repealed by legislation. The abandonment of the prohibition was so abrupt and so sweeping that when John Henry Wigmore edited the sixteenth edition of *Greenleaf on Evidence* in 1899, he wrote as if the attitudes supporting it had been nonsensical.

Shortly after repeal, the prohibition against party testimony had not only been discarded but also largely forgotten. It remains largely forgotten today. The episode thus illustrates a comparatively rare instance in which neither the filtering of external pressure to reframe a legal doctrine, nor the cloaking of changes that actually undermined a doctrine in the guise of doctrinal continuity, could occur. Instead, the entire intellectual apparatus supporting the doctrine—the premodern conception of the purposes of the civil trial—was discarded, and once discarded, "modern" techniques such as the cross-examination of witnesses and the hearsay rule were introduced which rested on a different conception of the function of a trial, that of a search for truth.

But such episodes are not, in our view, the rule. They are exceptional because they require a full abandonment not only of established doctrine but of the assumptions underlying that doctrine. Nonetheless, the fact that such episodes do occasionally occur underscores for us the power that external developments can bring to bear on established legal doctrines and practices, and cautions against too monolithic an emphasis on internal doctrinal frameworks and practices in explaining the process of judicially constructed change in common law fields.

A second pattern stands at the other extreme, in which the impetus for change is largely internal and comparatively uninfluenced by external pressure. Our principal example of this pattern involves Francis Bohlen's vision for the reconceptualization of tort while he served as the Reporter for the *Restatement of Torts*. There was no real external pressure for this reconceptualization. Rather, it represented an effort on Bohlen's part to escape the structure of the old forms of actions, motivated largely by a desire to bring an internal coherence to tort law that it lacked. As we showed in chapter 2, this effort was unsuccessful, at least in part because of the inevitable gravitational pull of history, reflected in the structure of the forms of action. Examples of this pattern are also rare.

The last pattern involving the interaction of external developments and internal doctrinal structure is in our view the predominant one. This is a pattern in which external developments influence the courts to make doctrinal changes, but because courts are constrained by history and precedent, and therefore labor to fit any changes they make within an existing doctrinal framework, the changes they construct seek to maintain continuity between the past and the future. Several of the episodes we examined fit this pattern. A principal example was the emergence of new torts in the first three decades of the twentieth century, such as various forms of privacy and intentional infliction of emotional distress. Early decisions allowing individuals to maintain tort actions in those areas needed to engage in cloaking because there was no received doctrinal framework acknowledging the existence of any of the torts. The courts drew analogies to existing actions, ranging from those protecting rights of personal property and assaults to rights afforded by state constitutions, such as the liberty of speech. The analogies were often contrived, but courts chose to make use of them because they recognized the normative weight attached to the wrongs in question, such as the disclosure of private information or the intentional subjecting of persons to emotional harm, that had become relatively common features of early twentieth-century life in America.

A second example of this pattern was reflected in the constitutionalization of defamation, certain of the privacy torts, and IIED in the period beginning with *New York Times v. Sullivan* in 1964. As we saw in chapter 4, this episode began with the pressure created by the civil rights movement for protection against liability for defamation for those criticizing government. The Supreme Court decisions extending the protections of the First Amendment then had to be harmonized with previous precedents in the common law of defamation. Although the common law of torts was openly modified, this was done so within the structure of that common law—for example, by characterizing the new limitations on liability as a constitutional privilege designed to create breathing space, analogous to prior, non-constitutional privileges creating breathing space.

Finally, we predicted that, if new torts regarding sexualized misconduct and cyber wrongdoing are created, they will follow this third, predominant pattern. They will be created only to redress wrongs with substantial normative weight due to cultural pressure, they will then be fitted into the existing doctrinal structure of other torts based on intentionally wrongful and negligent conduct, and they will involve awards of cognizable damages. They will therefore have the inevitable force of history behind them.

Lost History and Counter-History

We uncovered four examples of what might be considered "lost" history in our analysis. Those were the repeal of the prohibition on party testimony, Bohlen's failed effort to reconceptualize all of tort law, the proposed "unification" of the dignitary torts in the 1960s, and the failure of prima facie tort to find a meaningful place in tort law. All four episodes were lost to history because they ceased to be law, or never became law. That is certainly a common characteristic of most lost legal history.

To oversimplify, what becomes law is not lost to history, though the way it became law may be forgotten. What does not become law, however, is easily forgotten. It may also be that putative legal changes that never materialize are more likely to be lost to history if they involve matters that are largely internal to the law. All of our examples have this characteristic, although the repeal of the prohibition of party testimony obviously had far-reaching effects beyond the legal system.

There is in this respect a connection between lost history and counter-history worth noting. We have not spoken expressly in this book about counter-history, although counter-history was implicit in some of what we said, and we indulged in a bit of it in passing. The connection is this: if lost history, once rediscovered, is not part of a counternarrative of some sort, then it is nothing but newfound fact. Lost history has significance only as part of counter-history. We tried to imagine, for example, a tort law world in which the prohibition on party testimony was not repealed but instead endured into the twentieth century. But we could not do it. That world would have been so different from the actual history that materialized that it was difficult to picture. But that difficulty makes our point: repeal of the prohibition on party testimony is an episode of such extraordinary importance that we cannot imagine what tort law would have been like without it.

It is easier to imagine what would have happened if our other examples of lost history had materialized into law and therefore had not been forgotten. We think that they would ultimately have failed anyway. Bohlen's conceptual scheme would not have accounted for enough of tort law, and his *Restatement* would in that respect have been regarded as inadequate or irrelevant. The ostensible unification of the dignitary torts would have proved to be only ostensible because actual liabilities for causing dignitary harms would have devolved back into the existing, separate torts. And prima facie tort would have slowly wound down into oblivion, having become only slightly more than a historical footnote. In each instance, the deep structure of tort liability would have eventually generated the same history that actually occurred earlier. Much lost history is lost because it never had a chance of becoming, or staying, law to begin with.

Judicial versus Legislative Versions of Continuity and Change in Tort Law

We want to conclude by saying more about why our focus has been on decisions by courts—common law decisions—rather than on decisions by other authoritative legal institutions, notably legislatures. Our thesis about the inevitability of history should be understood as limited to tort law decisions made by courts, although we suspect it might apply to judicial decisions in other common law fields as well.

We have not advanced any normative view in this book about whether substantive doctrinal changes in tort law should primarily be made by courts or legislatures. There are examples of both sorts of changes in the history of American tort law, with legislatures taking the lead in such reforms as workers' compensation, comparative fault, limits on recoverable damages, and the apportionment of liability among multiple parties, and courts being the primary innovators in a host of other areas.

We do want to note, however, that the theory of the relationship among tort law, continuity, and change that we propound in this book seems most applicable to decisions made by courts. This is because, as we have indicated, legislatures always have the option of either retaining continuity with their existing laws and policies or making discontinuous substantive changes by the fiat of majority rule. Legislators are elected officials, and if voters do not like the fact that legislators have kept certain laws or policies in place, or do not like the changes legislators make, voters can elect other representatives who pledge to modify existing policies or to reverse them. Legislatures, in short, do not have to wrestle with the implications of making sudden changes in common law doctrines in the same fashion as do courts.

In contrast, every time a court fashions a substantive doctrinal change, it implicitly raises the question as to what gives it, often an unelected body, the authority to do so. This leads courts to consult the received doctrinal framework in which cases are decided, and to engage in filtering, and sometimes in cloaking, in the course of constructing substantive doctrinal changes. A good deal of the attention of our chapters has been directed to analyzing those activities by judges. That analysis has been designed to demonstrate that effectuating change in the orientation of tort law in the United States has been a complex process in which courts have repeatedly dealt with the interaction of external developments and received doctrinal rules, forms, and frameworks.

In addition, legislative retention of, or changes in, existing laws and policies does not typically take the same form as the potential judicial reconsideration of existing doctrine. Legislatures have established mechanisms for entertaining and responding to political, cultural, and social pressure, such as holding hearings, responding to lobbying groups and messages from constituents, and publicizing the interest of particular legislators in pursuing reforms of various kinds. But legislatures, as an initial matter, do not have to formally entertain external pressure at all, whereas trial courts, and many appellate courts, do not have discretion to decline to hear a case simply because they feel it might raise potentially thorny doctrinal issues. Legislators may receive some negative public response if they utterly fail to respond to what appear to be pressing social problems, but they nonetheless have the option not to do so. In that sense legislators may decline to maintain continuity with, or effectuate changes in, existing laws and policies by fiat. Courts, except on the rare occasions in which they can summarily dismiss a pending lawsuit, do not, and if they engage in such summary dismissals too frequently are likely to be criticized.

In short, pressure is not brought to bear on courts in the same fashion as it is on legislatures, nor do the different institutions tend to respond to its presence in the same fashion. When courts accomplish change in response to purportedly novel and urgent legal issues, they filter change through received doctrinal frameworks. It is those frameworks that provide the distinctive form of continuity with the past that partly characterizes the development of doctrine in common law fields over time. History, in the form of accumulated precedents containing established doctrinal propositions, is thus always an ingredient in the course of common law doctrines.

None of those features is necessarily present in legislative responses to external pressure. A current legislature has no obligation to maintain continuity with the laws and policies promulgated by its predecessors; it may discard those forms of history altogether. Legislatures do not need to filter external developments through received laws and policies because they can scuttle those laws and policies at any time. For political reasons legislators may want to cloak changes in laws and policies as being less, or more substantial than they in fact are, but they have no institutional pressure to do so simply to preserve the appearance of continuity with the past because they have no perceived obligation to retain the laws or policies of their predecessors. Courts, on the other hand, operate in a jurisprudential universe in which the past decisions of their predecessors are not regarded as simply outcomes reached by past judges with particular agendas but evidence that doctrinal propositions of law transcend the opinions of the judges who declare and apply them, and promote stability, predictability, and respect for law when they remain in place.

Thus, we are only claiming that the distinctive interaction of law, continuity, and change is limited to judicial decisions about tort law, although it may apply to other common law fields as well. We close by noting that in the voluminous commentary about tort law in America and its history that has appeared over the last three centuries, precious little has been directed toward the central issues we explore in this book. We hope that with an enhanced understanding of the factors affecting the judicial construction of change in tort law over time, and the ways those factors interact, others might pursue comparable studies of other common law fields. We hope that this work might serve to stimulate additional studies seeking to illuminate how judicial decisions in common law fields are made, and how doctrinal changes in those fields come into being and evolve.

NOTES

PREFACE

1. The articles are *The Transformation of the Civil Trial and the Emergence of American Tort Law*, 59 ARIZ. L. REV. 431 (2017); *The Puzzle of the Dignitary Torts*, 104 CORNELL L. REV. 317 (2019); *Torts without Names, New Torts, and the Future of Liability for Intangible Harm*, 68 AM. U. L. REV. 2089 (2019); *First Amendment Imperialism and the Constitutionalization of Tort Liability*, 98 TEX. L. REV. 813 (2020); and *Conceptualizing Tort Law: The Continuous (and Continuing) Struggle*, MD. L. REV. (2021).

INTRODUCTION

1. *See* Oliver Wendell Holmes, Jr., *The Path of the Law*, 10 HARV. L. REV. 457 (1897); BENJAMIN N. CARDOZO, THE NATURE OF THE JUDICIAL PROCESS (1921).
2. CARDOZO, *supra* note 1, at 25.
3. For this reason, we think, it is not easy to find tort cases in which a victim of racial wrongdoing succeeded in recovering until late in the period. *See, e.g.*, Bullock v. Tamiani Tours, Inc., 266 F. 2d 326 (5th Cir. 1959) (the defendant had a duty to warn Jamaican plaintiffs that they could face racial violence while riding on a bus in the segregated South); Fisher v. Carousel Motor Hotel, Inc., 424 S.W. 2d 627 (Tex. 1967) (the plaintiff, an African American NASA employee, was entitled to recover for assault and battery where his cafeteria tray was yanked away from him in an offensive manner because "he could not be served" there).
4. Kimberly A. Yurako & Ronen Avraham, *Valuing Black Lives: A Constitutional Challenge to the Use of Race-Based Tables*, 106 CAL. L. REV. 25 (2018).
5. *See, e.g.*, MARTHA CHAMALAS & JENNIFER B. WRIGGINS, THE MEASURE OF INJURY: RACE, GENDER, AND TORT LAW (2010); CATHERINE A. MAC-KINNON, SEXUAL HARASSMENT OF WORKING WOMEN 164–74 (1979).
6. Melissa Milewski, *From Slave to Litigant: African Americans in Court in the Postwar South*, 30 L. & HIST. REV. 723, 737 (2012).
7. *See, e.g.*, CHAMALAS & WRIGGINS, *supra* note 5; Jonathan Cardi *et al.*, *Do Black Injuries Matter? Implicit Bias and Jury Decision Making in Tort Cases*, 93 S. CAL. L. REV. 507 (2020); Camile A. Nelson, *Considering*

Tortious Racism, 9 DePaul J. Health Care L. 905 (2005); Regina Austin, *Employer Abuse, Worker Resistance, and the Tort of Intentional Infliction of Emotional Distress,* 41 Stan. L. Rev. 1 (1988); Richard Delgado, *Words That Wound: A Tort Action for Racial Insults, Epithets, and Name Calling,* 17 Harv. C.R.-C.L. L. Rev. 133 (1982).

8. Martha Chamalas, *Race and Tort Law,* Ohio State University Moritz College of Law Working Paper (July 27, 2020); Jennifer B. Wriggins, *Damages in Tort Litigation, Thoughts on Race and Remedies, 1865–2007,* 27 Rev. Lit. 37 (2007).

9. The rule in all but a few states now is "comparative negligence," under which a plaintiff's recovery is reduced in proportion to the amount of negligence attributable to that individual.

10. Oliver Wendell Holmes, Jr., *Law in Science and Science in Law,* 12 Harv. L. Rev. 443, 444 (1899).

11. One way of putting this point, as two prominent commentators have recently suggested, is that courts sometimes make a "loaded judgment" about the fit of a current decision within an existing doctrinal framework, and that in doing so they engage in "elucidation" of existing precedent. *See* John C. P. Goldberg & Benjamin C. Zipursky, Recognizing Wrongs 253–54 (2020).

12. For an account of these changes, see Kenneth S. Abraham & G. Edward White, *Rethinking the Development of Modern Tort Liability,* 101 B. U. L. Rev. 1289 (2021).

13. 111 N.E. 1050 (N.Y. 1916).

14. This process is recounted in Edward H. Levi's classic study An Introduction to Legal Reasoning (1948).

15. 192 P. 2d 1 (Cal. 1948).

16. 377 P. 2d 897 (Cal. 1963).

17. John Fabian Witt, The Accidental Republic (2004).

18. Risa L. Goluboff, The Lost Promise of Civil Rights (2007).

19. *See, e.g.,* Roscoe Pound, *The Economic Interpretation and the Law of Torts,* 53 Harv. L. Rev. 365, 366–67 (1940).

20. For some exceptions, *see* Alan Watson, Society and Legal Change (1977); Charles Fried, *The Artificial Reason of the Law,* 60 Tex. L. Rev. 35 (1981); Richard Epstein, *The Social Consequences of Common Law Rules,* 95 Harv. L. Rev. 717 (1982).

21. Lawrence M. Friedman, A History of American Law 10 (1973).

22. Examples include Harry Scheiber, *The Road to Munn: Eminent Domain and Public Purpose in the State Courts, in* 5 Perspectives in American History: Law in American History 329 (Donald Fleming & Bernard Bailyn eds., 1971); Charles W. McCurdy, *Justice Field and the Jurisprudence*

of Government-Business Relations, 61 J. AM. HIST. 970 (1975); and BARRY CUSHMAN, RETHINKING THE NEW DEAL COURT (1998).

23. The most influential historiographical treatment was Robert W. Gordon, *Critical Legal Histories,* 36 STAN. L. REV. 57, 101 (1984).

24. Compare Laura Kalman, *The Constitution, the Supreme Court, and the New Deal,* 110 AM. HIST. REV. 1052 (2005), with William E. Leuchtenberg, *Comment on Laura Kalman's Article, id.* at 1081, and with G. Edward White, *Constitutional Change and the New Deal: The Internalist Externalist Debate, id.* at 1094.

25. *See* KENNETH S. ABRAHAM, THE LIABILITY CENTURY: TORT LAW AND INSURANCE FROM THE PROGRESSIVE ERA TO 9/11 (2008).

26. The growth and forms of liability insurance that became available during the period considered in this book are examined in *id.*

27. Richard A. Posner, *Wealth Maximization and Tort Law: A Philosophical Inquiry, in* PHILOSOPHICAL FOUNDATIONS OF TORT LAW 99 (David G. Owen ed., 1995); STEVEN SHAVELL, ECONOMIC ANALYSIS OF ACCIDENT LAW (1987).

28. ERNEST J. WEINRIB, THE IDEA OF PRIVATE LAW (rev. ed. 2012); JULES L. COLEMAN, THE PRACTICE OF PRINCIPLE (2001).

29. GOLDBERG & ZIPURSKY, *supra* note 11.

1. THE EPISTEMOLOGY OF THE CIVIL TRIAL AND THE RISE OF MODERN TORT LIABILITY

1. LEON F. LITWACK, NORTH OF SLAVERY: THE NEGRO IN THE FREE STATES, 1790–1960 93 (1965); Paul Finkelman, *Prelude to the 14th Amendment: Black Legal Rights in the Antebellum North,* 17 RUTGERS L. J. 415, 424–25 (1986).

2. Victor B. Howard, *The Black Testimony Controversy in Kentucky, 1866–72,* 58 J. NEGRO HIST. 140 (1973).

3. *See, e.g.,* Bentley v. Cooke, 99 Eng. Rep. 729 (K.B. 1784).

4. The sole exception in all of torts scholarship that we have found is JOHN FABIAN WITT, THE ACCIDENTAL REPUBLIC 56–57 (2004), whose reference to the rule first led us into this subject. Outside the field of tort law, the principal source that mentions the rule is JOHN H. LANGBEIN ET AL., HISTORY OF THE COMMON LAW 247 (2009). We wrote about the rule in Kenneth S. Abraham, *The Common Law Prohibition of Party Testimony and the Development of Modern Tort Liability,* 95 VA. L. REV. 489 (2009), and Kenneth S. Abraham & G. Edward White, *The Transformation of the Civil Trial and the Emergence of American Tort Law,* 59 ARIZ. L. REV. 431 (2017). In the course of our work, we also encountered reference to the rule in

George Fisher, *The Jury's Rise as Lie Detector,* 107 YALE L. J. 575, 624–29 (1997), and Joel Bodansky, *The Abolition of the Party Witness Disqualification: An Historical Survey,* 70 KY. L. J. 92, 94 (1982). Bodansky wrote about the rule while he was a student in a seminar taught by Langbein.

5. The Holmes essays, in chronological order, were *The Theory of Torts,* 7 AM. L. REV. 652 (1873); *Common Carriers and the Common Law,* 13 AM. L. REV. 909 (1879); and *Trespass and Negligence,* 14 AM. L. REV. 1 (1880). For a discussion of each of the articles and Holmes's changing theories of how tort law should be understood, which culminated in his two chapters on torts in his 1881 book THE COMMON LAW, *see* G. EDWARD WHITE, JUSTICE OLIVER WENDELL HOLMES: LAW AND THE INNER SELF 123–24, 137–47 (1993). In THE COMMON LAW, Holmes's chapters on tort law were entitled "Torts: Trespass and Negligence" and "Fraud, Malice, and Intent: The Theory of Torts." *See* OLIVER WENDELL HOLMES, JR., THE COMMON LAW 71–147 (G. Edward White ed., 2009).

6. LAWRENCE M. FRIEDMAN, A HISTORY OF AMERICAN LAW (1973). An early vivid example of the approach Friedman would later take can be found in Charles O. Gregory, *Trespass to Negligence to Absolute Liability,* 37 VA. L. REV. 359 (1951), which contains the following passage suggesting an explanation for Chief Justice Lemuel Shaw's apparent holding, in Brown v. Kendall, 60 Mass. 292 (1850). In that case Shaw declared that either intent or fault should be the standard of care for bodily injury liability. Gregory wrote, "While it is pure speculation, one of Chief Justice Shaw's motives underlying his opinion appears to have been a desire to make risk-creating enterprises less hazardous to investors and entrepreneurs than it had been previously at common law. . . . Judicial subsidies of the sort to youthful enterprise removed pressure from the pocket-books of investors and gave incipient industry a chance to experiment on low-cost operations without the risk of losing its reserve in actions by injured employees. Such a policy . . . in a small way . . . probably helped to establish industry, which in turn was essential to the good society as Shaw envisaged it." Gregory, *supra,* at 368. The fact that there was not a shred of language in Shaw's opinion making any reference to risk-creating activities, or to industrial enterprise, and that the defendant in *Brown v. Kendall* was a dog owner who injured a stranger seeking to break up a dog fight, did not deter Gregory. He merely extrapolated Shaw's "motives" from the presence of "infant" industries in Massachusetts at the time.

7. As Friedman put it, "The explosion of tort law, and negligence in particular, has to be laid at the door of the industrial revolution. . . . From about 1840 on, one specific machine, the railroad locomotive, generated . . . more tort law than any other in the 19th century. . . . American law had

to work out some fresh scheme to distribute the burden of railroad accidents, among workers, citizens, companies, and state. . . . The law developed in a way which the power-holders of the day considered socially desirable. This way, in brief, was to frame rules friendly to the growth of young businesses; or at least rules the judges thought would foster such growth. The rules put limits on the liabilities of enterprises. This was the thrust of the developing law of negligence." LAWRENCE M. FRIEDMAN, A HISTORY OF AMERICAN LAW 223 (3d ed. 2007).

8. Friedman explained, "This is a social history of American law. . . . This book treats American law . . . not as a kingdom unto itself, not as a set of rules and concepts, not as the province of lawyers alone, but as a mirror of society. It takes nothing as historical accident, nothing as autonomous, everything as relative and molded by economy and society. This is the theme of every chapter and verse." FRIEDMAN, *supra* note 6, at 10.

In his third edition, referring to its connection with the earlier editions, Friedman said about the book, "It is still a *social* history of law. It still rejects any notion that law is autonomous. Law is a mirror of society. Perhaps it is a distorted mirror. Perhaps in some regards society mirrors law. Surely law and society interact. But the central point remains: Law is the product of social forces, working in society. If it has a life of its own, it is a narrow and restricted life." FRIEDMAN, *supra* note 7, at ix.

9. *See* G. Edward White, *The Intellectual Origins of Torts in America,* 86 YALE L. J. 671, 679–82 (1977). For a more extended version of the hypothesis, see G. EDWARD WHITE, TORT LAW IN AMERICA: AN INTELLECTUAL HISTORY 8–19 (expanded ed. 2003).

10. WITT, *supra* note 4, at 13–17.

11. One of us has defined modernism as "the actual world brought about by a combination of advanced industrial capitalism, increased participatory democracy, the weakening of a hierarchical class-based social order, and the emergence of science as an authoritative method of intellectual inquiry." G. EDWARD WHITE, THE CONSTITUTION AND THE NEW DEAL 5 (2000). For more detail on changing conceptions of causal agency, *see* DOROTHY ROSS, THE ORIGINS OF AMERICAN SOCIAL SCIENCE 3–17 (1990).

12. *See* WHITE, TORT LAW IN AMERICA, *supra* note 9, at 148–49. As late as 1881 Holmes invoked this attitude in a noteworthy passage in THE COMMON LAW in which he argued that liability in tort should be restricted to injuries that were the product of intentional or negligent conduct: "The general principle of our law is that loss from accident must lie where it falls, and this principle is not affected by the fact that a human being is the instrument of misfortune. . . . The state might conceivably make itself a mutual insurance company against accidents, and distribute the burden

of its citizens' mishaps among all its members. There might be a pension for paralytics, and state aid for those who suffered in person or estate from tempest or wild beasts. . . . The state does none of these things, however, and the prevailing view is that its cumbrous and expensive machinery ought not to be set in motion unless some other benefit is derived from disturbing the status quo. . . . It is no more justifiable to make me indemnify my neighbor against the consequences [of losses from accidents] than to make me do the same thing if I had fallen upon him in a fit, or to compel me to insure him against lightning." HOLMES, THE COMMON LAW, *supra* note 5, at 87–88.

    One of us has associated the late emergence of liability insurance in tort law and the resistance of late nineteenth-century courts and commentators to the idea that the tort system should be employed as a means of compensating injured persons to the persistence of an older "ethos of injury" in which injuries suffered by humans was attributed to bad luck, deficiencies of character, or the "costs of the struggle of life," rather than something for which "society bore some collective responsibility." WHITE, TORT LAW IN AMERICA, *supra* note 9, at xvii, 70. Recent work has uncovered examples of government-funded disaster relief as early as the late eighteenth century; *see generally* MICHELE LANDIS DAUBER, THE SYMPATHETIC STATE (2013), but the relation between these sporadic legislative actions and general cultural attitudes is unclear.

13. This was the case despite the premodern understanding that human beings were essentially self-interested creatures who coveted power and pursued their "interests," and that certain people, such as sovereigns or the masters of slaves, had a form of absolute power. Those power roles, however, were not treated as the result of *human* intervention but as gifts from God. For more detail, *see* WITT, *supra* note 4, at 6–16.

14. For discussions of premodern and modern epistemology, and the relationship of "modernist" attitudes toward causal agency, social organization, and the sources of knowledge to "modernity," *see* DOROTHY ROSS (ed.), MODERNIST IMPULSES IN THE HUMAN SCIENCES (1994), especially the essays by Ross, *Modernism Reconsidered* and *Modernist Social Science in the Land of the New/Old, in id.* at 1–25 and 171–89.

    We are associating a shift from premodern to modern epistemology with a massive change in attitudes toward the sources of causal agency in the universe that took place over the course of the nineteenth century in England and America. The shift amounted to a relocation of the locus of power to determine the destinies of humans and the course of a society's history from external causal agents, such as the "will" of an omnipotent deity, the relatively fixed hierarchy of social classes and orders, the forces of nature, and the purportedly inevitable cycles of history in which societies came into being, matured, and decayed, to humans holding power, exercising their wills, using science and technology to learn about and master the external world, altering the class structure of society, and making their futures better than their pasts. Early recognition of the ubiquity of this epistemological shift can be seen in J. G. A. Pocock's THE MACHIAVELLIAN MOMENT (1975). For efforts to link the shift to the emergence of the social sciences in America, *see* DOROTHY ROSS, THE ORIGINS OF AMERICAN SOCIAL SCIENCE (1991), and Ross's earlier article *Historical Consciousness in Nineteenth-Century America*, 89 AM. HIST. REV. 909 (1984). G. EDWARD WHITE, THE MARSHALL COURT AND CULTURAL CHANGE (1988), identified the consciousness of the Marshall Court, and the attitudes of its justices and early nineteenth-century commentators toward law and judging, as forming a stark contrast to "modern" attitudes but did not employ the term "premodern." For definitions of the terms "modernity" and "modernism," *see* G. EDWARD WHITE, THE CONSTITUTION AND THE NEW DEAL 5–10 (2000). *See also* Stephen M. Feldman's overview AMERICAN LEGAL THOUGHT FROM PREMODERNISM TO POSTMODERNISM (2000).

15. Addison's THE LAW OF TORTS was published in 1860. An American work on torts, Francis Hilliard's THE LAW OF TORTS, had appeared in two volumes in 1859.

16. *See, e.g.,* Nicholas St. John Green's preface to his 1870 abridgement of Addison, *supra* note 15, in which Green noted that "a large portion of the matter which [Addison's 1860 edition contained] included coverage of 'bailments, easements, patents, and copyrights,' as well as 'evidence' pleading, and practice.'" CHARLES G. ADDISON, THE LAW OF TORTS iii (1870). For more detail, *see* G. Edward White, *The Emergence and Doctrinal Development of Tort Law, 1870–1930*, 11 U. ST. THOMAS L. J. 403, 468 (2014).

17. Patrick Devlin, *Jury Trial of Complex Cases: English Practice at the Time of the Seventh Amendment*, 80 COLUM. L. REV. 43, 57–64 (1980).

18. The Massachusetts experience suggests that at least in some early American jurisdictions, the common law courts were inclined toward a more flexible interpretation of common law writ pleading. For more detail on early Massachusetts, *see* William J. Curran, *The Struggle for Equity Jurisdiction in Massachusetts*, 31 B. U. L. REV. 269 (1951); for more on New York, *see* HENRY W. SCOTT, THE COURTS OF THE STATE OF NEW YORK 259–62 (1909).

19. *See* THEOPHILUS PARSONS, TREATISE ON CONTRACTS (1853). An English treatise, John Joseph Powell's ESSAY ON THE LAW OF OBLIGATIONS AND CONTRACTS, had appeared as early as 1818, representing the culmination of work Powell had first published in 1790.

20. *See* ROBERT WYNESS MILLER, CIVIL PROCEDURE OF THE TRIAL COURT IN HISTORICAL PERSPECTIVE 52–57 (1952), demonstrating that the replacement of writ pleadings with a unitary civil action, first introduced in New York in 1848, was still not fully in place in 1912 in New Jersey and in 1915 in Michigan.

21. *See* WITT, *supra* note 4, at 12–17. It is striking how under-researched antebellum American attitudes about the causal origins of injury and suffering have been among historians. For a notable exception, see Thomas L. Haskell, *Capitalism and the Origins of Humanitarian Sensibility, in* THE ANTISLAVERY DEBATE 107–60 (Thomas Bender ed., 1992).

22. WHITE, TORT LAW IN AMERICA, *supra* note 9, at 148–49.

23. With the exception of James Oldham's retrieval of Lord Mansfield's civil trial notes, there has been no scholarship able to rely on civil trial court testimonial records, either in England or in America, for the period with which we are concerned. *See* JAMES OLDHAM, THE MANSFIELD MANUSCRIPTS AND THE GROWTH OF ENGLISH LAW IN THE EIGHTEENTH CENTURY (2 vols. 1992); James Oldham, *Truth Telling in the English Courtroom,* 12 L. & HIST. REV. 95 (1994). John H. Langbein's comparably important retrieval of the trial notes of eighteenth-century judge Dudley Ryder focuses on criminal cases. John H. Langbein, *Shaping the Eighteenth-Century Criminal Trial: A View from the Ryder Sources,* 50 U. CHI. L. REV. 1 (1983); John H. Langbein, *Historical Foundations of the Law of Evidence: A View from the Ryder Sources,* 96 COLUM. L. REV. 1168 (1996). *See also* JOHN H. LANGBEIN, THE ORIGINS OF ADVERSARY CRIMINAL TRIAL (2003), for a more general treatment, albeit focusing on criminal rather than civil proceedings. Oldham's transcriptions of Mansfield's trial notes in torts cases between 1756 and 1788 reveal that there was no witness testimony by either plaintiffs or defendants in the cases.

24. For the mid-nineteenth-century commentary, *see On the Testimony of Witnesses, Parties to the Record,* 10 MONTHLY L. MAG 50 (1841), an English publication. Connor Hanly, *The Decline of the Jury Trial in Nineteenth-Century England,* 26 J. LEGAL HIST. 253 (2005), collects a significant amount of early and mid-nineteenth-century articles and parliamentary debates about the efficacy of jury trials in civil disputes, commentary that was, in our view, highly relevant to the increasing professional dissatisfaction with the witness disqualification rule.

Abraham, *supra* note 4, at 490–93, collects the sources for more recent scholarship. LANGBEIN ET AL., *supra* note 4, at 247–48, take it for granted that what they call the application of "disqualification for interest" rules to parties as well as nonparties was in place "in the seventeenth century." *Id.*

at 247. They also suggest, without elaborating, that "testimonial disqualification retarded branches of the law, especially tort." *Id.* at 248.

25. George Fisher's important work on the history of the criminal jury describes its evolution and surveys the historical research that has been done on the subject, in both criminal and civil cases. *See generally* Fisher, *supra* note 4.

26. *Id.* at 591–94.

27. Oldham, *Truth Telling in the English Courtroom, supra* note 23, at 120.

28. The classic study of the dominant influence of squires on the voting practices of members of their households or village residents of lower social status is Thomas J. Wertenbaker, The Founding of American Civilization: The Middle Colonies (1938), an extension of Wertenbaker's Planters of Colonial Virginia (1922).

29. Both Mansfield and Ryder engaged in those practices. *See* Langbein, *Historical Foundations of the Law of Evidence, supra* note 23; 2 Oldham, The Mansfield Manuscripts, *supra* note 23, at App. E, 1541–1623.

30. Jeffrey Gilbert, The Law of Evidence 122 (1756), quoted by Fisher, *supra* note 4, at 625.

31. Fisher, *supra* note 4, at 624–25, 625 n. 204, cites Wigmore's conclusion that the parties were barred from testifying in civil cases by the mid-sixteenth century, and interested witnesses by the mid-seventeenth century, but suggests that this may simply have been because these were the earliest references Wigmore could find.

32. Fisher, *supra* note 4, at 584, 590, citing The Tryal of Slingsby Bethel Esq. (1681); Langbein, *Historical Foundations of the Law of Evidence, supra* note 23, at 1170; Fisher, *supra* note 4, at 584; Langbein et al., *supra* note 4, at 41, citing James B. Thayer, A Preliminary Treatise on the Law of Evidence at Common Law 90 (1898).

33. Fisher, *supra* note 4, at 606. We have seen nothing to indicate that there was an analogous practice of permitting the unsworn testimony of the parties in civil cases.

34. For more detail, *see generally* Heidi Brayman Hackel, Reading Material on Early Modern England (2009).

35. *See* Abraham, *supra* note 4, at 499–500.

36. Simon Greenleaf, A Treatise on the Law of Evidence (3 vols. 1842).

37. James Kent, Commentaries on American Law (4 vols. 1826–30). Story and Greenleaf were the two faculty members at the Harvard Law School at the time Greenleaf's treatise was issued. For more detail, *see* Daniel R. Coquillette & Bruce A Kimball, On the Battlefield of Merit: Harvard Law School, The First Century 166–73 (2015).

38. John H. Wigmore, A Treatise on the Anglo-American System of Evidence in Trials at Common Law (2 vols. 1904). Wigmore edited the first volume of the 16th edition of Greenleaf's A Treatise on the Law of Evidence (1899).

39. 1 Greenleaf, *supra* note 36, at 375–478.

40. *Id.* § 386 at 431–32.

41. *Id.* § 388 at 433. Emphasis in original.

42. Although the concept of an honorary obligation was perhaps heightened in the antebellum American South, for which *see* Bertram Wyatt-Brown, Southern Honor: Ethics and Behavior in the Old South (1982), it was entrenched in other areas of nineteenth-century America as well. *See* Ryan Chamberlain, Pistols, Politics and the Press (2008); Andrew Porwancher, The Devil Himself (2016).

43. The most extensive discussion of the transformation of evidence law in England between the 1780s and 1820s is T. P. Gallanis, *The Rise of Modern Evidence Law*, 84 Iowa L. Rev. 499 (1999). Oldham, *Truth Telling in the English Courtroom*, *supra* note 23; Fisher, *supra* note 4; and Langbein et al., *supra* note 4, at 452–56, agree that in the decades on which Gallanis focuses, and most particularly between the 1820s and the 1850s, when the witness rules began to be abolished in both England and America, prohibitions against hearsay evidence were tightened and cross-examination of witnesses in both criminal and civil trials became routine.

44. As Wigmore put it, cross-examination was "the greatest legal engine ever invented for the discovery of truth." 2 Wigmore, *supra* note 38, § 1367 at 1697.

45. A standard reference on the origins of the chancery courts in England is T. F. T. Plucknett, A Concise History of the Common Law 178–81 (5th ed. 1956).

46. *See* Patrick Devlin, *Jury Trial of Complex Cases at the Time of the Seventh Amendment*, 80 Colum. L. Rev. 43, 58–59 (1980). The case was Chapman v. Graves (1810), quoted in full in Stevens v. Lynch, 2 Camp. 333, n. 2 (1809).

47. *On the Testimony of Witnesses, Parties to the Record*, *supra* note 24, at 54 (italics in original).

48. *Id.*

49. 1 Car. & P. 577 (1824).

50. *On the Testimony of Witnesses, Parties to the Record*, *supra* note 24, at 54.

51. Jeremy Bentham, *Rationale of Judicial Evidence Part 2*, *in* Works of Jeremy Bentham 564–66 (rept. ed. 1962) (1843). The contemporary account in *On the Testimony of Witnesses, Parties to the Record*, *supra* note 24, at

52–58, lists several cases in which the question of whether a particular witness should be disqualified was litigated in the courts of Westminster.

52. St. 14 & 15 Vict., c. 99, § 1.

53. GREENLEAF, *supra* note 36, § 396 at 442.

54. For discussion of the various sources of attack, *see* Bodansky, *supra* note 4, at 94.

55. *Of the Disqualification of the Parties as Witnesses*, AM. L. REG. 259–64 (1857). Although we are writing about the effect of the witness disqualification rule on the rise of tort liability, it would be a mistake to suppose that pressure for reform arose because of a felt need to facilitate bringing bodily injury suits in particular. We have found no evidence that this was the case, and the applicability of the rule to all lawsuits makes this very unlikely.

56. 2 WIGMORE, *supra* note 38, § 578 at 707.

57. 365 U.S. 570 (1961).

58. GREENLEAF, *supra* note 36, § 396 at 442.

59. *See, e.g.*, FRIEDMAN, *supra* note 7, at 262 ("The law developed in a way that the power-holders of the day considered socially desirable"); MORTON HORWITZ, THE TRANSFORMATION OF AMERICAN LAW, 1780–1860 99–101 (1977) ("Common law doctrines were transformed to create immunities from liability and thereby to provide substantial subsidies to those who undertook economic development").

60. William Blackstone took a different view, but he was writing in an era when there were few tort actions: "Experience will abundantly show, that above a hundred of our lawsuits arise from disputed facts, for one where the law is doubted of." 3 WILLIAM BLACKSTONE, COMMENTARIES ON THE LAWS OF ENGLAND 330 (4 vols. 1765–69).

61. If the hearsay rule were already in force, this evidence would have been admitted under the *res gestae* exception to the hearsay rule, as part of the surrounding circumstances. GREENLEAF, *supra* note 36, § 108 at 120.

62. WILLIAM E. NELSON, THE AMERICANIZATION OF THE COMMON LAW 25, 192 n. 121 (1975), cited in Langbein, *Historical Foundations of the Law of Evidence, supra* note 23, at 1187 n. 94.

63. Langbein, *Historical Foundations of the Law of Evidence, supra* note 23, at 1185.

64. 2 WIGMORE, *supra* note 38, § 1367 at 1697, suggests that the possibility of cross-examination dates to the beginning of the eighteenth century. But how frequent the practice was is another matter. For example, Langbein, *Historical Foundations of the Law of Evidence, supra* note 23, at 1199, indicates that in the early nineteenth century cross-examination was observed

to be displacing the role of the judge and that the other hallmarks of lawyer-driven criminal procedure fell into place in these years.

65. This is in essence Langbein's view. *See* Langbein, *Historical Foundations of the Law of Evidence, supra* note 23, at 1200.

66. The most substantial repository of trial records appears to be the Salt Lake City Genealogical Library, which has a collection of microfilmed trial court records from the nineteenth century. The Library of Virginia is a repository of Virginia trial court records. We reviewed microfilm records of Kanawah County, West Virginia; Marion County, Indiana; and Austin County, Texas, supplied by the Genealogical Library for selected years pre- and post-repeal in these localities. The Kanawah County records were simply case captions, sometimes but not always indicating the nature of the case. This made quantitative comparison of filings before and after repeal unreliable and qualitative assessment impossible. It turned out that the Austin County records filmed only selective types of cases, and neither tort nor any subset of tort were included. The Marion County records were handwritten orders and judgments of a wide variety by a judge or judges in the Marion County Court. Because we were unable to determine what percentage of filed cases these orders, judgments, and opinions represented, quantitative assessment of what they signified would not have been meaningful or reliable.

The Library of Virginia microfilm records were similarly unhelpful. We reviewed records for the Hustings court of Richmond and of the Albemarle County Circuit Court. These records consisted of thousands of pages of handwritten summaries of trial court orders and actions, without sufficient information to be useful.

It is possible that a more systematic review of all the trial court records available from the Salt Lake City Genealogical Library would reveal more than we have discovered. A more important fact about the records that seem to exist, however, is that they can give us only a very limited glimpse into the nature of trials in the first half of the nineteenth century because they are not records of trials. Rather, they are records of actions taken by courts in connection with lawsuits.

67. Oswald M. T. Ratteray, *Verbatim Reporting Comes of Age,* 56 JUDICATURE 368, 369–70 (1973).

68. Abraham & White, *supra* note 4, at 465–68.

69. *See, e.g.,* JOHN J. DUFF, A. LINCOLN, PRAIRIE LAWYER 56 n. 12 (1960); *see generally* MARK E. STEINER, AN HONEST CALLING: THE LAW PRACTICE OF ABRAHAM LINCOLN (2006).

70. The Law Practice of Abraham Lincoln, 2nd edition, http://www.law practiceofabrahamlincoln.org/Results.aspx. The search we conducted was

for all cases classified as involving "negligence." This yielded twenty-four cases, two of which were duplicates and one of which involved breach of contract.

71. Ferdinand Fairfax Stone, *The Record on Appeal in Civil Cases*, 23 VA. L. REV. 766, 775 (1936); Frank O. Bowman, III, *Stories of Crimes, Trials, and Appeals in Civil War Era Missouri*, 93 MARQ. L. REV. 349, 361–67 (2009) (describing the situation in Missouri after 1836).

72. Ratteray, *supra* note 67, at 369.

73. Langbein, *Historical Foundations of the Law of Evidence*, *supra* note 23, at 1178–79. Langbein suggested that some other features of eighteenth-century English law may have functioned to limit the number of tort actions, such as the lack of liability insurance, the underdeveloped state of the law of vicarious liability, and the *action moritur* doctrine, which extinguished tort claims on the death of the prospective claimant. *See id.* at 1179. Norma Landau's research, however, suggests that in eighteenth-century England, misdemeanor prosecutions were often converted into tort actions. Norma Landau, *Indictment for Fun and Profit: A Prosecutor's Reward at Eighteenth-Century Quarter Sessions*, 17 L. & HIST. REV. 507 (1999).

74. FRIEDMAN, *supra* note 6, at 350.

75. To obtain a very rough and not necessarily representative sense of the impact of the change in the rules that began to occur in the 1850s, we conducted Westlaw searches to identify all reported federal and state decisions between 1800 and 1880 that used the phrase "the plaintiff testified" or "the defendant testified," whenever each phrase appeared in an opinion that also used the word "negligence." Before 1850 there were virtually no such cases. In the 1850s there were 13 of the former and 9 of the latter. In contrast, in the 1870s—a decade before the escalation in tort filings is generally understood to have occurred—there were 264 of the former and 80 of the latter—20-fold and 8.5-fold increases, respectively. These are obviously general results. Nonetheless, the results may tell us something about the change that took place after repeal: a massive increase in the number of appellate cases involving negligence in which one or both of the parties had testified at trial. There were so many other forces at work during these periods that it would be reckless to try to identify repeal as the sole cause of change, but the fact that this very marked change did occur after repeal is noteworthy.

For the former, the search inquiry was as follows: advanced: "plaintiff testified" & DA(180*) [by decade] % "#for the plaintiff testified" "#for plaintiff testified" "#of the plaintiff testified" "#of plaintiff testified" "#by the plaintiff testified" "#by plaintiff testified." For the latter, the search inquiry was as follows: advanced: "defendant testified" & "negligence" & DA(180*) [by decade] % "#for the defendant testified" "#for defendant testified" "#of the defendant testified" "#of defendant."

76. *See, e.g.,* Derwort & Wife v. Loomer, 21 Conn. 245, 247 (1851); Hood v. New York & N.H. R. Co., 22 Conn. 1, 3 (1852); Stover v. Bluehill, 51 Me. 439 (1863); Brown v. Perkins, 83 Mass. 89 (1861).

77. Bacon v. Charlton, 61 Mass. 581, 586 (1851). See also Lund v. Tyngsborough, 63 Mass 36 (1851) (elucidating the *res gestae* rule on which the distinction in *Bacon* was based).

78. *See* John C. P. Goldberg, *Two Conceptions of Tort Damages: Fair v. Full Compensation,* 55 DePaul L. Rev. 435 (2006) (noting throughout that pain and suffering was not an express component of damages awards); Abraham, *supra* note 4, at 508–9 (discussing the same issue).

79. Seger v. Town of Barkamsted, 22 Conn. 290, 298 (1853).

80. Some evidence of this development can be seen in the treatment of damages for pain and suffering in one of the leading post–Civil War treatises on the law of negligence. In the first edition of this treatise there was no separate section on pain and suffering damages—only half a sentence in the section on damages for personal injury. *See* Thomas G. Shearman & Amasa G. Redfield, A Treatise on the Law of Negligence § 606 at 662 (1869). Two decades later, the treatise contained a separate section on pain and suffering and cited more than a dozen cases on the subject. *See* 2 Thomas G. Shearman & Amasa G. Redfield, A Treatise on the Law of Negligence § 761 at 657–58 (2 vols., 4th ed. 1888).

81. Warren v. Fitchburg Railroad Co., 90 Mass. 227, 228 (1864).

82. *See* George Rogers Taylor, The Transportation Revolution, 1815–1860 (1951).

83. *See, e.g.,* Bradley v. Boston & Maine Railroad Co., 56 Mass. 539 (1848); Sherwood v. Town of Weston, 18 Conn. 32 (1846); Chidsey v. Town of Canton, 17 Conn. 475 (1846); Perkins v. E.R.R. Co. and Boston & Maine R.R. Co., 29 Me. 307 (1849).

84. Department of the Interior, Statistics of the United States in 1860; Complied from the Original Returns and Being the Final Exhibit of the Eighth Census, 333 (1866).

85. *See, e.g.,* Randolph E. Bergstrom, Courting Danger: Injury and Law in New York City, 1870–1910 (1992); Robert A. Silverman, Law and Urban Growth: Civil Litigation in Boston Trial Courts, 1880–1900 (1981); Lawrence M. Friedman, *Civil Wrongs: Personal Injury Law in the Late 19th Century,* 1987 Am. Bar Found. L. J. 351.

86. *See* Bergstrom, *supra* note 85, at 17.

87. *See* Holmes, The Common Law, *supra* note 5, at 88.

88. WILLIAM L. PROSSER, HANDBOOK OF THE LAW OF TORTS (1941).

89. FOWLER V. HARPER & FLEMING JAMES, JR., THE LAW OF TORTS (2 vols. 1956).

90. The notable exception among torts scholars is WITT, *supra* note 4, 56–57, whose reference to the rule first acquainted us with it.

91. *See, e.g.,* Julia Simon-Kerr, *Unchaste and Incredible: The Use of Gendered Conceptions of Honor in Impeachment,* 117 YALE L. J. 1854, 1888 (2008).

92. 2 WIGMORE, *supra* note 38, at § 575 at 696.

93. The historical sources Wigmore cited did not demonstrate that the oaths of parties were "necessarily excluded" in jury trials; we do not know whether medieval civil trials had juries or not. The term "modern witnesses" for trials in the 1400s and 1500s equates "modern" with "trials not governed by the oath regime," and at any rate Wigmore did not know whether trials in the 1400s were governed by the oath regime or not (recent historical research suggests they were). Why would a party "naturally" be "deemed incapable of being a witness" in the 1400s and 1500s? That would seem a question that Wigmore, or the sources he cited, were incapable of answering, given the absence of data. On what basis could Wigmore claim that "otherwise no rule or disqualification for interested persons was recognized in the earlier days of witnesses"? His insight may well have been accurate, not because disqualification for "interest" was regarded as unnecessary but because taking an oath was regarded as a sufficient deterrent to perjury. Finally, although the seventeenth-century cases Wigmore cited made it plain that interested *persons,* not just interested parties, were being regularly disqualified under the witness rule, Wigmore claimed that that development was probably due to the (sinister?) influence of Sir Edward Coke. He had no basis for that claim other than Coke's statements that the rule was in place and its object was to protect against perjury.

94. THOMAS STARKIE, A PRACTICAL TREATISE ON THE LAW OF EVIDENCE (1824).

95. *Id.* at 83, quoted in 2 WIGMORE, *supra* note 38, § 576 at 699.

96. 2 WIGMORE, *supra* note 38, at 699–700.

97. *Id.* at 701–3.

98. *Id.* at 703.

99. *Id.* § 1367 at 1697.

100. *Id.* at 704.

2. CONCEPTUALIZING TORT LAW—THE CONTINUOUS (AND CONTINUING) STRUGGLE

1. Oliver Wendell Holmes, Jr., *Book Review,* 5 AM. L. REV. 340, 341 (1871). The review was unsigned; Mark DeWolfe Howe attributed it to Holmes

after finding a copy of the review in Holmes's papers. *See* MARK DEWOLFE HOWE, JUSTICE OLIVER WENDELL HOLMES: THE PROVING YEARS (1964). Holmes was born in March 1841, so he was at most thirty years old when he wrote the quoted passage.

2. Oliver Wendell Holmes, Jr., *The Theory of Torts*, 7 AM. L. REV. 652, 659–60 (1873) (concluding that enumerating actions that were successful and ones that failed might be sufficient to give the subject of torts an identity). As above, Howe attributes this unsigned article to Holmes; *see* HOWE, *supra* note 1, at 64. OLIVER WENDELL HOLMES, JR., THE COMMON LAW 77–163 (1881).

3. It is perhaps ironic, given his first thoughts about the propriety of treating torts as a separate subject, that this phrase has sometimes been attributed to Holmes. *See, e.g.,* JOHN WITTE JR., RELIGION AND THE AMERICAN CONSTITUTIONAL EXPERIMENT 225 (2d ed. 2005).

4. *See generally* FREDERICK W. MAITLAND, THE FORMS OF ACTION AT COMMON LAW (A. H. Chaygtort & W. J. Whitaker eds., 1909).

5. *Id.* at viii.

6. George E. Woodbine, *The Origins of the Action of Trespass*, 34 YALE L. J. 343, 368–69 (1925).

7. *Id.* at 369–70.

8. R. C. VAN CAENEGEM, ROYAL WRITS IN ENGLAND FROM THE CONQUEST TO GLANVILL 240–44 (1959).

9. MAITLAND, *supra* note 4, at 42.

10. *Id.*

11. *Id.* at x; J. H. BAKER, AN INTRODUCTION TO ENGLISH LEGAL HISTORY 6–63 (4th ed. 2002).

12. MAITLAND, *supra* note 4, at 4–5.

13. G. EDWARD WHITE, TORT LAW IN AMERICA: AN INTELLECTUAL HISTORY 13–14 (2d ed. 2003); S. F. C. MILSOM, HISTORICAL FOUNDATIONS OF THE COMMON LAW 254–56, 269–70, 346–51 (1969).

14. HENRY MAINE, EARLY LAW AND CUSTOM 389 (1907).

15. 1 FRANCIS HILLIARD, THE LAW OF TORTS OR PRIVATE WRONGS v–vi (2 vols. 1859). Emphasis in original.

16. *See* Holmes, *supra* note 1.

17. *Id.* This stance was echoed by Holmes's friend and colleague Nicholas St. John Green in his preface to an 1870 abridged edition of Charles G. Addison's 1860 English treatise, THE LAW OF TORTS, which Green used in his torts course at Harvard. He noted that torts was "usually treated of under the titles of the various forms of action which lie for the infringement of . . . rights which avail against other persons generally, or against all mankind." Such an emphasis, he felt, tended "to confuse those

fundamental principles which should be kept distinct in the mind of the student." Nicholas St. John Green, *preface, in* CHARLES ADDISON, WRONGS AND REMEDIES, ABRIDGED FOR USE IN THE LAW SCHOOL OF HARVARD UNIVERSITY iii (Nicholas St. John Green ed., 1870).

18. For more detail, *see* G. EDWARD WHITE, LAW IN AMERICAN HISTORY: FROM THE COLONIAL YEARS THROUGH THE CIVIL WAR 248–60, 271–78 (2012).

19. For more detail, *see id.*, 285–87; Jack Nortrup, *The Education of a Western Lawyer*, 12 AM. J. LEGAL HIST. 294 (1968).

20. On the nineteenth-century codification movement in America, *see* CHARLES W. COOK, THE AMERICAN CODIFICATION MOVEMENT (1981); Robert W. Gordon, *The American Codification Movement*, 36 VAND. L. REV. 431 (1983).

21. Charles E. Clark, *History, Systems, and Functions of Pleading*, 11 VA. L. REV. 517, 533 (1925); CHARLES M. HEPBURN, THE DEVELOPMENT OF CODE PLEADING 114, 124 (1867).

22. Cal. Code of Civil Procedure § 307, Practice Act of 1851 (providing that "there is in this State but one form of civil actions for the enforcement or protection of private rights and the redress or prevention of private wrongs").

23. Clark, *supra* note 21, at 534.

24. Holmes, *supra* note 1, at 341.

25. *Id.*

26. *See* GEORGE FREDRICKSON, THE INNER CIVIL WAR: NORTHERN INTELLECTUALS AND THE CRISIS OF THE UNION (1965); ROBERT WIEBE, THE SEARCH FOR ORDER, 1877–1920 (1967).

27. See FREDRICKSON, *supra* note 26, at 199–216; LAWRENCE VEYSEY, THE EMERGENCE OF THE AMERICAN UNIVERSITY 21–56 (1965).

28. C. C. LANGDELL, A SELECTION OF CASES ON THE LAW OF CONTRACTS vi (1871).

29. 1 HILLIARD, *supra* note 15, at vii.

30. *Id.* at x (italics in original).

31. Illustrations are chapters on bailments, patents, and copyrights, and in a chapter on slander, evidence, and damages. See *id.* at viii, xx.

32. *Id.* at xiv.

33. *Id.* at xv–xix.

34. *Id.* at ii–vii.

35. *Id.* at xvi–xvii.

36. *Id.* at 119–21.

37. CHARLES G. ADDISON, THE LAW OF TORTS 2, 43 (1860).

38. 1 THOMAS G. SHEARMAN & AMASA REDFIELD, A TREATISE ON THE LAW OF NEGLIGENCE 3 (2 vols. 1869).

39. Thomas M. Cooley, A Treatise on the Law of Wrongs; or, The Wrongs Which Arise Independent of Contract 80–81 (1879).

40. The state, Holmes suggested, "might conceivably make itself a mutual insurance company against accidents, and distribute the burden of its citizens' mishaps among its members. . . . As between individuals it might adopt the mutual insurance principle . . . and divide damages when both were in fault . . . or it might throw all loss upon the actor irrespective of fault. The state does none of these things, however, and the prevailing view is that its cumbersome and expensive machinery ought not to be set in motion unless some clear benefit is derived from disturbing the *status quo*. State interference is an evil, where it cannot be shown to be a good." Holmes, *supra* note 2, at 88.

41. Blackstone had characterized some wrongs as "injuries to personal security," others as "injuries to the limbs and body," and still others as "injuries to personal liberty." 3 William Blackstone, Commentaries on the Law of England 115, 130–48 (4 vols. 1765–70).

42. Cooley, *supra* note 39, at vii.

43. John C. P. Goldberg and Benjamin C. Zipursky describe this as a rights and wrongs approach. *See* John C. P. Goldberg & Benjamin C. Zipursky, *Thomas McIntyre Cooley (1824–1898) and Oliver Wendell Holmes (1841–1935): The Arc of American Tort Theory, in* Scholars of Tort Law 48–53 (James Gouldcamp & Donal Nolan eds., 2019).

44. *See, e.g.,* Francis Burdick, The Law of Torts xiii–xiv (1905), referring to "the Right Invaded by an Assault," "the Right Invaded by Battery," and "the Right Invaded by Defamation."

45. Cooley, *supra* note 39, at vii.

46. *Id.* at vii–x.

47. *Id.* at xv.

48. Holmes, *supra* note 2, at 120, 118.

49. Melville M. Bigelow, Elements of the Law of Torts iv–v (1878).

50. This included "duties, which govern the relations of individuals to each other 1) as mere members of the State; or 2) as occupying some special situation toward each other not produced by agreement . . . or 3) as occupying some special situation of agreement between them . . . which affords occasion for breaches of duty between them that need not be treated as breaches of contract." *Id.* at 3.

51. *Id.* at 5–6. Emphasis in original.

52. *Id.* at 5.

53. *Id.* at 5–6.

54. *Id.* at 6.

55. FREDERICK POLLOCK, THE LAW OF TORTS (1887). For a discussion of Pollock's adoption of the tripartite approach, *see* Robert Stevens, *Professor Sir Frederick Pollock (1845–1937): Jurist as Mayfly, in* SCHOLARS OF TORT LAW, *supra* note 43, at 75–102.

56. *See* POLLOCK, *supra* note 55, at 11–12.

57. JOHN HENRY WIGMORE, SELECT CASES ON THE LAW OF TORTS (2 vols. 1912).

58. John Henry Wigmore, *Responsibility for Tortious Acts: Its History,* 7 HARV. L. REV. 315 (1894); *Responsibility for Tortious Acts: Its History—II,* 7 HARV. L. REV. 383 (1894); *Responsibility for Tortious Act: Its History—III,* 7 HARV. L. REV. 441 (1894); *The Tripartite Division of Torts,* 8 HARV. L. REV. 200 (1894).

59. Wigmore, *The Tripartite Division of Torts, supra* note 58, at 206.

60. JAMES BARR AMES, A SELECTION OF CASES ON THE LAW OF TORTS (1874). In the 1893 and 1905 editions of Ames's casebook Jeremiah Smith was a co-author.

61. MELVILLE M. BIGELOW, LEADING CASES ON THE LAW OF TORTS (1875).

62. FRANCIS M. BURDICK, CASES ON TORTS SELECTED AND ARRANGED FOR THE USE OF LAW STUDENTS IN CONNECTION WITH POLLOCK ON TORTS (1891).

63. GEORGE CHASE, LEADING CASES UPON THE LAW OF TORTS (1892); JAMES PAIGE, ILLUSTRATIVE CASES IN TORTS (1896); FRANK A. ERWIN, CASES ON TORTS (1900); FRANK LESLIE SIMPSON, CASES ON TORTS (1908); WILLIAM DRAPER LEWIS & MIRIAM MCCONNELL, EQUITY JURISDICTION, TORTS: A COLLECTION OF CASES WITH NOTES (1908); JOHN HENRY WIGMORE, SELECT CASES ON THE LAW OF TORTS (1912); RICHARD D. CURRIER & OSCAR M. BATE, CASES ON TORTS (1914); CHARLES M. HEPBURN, CASES ON THE LAW OF TORTS (1915); CHARLES A. KEIGWIN, CASES ON TORTS (1915).

64. FRANCIS H. BOHLEN, CASES ON THE LAW OF TORTS (2 vols. 1915).

65. *Id.* at iii.

66. *Id.*

67. *Id.* at iv.

68. *Id.*

69. *Id.*

70. *Id.*

71. *Id.*

72. *Id.* at vi.

73. *Id.* at vi–vii.

74. *Id.* at vii.

75. Francis H. Bohlen, *The Rule in Rylands v. Fletcher, in* FRANCIS H. BOHLEN, STUDIES IN THE LAW OF TORTS 366–67 (1926). In that essay Bohlen maintained that "the most important function of modern tort law" was "to apply fundamental and traditional conceptions of justice to the solution of new social and economic problems," in which "the interests of one person or class conflict with the interests of another person or class." *Id.*

76. 1 BOHLEN, *supra* note 64, at xii–xiv, xv.

77. A glance at the table of contents of AMES, *supra* note 60, and BIGELOW, *supra* note 61, reveal that the organization of both those casebooks also was a combination of writ-based and miscellaneous classifications of tort actions.

78. 1 RESTATEMENT OF THE LAW, TORTS viii (4 vols. 1934). *See also* "The Story of ALI," https://www.ali.org/about-ali/story-line/.

79. RESTATEMENT, *supra* note 78, at ix.

80. *Id.* at x.

81. At the time the early *Restatements* were published, there were a number of other criticisms that fall outside of our concerns in this chapter, involving (among other things) the deceptive putative certainty associated with formulating black-letter rules. *See generally* G. Edward White, *The American Law Institute and the Triumph of Modernist Jurisprudence,* 15 L. & HIST. REV. 1 (1997).

82. *See generally* RESTATEMENT OF CONTRACTS (1932).

83. *See generally* RESTATEMENT OF PROPERTY (1936–44).

84. *See* BOHLEN, *supra* note 64.

85. Torts: Restatement No. 1 (April 5, 1925) (hereinafter "Tentative Draft No. 1"). The early ALI nomenclature was not completely consistent, and it is complicated by the nomenclature used by HeinOnline, where the drafts are available in the HeinOnline database. For the most part, during the years with which we are concerned, it appears from their title pages that drafts submitted to the Council—the board of the ALI—tended to be termed "Tentative Drafts" and were sometimes simply identified by the abbreviation "T.D." followed by a number. Drafts submitted to the full membership at the "Annual Meeting" tended to be referred to as "Preliminary Draft No. __." A statement on the title page of Tentative Draft No. 1 indicates that the same draft was submitted first to the Council and then to the Annual Meeting. This draft had neither the Tentative Draft nor Preliminary Draft designation on its title page. It is accessible in the HeinOnline American Law Institute Library directory "Restatements and Principles of the Law" > "Torts" > "Restatement of the Law Torts (1923–2019)" database as "Tentative Draft No. 1." That is how we cite it. We cite other drafts in the same manner simply by using the name that renders them accessible in the HeinOnline database.

86. Proceedings at Fourth Annual Meeting 189–91 (Am. Law Inst., April 29–May 1, 1926). Although Bohlen's phrase "first of all" implies that he had a second point to make about his approach, he did not make it.

87. Although this first draft used the terms "right" and "rights," the final version substituted the terms "interest" and "interests." At least as early as the publication of a collection of his previously published articles, Studies in the Law of Torts (1926), Bohlen had said that terms such as "right," "duty," and "wrong were, at the time these articles were written, regarded as sufficiently accurate. Today . . . an attempt is made to find new and, it is to be hoped, more exact terms. Thus, what in the earlier articles is termed a 'right' is in the later articles called a 'legally protected interest.'" Id. at vi. Bohlen thought that the use of the term "interest" signified "a very distinct alteration in the judicial view as to the protection which should be given to various interests by the imposition of liability for acts which invaded them." Id. Perhaps the most visible proponent of "interest analysis" of this sort was Roscoe Pound, who coined the term "sociological jurisprudence" to emphasize that judicial decisions needed to be attentive to "social interests." Roscoe Pound, The Theory of Judicial Decision, 36 Harv. L. Rev. 641, 802, 940 (1923). Consequently, we think that Bohlen was probably thinking of "interests" even when he used the term "rights" in Tentative Draft No. 1, though we cannot explain why he did not substitute that term until the draft was revised. It may be that it took more time to persuade his advisors that it made sense to do so.

88. Tentative Draft No. 1, supra note 85, at 5. This was indicated to be "Part II," though there was no part 1. That was left open for a list of definitions, which eventually were included in the final draft.

89. Id. at 5.

90. In an earlier document containing no black-letter material, submitted to his advisors only, Bohlen had toyed with including other interests in the "Rights of Personality," including the "right to reputation" and the "right to privacy." Restatement T.D. No. 1, at 5 (12-10-23), supra note 85, accessible in HeinOnline as "[Preliminary] Draft 1 (December 23, 1923)" but bearing the initials "T.D." But there was no discussion of "personality" in this document either, and those references had dropped out when Bohlen's first draft was presented to the Annual Meeting.

91. The absence of explanation or elaboration probably foreshadowed the difficulty Bohlen later faced in extending interest analysis to the remainder of tort law.

92. See, e.g., Barbara Young Welke, Recasting American Liberty: Gender, Race, Law, and the Railroad Revolution, 1865–1920 125–32

(2001); Martha Chamalas & Jennifer B. Wriggins, the Measure of Injury: Race, Gender, and Tort Law 35–51 (2010).

93. Welke, *supra* note 92, at 155–70.

94. Restatement T.D. No. 1, *supra* note 90, at sec. 2, 8. We quote those sections below so that the reader may appreciate the way in which the draft treated battery as a sub-subdivision of the more general right to personality, and of its subdivision, the right to freedom from bodily harm:

> Part II.
> CONDUCT VIOLATING RIGHTS OF PERSONALITY.
> The rights of personality are:
> 1. Right to freedom from bodily harm;
> 2. Right to freedom from offensive bodily touchings;
> 3. Right to freedom from apprehension of a harmful or offensive bodily touching;
> 4. Right to freedom from confinement;
> 5. Right to freedom from disagreeable emotions.
> Chapter I.
> CONDUCT VIOLATING THE RIGHT TO FREEDOM FROM BODILY HARM.
> Subchapter 1—General Principles
> Section 1. Causing bodily harm to another, unless privileged, subjects the one causing it to a liability to the other, if:
> {here the four bases of liability are specified: intent, negligence, strict liability, and breach of duty}
> Subchapter 2—The Intentional Violation of the Right to Freedom from Bodily Harm [Battery]
> {here the elements of battery are stated}

95. *Id.* at sec. 1, 6.

96. *Id.* at ch. 3, secs. 27–48; ch. 4, secs. 49–65.

97. However, the initial assault and false imprisonment sections did each reference breach of duty to protect another from such harm, apart from negligence, as a basis of liability. See *id.* at sec. 27 (b) (ii) (assault) and sec. 49 (b) (ii) (false imprisonment).

98. Preliminary Draft No. 20, sec. 165 (May 18, 1928).

99. *Id.*

100. 2 Restatement of Torts, chap. 18 at 1287 (1965).

101. For discussion of this change in terminology, *see supra* note 87.

102. *Id.* That is how the final product read as well. 2 Restatement of Torts, *supra* note 100, at 25.

103. Proposed Final Draft No. 1, *supra* note 85, at 41.

104. PROCEEDINGS AT ELEVENTH ANNUAL MEETING 477 (Am. Law Inst., July 1, 1932–June 30, 1934).

105. The University of Pennsylvania Law Library maintains the ALI archives and contains not only drafts but also some minutes and other less formal material. For the contents, *see* http://dla.library.upenn.edu/dla/ead/ead .html?q=bohlen&id=EAD_upenn_biddle_USPULPULALI04001&.

106. Michael D. Green, one of the Reporters for the Third *Restatement*, observes that Bohlen provided "structure and organization to the topic" of torts. Michael D. Green, *Professor Frances Hermann Bohlen (1869-1942)*, *in* SCHOLARS OF TORT LAW, *supra* note 43, at 135. But he then observes that the First *Restatement* "relied predominately on a combination of legally protected interests and specific types of wrongful conduct," which is not the way we have described it. *Id.* at 155. Learned Hand praised Bohlen for "trying to impose some pattern upon the amorphous material" of torts. Learned Hand, *Francis Hermann Bohlen*, 91 U. PENN. L. REV. 386, 386 (1943). Notably, however, Hand did not indicate that Bohlen succeeded in doing so. Although Patrick Kelley does not express an opinion on the issue, he argues that "Bohlen was not a systematic thinker. . . . [He] was a master of 'microtheory.'" Patrick J. Kelley, *The First Restatement of Torts: Reform by Descriptive Theory*, 32 S. ILL. L. J. 93, 123–24 (2007).

107. 1 RESTATEMENT OF TORTS, *supra* note 78, at xxvi; 2 RESTATEMENT OF TORTS, *supra* note 100, at 137.

108. 2 RESTATEMENT OF TORTS, *supra* note 100, at topic 2, p. 565; topic 3, p. 572.

109. Michael Green made a search for Bohlen's private papers in various sources but was unable to locate any. *See* Green, *supra* note 106, at 133–34.

110. FRANCIS H. BOHLEN, CASES ON THE LAW OF TORTS (2d ed. 1925).

111. *Id.* at 158–890.

112. Bohlen became ill toward the end of the process, and others finished up the last of the project. *See* Green, *supra* note 106, at 138.

113. *See* WILLIAM L. PROSSER, HANDBOOK ON THE LAW OF TORTS (1941).

114. *Id.* at 35.

115. *See* FOWLER VINCENT HARPER, A TREATISE ON THE LAW OF TORTS (1933).

116. *See, e.g.,* WILLIAM L. PROSSER & W. PAGE KEETON *ET AL.*, PROSSER AND KEETON ON TORTS (5th ed. 1984).

117. WILLIAM L. PROSSER & YOUNG B. SMITH, CASES AND MATERIALS ON TORTS (1951). The most recent edition of that casebook is PROSSER, WADE, AND SCHWARTZ'S TORTS: CASES AND MATERIALS (Victor E. Schwartz, Kathryn Kelly, & David F. Partlett eds., 2020).

118. *See* SCHWARTZ *ET AL.*, TORTS: CASES AND MATERIALS, *supra* note 117.

119. *See* CHARLES O. GREGORY & HARRY KALVEN, JR., CASES AND MATERI-
     ALS ON TORTS (1959). Only the casebook produced by Harry Shulman
     and Fleming James, which deliberately sets out to call negligence liability
     into question, follows a different sequence. It begins with strict liability,
     then moves to negligence, then to freestanding torts, and concludes with
     a chapter reflecting interest analysis and addressing assault, battery, false
     imprisonment, and malicious prosecution, without employing any gen-
     eralizing title for that chapter. HARRY SHULMAN & FLEMING JAMES, JR.,
     CASES AND MATERIALS ON THE LAW OF TORTS (1942).
120. *See* DAN B. DOBBS, THE LAW OF TORTS xvi–xxviii (2000).
121. For an account of the positions of the major figures, *see* George L Priest,
     *The Invention of Enterprise Liability: A Critical History of the Intellectual
     Foundations of Modern Tort Law,* 14 J. LEGAL STUD. 461 (1985).
122. *See generally* Priest, *supra* note 121. For products liability, *see, e.g.,* Marcus
     L. Plant, *Strict Liability of Manufacturers for Injuries Caused by Defects
     in Products—An Opposing View,* 24 TENN. L. REV. 938 (1957); William L.
     Prosser, *The Assault upon the Citadel: Strict Liability to the Consumer,* 69
     YALE L. J. 1089 (1960). For auto liability, *see, e.g.,* ROBERT E. KEETON & JEF-
     FREY O'CONNELL, BASIC PROTECTION FOR THE TRAFFIC VICTIM (1965).
123. *See* Guido Calabresi, *Some Thoughts on Risk Distribution and the Law of
     Torts,* 70 YALE L. J. 499 (1961); Ronald H. Coase, *The Problem of Social
     Cost,* 3 J. L. & ECON. 138 (1960); Richard A. Posner, *A Theory of Negligence,*
     1 J. LEGAL STUD. 29 (1972); Steven Shavell, *Strict Liability versus Negli-
     gence,* 9 J. LEGAL STUD. 1 (1980), among others.
124. *See, e.g.,* ERNEST J. WEINRIB, THE IDEA OF PRIVATE LAW (1995); JULES L.
     COLEMAN, RISKS AND WRONGS (1992); John C. P. Goldberg & Benjamin
     C. Zipursky, *Torts as Wrongs,* 88 TEX. L. REV. 917 (1910).
125. *See* RESTATEMENT (THIRD) OF TORTS: APPORTIONMENT OF LIABILITY
     (1999).
126. *See* https://www.ali.org/projects/show/torts-concluding-provisions/.
127. MAITLAND, *supra* note 4, at 1.
128. For an argument about the factors that necessitate each separate tort being
     distinctive, *see* JOHN C. P. GOLDBERG & BENJAMIN C. ZIPURSKY, RECOG-
     NIZING WRONGS 4, 234 (2020).
129. *See* BLACKSTONE, *supra* note 41, at 120–21.
130. *See* COOLEY, *supra* note 39, at vii.
131. *See* AMES & SMITH, *supra* note 60, at vi (1905 ed.).
132. PROSSER, *supra* note 113, at 34.

3. THE PROBLEM OF THE DIGNITARY TORTS

1. Caroll Smith-Rosenberg, *The Hysterical Woman: Sex Roles and Role Conflict in Nineteenth-Century America*, in DISORDERLY CONDUCT: VISIONS OF GENDER IN VICTORIAN AMERICA 197 (2005).
2. Martha Chamalas & Linda Kerber, *Women, Mothers, and the Law of Fright: A History*, 88 MICH. L. REV. 814, 847 (1990).
3. *See* MICHAEL ROSEN, DIGNITY: ITS HISTORY AND MEANING 19 (2012).
4. *See id.* at 19–21.
5. *See id.* at 30–31.
6. An earlier conception of dignity had associated it with rank or status. The "dignity" of a member of the nobility was acknowledged though public gestures of respect or obeisance by persons of lower status, such as doffing hats, bowing, or touching forelocks. *See* DIGNITY, RANK, AND RIGHTS 30–33 (Jeremy Waldron ed., 2012).
7. *See* Christopher McCrudden, *Human Dignity and Judicial Interpretation of Human Rights*, 19 EUR. J. INT'L. L. 665 (2008). Other scholars who have written on dignity include, in addition to Michael Rosen, *supra* note 3, Wai Chee Dimock, Donald Herzog, and Jeremy Waldron, in DIGNITY, RANK, AND RIGHTS, *supra* note 6.
8. McCrudden, *supra* note 7, at 680.
9. *See* Michael Rosen, *Dignity: The Case Against*, in UNDERSTANDING HUMAN DIGNITY, 146–154 (Christopher McCrudden ed., 2013).
10. McCrudden, *supra* note 7, at 679.
11. *Id.*
12. *Id.*
13. *Id.* at 680.
14. In DAN B. DOBBS & ELLEN M. BUBLICK, ADVANCED TORTS: CASES AND MATERIALS 1–3 (2006), to take a prominent example, there is an introduction entitled "What Are Economic and Dignitary Torts?" The closest the authors come to explaining what interests "dignitary torts" might protect is one sentence in which they describe a "dignitary loss" as "a damage to one's rights of personality." *Id.* at 1. We refer to such unanalyzed references to dignity as "placeholders" because we suspect that those making the references have a sense of what "dignity" might entail but are disinclined to articulate the concept more precisely.
15. *See* J. H. BAKER, AN INTRODUCTION TO ENGLISH LEGAL HISTORY 402–3 (4th ed. 2002).
16. *See id.* at 25–26.
17. *See* BAKER, *supra* note 15, at 436–46.

18. *See* Marc A. Franklin, *The Origins and Constitutionality of Limitations on Truth as a Defense in Tort Law*, 16 STAN. L. REV. 789, 820 (1964).
19. *See* BAKER, *supra* note 15, at 443–44.
20. G. EDWARD WHITE, TORT LAW IN AMERICA: AN INTELLECTUAL HISTORY 103 (expanded ed. 2003).
21. *Id.* at 105.
22. BARBARA YOUNG WELKE, RECASTING AMERICAN LIBERTY: GENDER, RACE, LAW, AND THE RAILROAD REVOLUTION, 1865–1920 (2001); Margo Schlanger, *Injured Women before Common Law Courts, 1860–1930*, 21 HARV. WOMEN'S L. J. 79 (1998).
23. 70 N.E. 857 (N.Y. 1904).
24. *Id.* at 858.
25. *Id.* at 858–59.
26. *See, e.g.,* Knoxville Traction Co. v. Lane, 53 S.W. 557 (Tenn. 1899); Lamson v. Great Northern Ry. Co., 130 N.W. 945 (Minn. 1911).
27. *See, e.g.,* Emmke v. DeSilva, 293 F. 17, 20 (8th Cir. 1923) (noting that there was a difference among courts as to whether the action was for breach of contract or tort).
28. *See, e.g.,* Nickerson v. Hodges, 84 So. 37 (La. 1920); Great Atlantic & Pacific Tea Co. v. Roch, 153 A. 22 (Md. 1930).
29. *See* WELKE, *supra* note 22; MARTHA CHAMALAS & JENNIFER B. WRIGGINS, THE MEASURE OF INJURY: RACE, GENDER, AND TORT LAW (2010).
30. Gulf, Colorado & Santa Fe Ry. Co. v. Luther, 90 S.W. 44 (Tex. Civ. App. 1905).
31. RESTATEMENT OF TORTS § 48 (1934).
32. WILLIAM L. PROSSER, HANDBOOK OF THE LAW OF TORTS (1941).
33. We have discussed the reviews of Prosser's treatise in Kenneth S. Abraham & G. Edward White, *Prosser and His Influence*, 6 J. TORT LAW 27 (2013).
34. PROSSER, *supra* note 32, at 54.
35. *Id.*
36. William L. Prosser, *Intentional Infliction of Mental Suffering*, 37 MICH. L. REV. 874 (1939).
37. PROSSER, *supra* note 32, at 54.
38. *Id.* at 874.
39. *Id.* at 59–62.
40. *See id.* at 59 n. 39.
41. *Id.* at 60 (footnotes omitted).
42. *Id.* at 65.
43. *Id.* at 59 n. 34, 62 nn. 58–62.
44. RESTATEMENT (SECOND) OF TORTS § 46 (1965).

45. On the history of journalism in America, *see* CHRISTOPHER B. DALY, COVERING AMERICA (2012).

46. Samuel D. Warren & Louis D. Brandeis, *The Right of Privacy,* 4 HARV. L. REV. 193 (1890).

47. Two recent articles have suggested that Warren could not have been motivated by a concern about his sister's wedding because she was only seven at the time *The Right of Privacy* article appeared, and that Warren's concern may have been in shielding his bother Ned from press coverage since his brother was gay and revelation of that fact would have been stigmatic in the Warrens's social circles. See Amy Gajda, *What If Samael D. Warren Hadn't Married a Senator's Daughter?* 2008 MICH. ST. L. J. 36 (2008); Charles E. Colmna, *About Ned,* 128 HARV. L. REV. F. 129, 135 (2016).

48. 229 S.W. 967 (Ky Ct. App. 1927).

49. 149 S.W. 849 (Ky. Ct. App. 1912).

50. 229 S.W. at 971.

51. RESTATEMENT (SECOND) OF TORTS § 652D (1977).

52. *See* Haynes v. Alfred A. Knopf, Inc., 8 F. 3d 1222, 1228–30 (7th Cir. 1993) (Posner, J.).

53. *See* Anita L. Allen & Erin Mack, *How Privacy Got Its Gender,* 19 N. ILL. U. L. REV. 441 (1991).

54. 37 S.W. 2d 46 (Ky. Ct. App. 1931).

55. *See supra,* at notes 48 and 49.

56. RESTATEMENT (SECOND) OF TORTS § 652B (1977).

57. *See, e.g.,* Hamberger v. Eastman, 206 A. 2d 239, 241 (N.H. 1964) (considering the bugging of a tenant's apartment by the landlord); Koeppel v. Speirs, 808 N.W. 2d 177, 178–82 (Iowa 2011) (considering a video camera installed in a bathroom).

58. *See, e.g.,* Nader v. General Motors Corp., 255 N.E. 2d 765, 768–69 (N.Y. 1970).

59. *See, e.g., id.* at 769–71 (noting that "privacy is invaded only if the information sought is of a confidential nature and the defendant's conduct was unreasonably intrusive").

60. See EDD APPLEGATE, THE RISE OF ADVERTISING IN THE UNITED STATES (2012).

61. *See* KENNETH S. ABRAHAM, THE FORMS AND FUNCTIONS OF TORT LAW 308 (5th ed. 2017); *see also* PROSSER, *supra* note 32, at 1056–57.

62. 50 S.E. 68 (Ga. 1905).

63. Id. at 70 (citing Wallace v. Georgia, C. & N. Ry. Co., 22 S.E. 579 [Ga. 1894]).

64. 50 S.E. at 68.

65. *See* Fairfield v. American Photocopy Equipment Co., 291 P. 2d 194, 197 (Cal. 1955); *see also* ABRAHAM, *supra* note 61, at 309; PROSSER, *supra* note

32, at 1056 ("Although the protection of his personal feelings is still highly important in such a case, the right invaded has also a commercial value").

66. See Pavesich v. New England Life Ins. Co., 50 S.E. 68 (Ga. 1904) ("It cannot be that the mere fact that a man aspires to public office or holds public office subjects him to the humiliation and mortification of having his picture displayed in places where he would never go to be gazed upon").

67. 385 U.S. 374 (1967).

68. RESTATEMENT (SECOND) OF TORTS § 652E (1977).

69. See Cantrell v. Forest City Pub. Co., 419 U.S. 245, 247–48 (1974).

70. See id. at 246

71. PROSSER, supra note 32, at 1050.

72. Id.

73. There were few if any cases involving what we now call false light until after the first edition was published. By the time of the second edition there had been some such cases, and in that edition Prosser recognized false light as a fourth category. In response to Roberson v. Rochester Folding Box Co., note 137, infra, 64 N.E. 442 (N.Y. 1902), denying recovery for the unconsented to use of the plaintiff's picture in an advertisement, New York enacted a statute that might have been construed to permit recovery for false light. See N.Y. Sess. Laws 1903, ch. 132, §§ 1–2, now N.Y. Civil Rights Law §§ 50–51. But the statute does not appear to have been the basis of false-light claims until much later.

74. See Warren & Brandeis, supra note 46.

75. 64 N.E. 442 (N.Y. 1902).

76. Pavesich, supra note 66.

77. PROSSER, supra note 32, at 1052–53.

78. Id. at 1053–54.

79. Id. at 1054.

80. Id. at notes 41–43, citing Byfield v. Candler, 125 S.E. 905 (Ga. 1924); Rhodes v. Graham, 37 S.W. 46 (Ky. 1931); and McDaniel v. Atlanta Coca-Cola Bottling Co., 2 S.E. 2d 810 (Ga. App. 1939).

81. Id. at 1055–56 nn. 50–55. In our view, of several cases Prosser cited in note 55, only Iskovitch v. Whitaker, 115 La. 479 (1905), and Schulman v. Whitaker, 117 La. 704 (1906), directly support the statement in his text.

82. PROSSER, supra note 32, at 1050.

83. Id.

84. Id. at 636 (2d ed. 1955).

85. Id. at 637.

86. Id. at 638.

87. See Christopher J. Robinette, The Prosser Notebook: Classroom as Biography and Intellectual History, U. ILL. L. REV. 578, 602 n. 274 (2010), quoting

Phillip P. Frickey, *Transcending Transcendental Nonsense: Toward a New Realism in Federal Indian Law*, 38 CONN. L. REV. 649, 653–54 (2006).

88. *See, e.g.,* George L. Priest, *The Invention of Enterprise Liability: A Critical History of the Intellectual Foundations of Modern Tort Law*, 14 J. LEGAL STUD. 461, 512–18 (1985).

89. *See* WHITE, *supra* note 20, at 12–15, 104–10 (expanded ed. 2003).

90. *See id.* at 106–12.

91. *See id.* at 104–10.

92. *See id.* at 146; *see also* Albert Ehrenzweig, *Loss-Shifting and Quasi-Negligence: A New Interpretation of the* Palsgraf *Case*, 8 U. CHI. L. REV. 729, 729–30 (1941); Fleming James, Jr., *Accident Liability Reconsidered: The Impact of Liability Insurance*, 57 YALE L. J. 549, 549–51 (1948). Even by the mid-twentieth century, for example, there was no general cause of action for loss caused by negligence. Negligence was a cause of action mainly for bodily injury and property damage, and even that cause of action was constrained by strong limitations, mostly in the form of no-duty and limited-duty constraints on the imposition of liability. There was limited liability for bodily injury arising out of negligently maintained premises, limited liability for negligently manufactured products, limited liability for negligently inflicted emotional distress, limited liability for "wrongful birth," and virtually no liability for negligently caused economic loss, to name just a few such doctrinal limitations. *See* ABRAHAM, *supra* note 61, at 104–269.

93. *See generally* ROBERT E. KEETON, COMPENSATION SYSTEMS: THE SEARCH FOR A VIABLE ALTERNATIVE TO NEGLIGENCE LAW (1969) (providing a summary of this attitude).

94. *Id.* at 1050–54.

95. *Id.* at 1054.

96. *See* Fowler V. Harper & Mary Coate McNeely, *A Re-Examination of the Basis for Liability for Emotional Distress*, 1938 WIS. L. REV. 426, 426–27 (1938); *see also* Leon Green, *The Right of Privacy*, 27 ILL. L. REV. 237, 239 (1932) (similarly emphasizing the "interests" at stake in emotional harm cases and concluding that many cases described as "privacy" actions were actually attempts to protect an interest in "personality").

97. *See* Harper & McNeely, *supra* note 96, at 426–27.

98. *See id.* at 427–45.

99. *Id.* at 427–45.

100. *See id.* at 463–64.

101. *Id.* at 451.

102. *Id.*

103. *See id.* at 452–58.

104. *See id.*
105. *See id.* at 453.
106. Harry Kalven, Jr., *Recent Books*, 32 TEX. L. REV. 629, 629 (1954) (reviewing CLARENCE MORRIS, MORRIS ON TORTS [1953]); CHARLES O. GREGORY & HARRY KALVEN, JR., CASES AND MATERIALS ON TORTS, 848 (1959).
107. *See* WHITE, *supra* note 20, at 104–13.
108. *See* William L. Prosser, *Privacy*, 48 CALIF. L. REV. 383, 389 (1960).
109. Ronald J. Rychlak, *John Wade: Teacher, Lawyer, Scholar*, 65 MISS. L. J. 1, 1 (1995).
110. John W. Wade, *Defamation and the Right of Privacy*, 15 VAND. L. REV. 1093, 1094 (1962).
111. *Id.* at 1109–20.
112. *Id.* at 1095–96.
113. *Id.* at 1098.
114. *Id.* at 1095.
115. *Id.* at 1121.
116. *Id.* at 1121.
117. *Id.* at 1121–22.
118. *Id.* at 1122.
119. *Id.*
120. *Id.* at 1124–25.
121. Edward J. Bloustein, *Privacy as an Aspect of Human Dignity: An Answer to Dean Prosser*, 39 N.Y.U. L. REV. 962 (1964).
122. *Id.* at 971–72.
123. *Id.* at 971.
124. *Id.* at 970.
125. *Id.* at 972–92.
126. *Id.* at 973.
127. *Id.* at 973–74.
128. *Id.* at 978.
129. *Id.*, quoting Warren & Brandeis, *supra* note 46, at 218.
130. *Id.* at 985–91.
131. *Id.* at 986. Although some cases involved "special circumstances" where, because the plaintiff was "a public figure, the use of his likeness or name for commercial purposes involves the appropriation of a thing of value," the gravamen of the action, Bloustein believed, was that "the very commercialization of a name or photograph . . . does injury to the sense of personal dignity." *Id.* at 988.
132. *Id.* He noted two California cases, based on the same episode, in which a married couple was photographed embracing in their place of business. The photograph was then published in two different articles on the subject

of love. One article attached a caption to the photograph that stated it was an example of "the wrong kind of love," consisting "wholly of sexual attraction and nothing else." The other article merely included the photograph without comment. The plaintiffs sued both publishers. Gill v. Curtis Publishing Co., 38 Cal. 2d 273 (1952); Gill v. Hearst Publishing Co., 40 Cal. 2d 224 (1953). In the case with the caption, the court upheld an action in false-light privacy; in the other case the complaint was dismissed on the ground that by embracing in public the plaintiffs implicitly consented to having their photograph taken. Bloustein argued that in the first case publication of the photograph, combined with the caption, "turn[ed] the otherwise inoffensive publication into one which is an undue and reasonable insult to personality." The "false and stigmatic comment on character" that accompanied the photograph "constitute[d] the actionable wrong." Bloustein felt that publication of the photograph with the misleading caption "serve[d] the same function" as an unconsented "use of [a] photograph for advertising purposes." In that respect false-light cases were protecting the same interest as name and likeness cases. "Once it is recognized that the user of a name for advertising reasons is wrongful because it is an affront to personal dignity," Bloustein maintained, "the underlying similarity between the advertising and 'false light' cases becomes apparent. The 'false light' and the advertising use are merely two different means of publishing a person's name or likeness so as to offend his dignity as an individual." *Id.* at 992.

133. Wade, *supra* note 110, at 1125.
134. *See* Abraham & White, *supra* note 33, at 35–40 (2013) (recounting Prosser's career in the 1960s); Vincent Blasi, *Harry Kalven, Jr.,* 61 J. LEGAL EDUC. 301, 302–3 (2011) (discussing Kalven's career and referencing his "most important law review article," published in 1964); Hardy C. Dillard, *A Tribute to Charles O. Gregory: Foreword,* 53 VA. L. REV. 759 (1967) (discussing Gregory's influence in the wake of his death); Rychlak, *supra* note 109 (discussing Wade's professional career).
135. Thomas J. Frusciano, *Leadership on the Banks: Rutgers' Presidents, 1766–1991,* 53 J. RUTGERS U. LIBR. 1, 36 (1991).
136. *See id.* at 36; *see also, e.g.,* Edward J. Bloustein, *Privacy, Tort Law, and the Constitution: Is Warren and Brandeis' Tort Petty and Unconstitutional as Well?* 46 TEX. L. REV. 611 (1968).
137. RESTATEMENT (SECOND) OF TORTS § 19 (1965).
138. *See, e.g.,* Alcorn v. Mitchell, 63 Ill. 553, 554 (1872) (noting that spitting in a person's face is an act of indignity); Draper v. Baker, 21 N.W. 527 (Wis. 1884) (holding that a jury verdict rendered against a defendant who spat in a woman's face was not excessive).

139. *See, e.g.,* Koeppel v. Speirs, 808 N.W. 2d 177 (Iowa 2011) (holding that recording equipment did not have to be functional for the intrusion to be actionable).

140. Pavesich, *supra* note 66, is a classic example of this form of appropriation. For modern examples, *see* Faegre & Benson, LLP v. Purdy, 447 F. Supp. 2d 1008 (D. Minn., 2006) (an anti-abortion activist registered domain names incorporating the names of his opponents); Felsher v. University of Evansville, 755 N.E. 2d 589 (2001) (a professor created noncommercial websites and email accounts employing the names of his former colleagues, then sent emails to a number of universities nominating those persons for academic positions and directing readers to the websites, which contained critical posts about the nominated individuals).

141. For a collection of the early cases, *see* PROSSER, *supra* note 32, at 57–62. The modern cases involve various forms of ridicule, harassment, and repeated efforts at debt collection, among other things. *See, e.g.,* Slocum v. Food Fair Stores of Florida, 100 So. 2d 396, 397 (Fl. 1958) (saying to a customer, "you stink to me"); Taggart v. Drake Univ., 549 N.W. 2d 796, 802 (Iowa 1996) (a faculty member referring to the plaintiff in a "sexist and condescending manner"); Harris v. Jones, 380 A. 2d 611, 562–63 (Md. 1977) (ridiculing a plaintiff's stuttering); Samms v. Eccles, 358 P. 2d 344, 345 (Utah 1961) (a debt collector making late night telephone calls over a six-month period and engaging in indecent exposure); Womack v. Eldridge, 210 S.E. 2d 145, 146–47 (Va. 1974) (taking the plaintiff's photograph under false pretenses and then misleadingly using it at a trial to imply that he may have committed a crime).

142. *See, e.g.,* Womack v. Eldridge, *supra* note 141 (fear of being accused of a crime); State Rubbish Collectors Ass'n. v. Siliznoff, 240 P. 2d 282, 284 (Cal. 1952) (fear of being physically harmed); Russo v. White, 400 S.E. 2d 160, 163 (Va. 1991) (extreme irritation resulting from 340 hang-up calls by a disappointed suitor).

143. Gertz v. Robert Welch, Inc., 418 U.S. 323, 341 (1974) (quoting Rosenblatt v. Baer, 383 U.S. 75, 92 [1966]).

144. *See, e.g.,* Haynes v. Alfred A. Knopf, Inc., 8 F. 3d 1222, 1233–34 (holding that depiction of the plaintiff as a man who drank heavily, neglected his children, and was pathetically amorous when drunk was not highly offensive).

145. Two of many illustrations are John W. Wade, *Tort Liability for Abusive and Insulting Words,* 4 VAND. L. REV. 63, 76–79 (1951), and LAWRENCE McNAMARA, REPUTATION AND DEFAMATION 162–89 (2007).

146. For some evidence consistent with that suggestion, *see* Lee Rainie & Janna Anderson, *The Future of Privacy,* Pew Research Center (December 18, 2014), http://www.pewinternet.org/2014/12/18/future-of-privacy/

[https://perma.cc/8FE8-3AR3]; Irina Raicu, *Are Attitudes About Privacy Changing?* Markkula Center for Applied Ethics, Santa Clara U. (June 1, 2012), https://perma.cc/5BEW-ZY7P.

147. While a candidate for president, Bill Clinton answered the question, "boxers or briefs?" by saying, "usually briefs." Richard Lei, *The Commander in Briefs,* WASH. POST, April 20, 1994, at https://www.washingtonpost.com /archive/lifestyle/1994/04/20/the-commander-in-briefs/04219ef3-aa61 -4f28-8869-6217476c1b47/?utm_term=.1307ce1f0ba4 [https://perma.cc /ZM73-EMCB].

148. *See* PROSSER, *supra* note 32, at 383, 389–98, 422 (privacy).

149. *Id.* at 389. *See also* GREGORY & KALVEN, *supra* note 106, at 883–84 (mentioning Prosser's assertion that most privacy torts would be absorbed into the IIED tort); Bloustein, *supra* note 121, at 971–72 (discussing Prosser's opinion that there is no single privacy tort).

150. PROSSER, *supra* note 32, at 45; WHITE, *supra* note 20, at 104; Warren & Brandeis, *supra* note 46, at 195–98.

151. RESTATEMENT (SECOND) OF TORTS § 652B (1977); RESTATEMENT (SECOND) OF TORTS § 46 (1965); ABRAHAM, *supra* note 61, at 308–10; Andrew L. Merritt, *Damages for Emotional Distress in Fraud Litigation,* 42 VAND. L. REV. 1, 15–16, 21 (1989).

152. PROSSER, *supra* note 32, at 45; WHITE, *supra* note 20, at 104; Prosser, *supra* note 108, at 389; Warren & Brandeis, *supra* note 46, at 195–98.

4. THE FIRST AMENDMENT AND THE CONSTITUTIONALIZATION OF TORT LIABILITY

1. Chaplinsky v. New Hampshire, 315 U.S. 568, 571–72 (1942).

2. Commentators noting this tendency in the U.S. Supreme Court's First Amendment jurisprudence have focused on different points of emphasis and given that tendency different labels. As early as 2002 Frederick Schauer identified a growing interest by litigators in advancing novel First Amendment challenges to government regulations and associated that interest with a perception that the courts were increasingly receptive to First Amendment arguments. He labeled the surfacing of that perception "First Amendment opportunism." Frederick Schauer, *First Amendment Opportunism, in* ETERNALLY VIGILANT: FREE SPEECH IN THE MODERN ERA 176 (Lee C. Bollinger & Geoffrey Stone eds., 2002). Recently Leslie Kendrick, emphasizing the growing "level of success" of First Amendment challenges in the courts, has described that trend as "First Amendment expansionism." Leslie Kendrick, *First Amendment Expansionism,* 56 WM. & MARY L. REV. 1099 (2015). As early as 1979 Thomas

Jackson and John Jeffries spotted and criticized the tendency without giving it a label. Thomas Jackson & John C. Jeffries, *Commercial Speech: Economic Due Process and the First Amendment*, 65 VA. L. REV. 1 (1979).

3. Cohen v. California, 403 U.S. 15 (1971).

4. Buckley v. Valeo, 424 U.S. 1 (1976).

5. Virginia St. Bd. of Pharmacy v. Virginia Citizens Council, 425 U.S. 748 (1976).

6. Rubin v. Coors Brewing Co., 514 U.S. 476 (1976).

7. U.S. v. Stevens, 559 U.S. 460 (2010).

8. Brown v. Ent. Merch. Ass'n., 564 U.S. 786 (2011).

9. Expressions Hair Design v. Schneiderman, 137 S. Ct. 1144 (2017).

10. U.S. v. Alvarez, 132 S. Ct. 2537 (2012).

11. *See* Frederick Schauer, *Out of Range: On Patently Uncovered Speech*, 128 HARV. L. REV. F. 346 (2015) (asserting "for example . . . it is laughable to suppose that all, most, or even much of contract law in any way implicates the First Amendment").

12. Janus v. State, County, & Mun. Emps., 138 S. Ct. 2448, 2501–2 (2018) (Kagan, J., dissenting).

13. To take just one of numerous examples, see GEOFFREY R. STONE ET AL., THE FIRST AMENDMENT 88, 133–34 (5th ed. 2016). An illustration of the distinction between coverage and protection in First Amendment jurisprudence is the treatment of "commercial speech," defined as proposing a commercial transaction. As we subsequently note, commercial speech was originally thought to lie outside the coverage of the First Amendment altogether; then, in 1976 it was brought within that coverage. But commercial speech has never been afforded the level of protection given to many other forms of speech, so that the justifications for restricting it need not be as weighty as those required for, say, political speech. In the vocabulary of First Amendment jurisprudence, true and accurate commercial speech is treated as a "lower" form of speech, referring to its level of protection. In contrast, false and misleading commercial speech remains outside the ambit of the amendment's coverage and consequently receives *no* protection.

14. *See* Schenck v. United States, 249 U.S. 47 (1919); Abrams v. United States, 250 U.S. 616 (1919).

15. That language was from Justice Oliver Wendell Holmes's opinion for a unanimous Court in Schenck v. United States, 249 U.S. 47 (1919), even though it was accompanied by the statement that "the question in every case is whether the words used are used in such circumstances and are of such a nature as to create a clear and present danger" that they would bring about substantive evils. In two cases decided along with Schenck, Frohwerk v. United States, 249 U.S. 204 (1919), and Debs v. United States,

249 U.S. 211 (1919), Holmes, in the course of upholding convictions under the Espionage Act of 1917, referred to the "tendency" of expressions to obstruct the war effort without using the "clear and present danger" language. In Gitlow v. New York, 268 U.S. 652, 671 (1925), the Court restated the test as a "natural tendency and probable effect . . . to bring about the substantive evil which the legislative body might prevent."

16. 315 U.S. 568 (1942).

17. *Id.* at 571–72.

18. *Id.*

19. Yates v. United States, 354 U.S. 298 (1957); Scales v. United States, 367 U.S. 203 (1961); Bond v. Floyd, 385 U.S. 116 (1966).

20. Brandenburg v. Ohio, 395 U.S. 444, 447 (1969).

21. For illustrations, *see* Gerald Gunther, *Learned Hand and the Origins of Modern First Amendment Doctrine*, 27 STAN. L. REV. 719, 754–55 (1975); JOHN HART ELY, DEMOCRACY AND DISTRUST 115 (1980).

22. Brandenburg v. Ohio, *supra* note 20, at 447.

23. The decision was Dennis v. United States, 341 U.S. 494, 507 (1951).

24. Brandenburg v. Ohio, *supra* note 20, at 447.

25. An example was the Court's majority opinion in Gitlow v. New York, 268 U.S. 652, 668 (1925).

26. In Bridges v. California, 314 U.S. 252 (1941), Justice Felix Frankfurter, joined by Chief Justice Harlan Fiske Stone and Justice Owen Roberts, would have found a telegram labor leader Harry Bridges sent to the secretary of labor, suggesting that if a judge's decision in litigation between two rival unions was enforced, his union would call a strike affecting the port of Los Angeles, a "true threat." *Id.* at 303–4.

27. Teminiello v. Chicago, 337 U.S. 1 (1949).

28. Valentine v. Chrestensen, 316 U.S. 52 (1942); Breard v. Alexandria, 341 U.S.622 (1951).

29. *See* SIMON HALL, PEACE AND FREEDOM: THE CIVIL RIGHTS AND ANTI-WAR MOVEMENTS IN THE 1960S (2006).

30. *See, e.g.,* Cox v. Louisiana, 379 U.S. 536 (1965), where a group of students challenged their convictions for a breach of the peace based on their having picketed a courthouse as a protest against some civil rights arrests.

31. Louis Henkin called the distinction "specious," asserting that "speech *is* conduct, and actions speak," and arguing that the "meaningful constitutional distinction is not between speech and conduct but between conduct that speaks, communicates, and other kinds of conduct." Louis Henkin, *On Drawing Lines,* 82 HARV. L. REV. 63, 79–80 (1968).

32. United States v. O'Brien, 391 U.S. 367 (1968).

33. Tinker v. Des Moines Indep. Cnty. Sch. Dist., 393 U.S. 509 (1969).

34. Schacht v. United States, 398 U.S. 58 (1970).
35. Street v. New York, 394 U.S. 576 (1969). Subsequently, after Black left the Court in the fall of 1971, two persons had their convictions for "contemptuous treatment" of the flag and "flag misuse" overturned by Court majorities. The first case involved wearing a replica of the flag sewn to the seat of trousers, and the second the public display of a privately owned flag with a peace symbol affixed to it with removable tape. Smith v. Goguen, 415 U.S. 566 (1974); Spence v. Washington, 418 U.S. 405 (1974).
36. 403 U.S. 15 (1971).
37. *Id.* at 20. The Court's then current definition of obscenity had been set forth in Roth v. United States, 354 U.S. 476 (1957).
38. The petitioner, Paul Robert Cohen, was given thirty days in jail for violating a California statute prohibiting individuals from "maliciously and willfully disturbing the peace of . . . any . . . person . . . by . . . offensive conduct." 403 U.S. at 16.
39. *Id.* at 24–25.
40. Justice Harry Blackmun, joined by Chief Justice Warren Burger and Justice Hugo Black, dissented in *Cohen* on the ground that the defendant's expression was "mainly conduct, and little speech" and thus "well within the sphere of *Chaplinsky v New Hampshire.*" 403 U.S. at 27.
41. 86 Stat. 3 (1972); 88 Stat. 1263 (1974).
42. 424 U.S. 1 (1976).
43. *Id.* at 16.
44. *Id* at 22, 19.
45. *Id.* at 48–49.
46. 558 U.S. 310 (2010).
47. *Id.* at 441.
48. Valentine v. Chrestensen and Breard v. Alexandria, *supra* note 28.
49. Martin v. Struthers, 319 U.S. 141, 142–43 (1943).
50. Smith v. California, 361 U.S. 147, 150 (1959); Bantam Books v. Sullivan, 372 U.S. 58, 64 n.6 (1963).
51. 425 U.S. 748 (1976).
52. *Id.* at 756–57.
53. *Id.* at 763.
54. *Id* at 763–64.
55. *Id.* at 762.
56. *Id.* at 765.
57. Cent. Hudson Gas v. Public Serv. Comm'n of N.Y., 447 U.S. 557, 567 n. 9 (1980). The majority opinion in *Virginia Pharmacy* had anticipated that "false and misleading" commercial speech might constitutionally be regulated, stating that "the greater objectivity and hardiness of commercial

speech" may "make it less necessary to tolerate inaccurate statements for fear of silencing the speaker," and "may also make it appropriate . . . to require that a commercial message . . . include such additional information, warnings, and disclaimers, as are necessary to prevent its being deceptive." 425 U.S. 748, 773 n. 24.

58. *See* WILLIAM L. PROSSER, HANDBOOK OF THE LAW OF TORTS 572 (2d ed. 1955) (indicating that the state of defamation law is a product of "historical accident and survival").

59. *Id.* at 606–13.

60. *Id.* at 618–19.

61. *Id.* at 619–21

62. *Id.* at 621.

63. *See, e.g.,* Coleman v. MacLennan, 98 P. 281 (Kan. 1908).

64. KENNETH S. ABRAHAM, THE FORMS AND FUNCTIONS OF TORT LAW 301 (5th ed. 2017).

65. 376 U.S. 254 (1964).

66. *Id.* at 258–259. Sullivan made no effort to prove that he suffered actual pecuniary loss as a result of the ad, but he did make a demand for a retraction from each of the named defendants in his suit, a necessary step to recovery in punitive damages under Alabama law. None of the defendants issued a retraction, and the *Times* wrote Sullivan that it failed to see how the ad referred to him. *Id.* at 260–61.

67. Alabama defamation law adopted the conclusion in Post Publishing v. Hallam, 59 F. 530 (6th Cir. 1893), that in order for criticism of public officials to be privileged, it must be based on true underlying facts. As the case progressed through the Alabama courts, those courts ruled that false written statements of fact made about a person with respect to his business or profession were libelous *per se,* not requiring proof of actual damages. They followed then-existing Alabama law in ruling that a statement had to be factually accurate to trigger the common law privilege of fair comment on matters of public concern, and that any claim that statements were true had to demonstrate they were true in all their particulars. The Alabama courts ruled that the mere fact of publication of a libel *per se* created a presumption that it was false and malicious, allowing punitive as well as presumed damages. They did not require the jury to separate compensatory from punitive damages in its award of $500,000. They ruled that the jury could have found that the statements about "police," "Southern violators," and "They" were "of and concerning" Sullivan because it was "common knowledge" to the average citizen that the police were "under the direction and control of a single commissioner." And they did not find the damages "excessive," stating that the *Times* had been "irresponsible"

258 NOTES TO PAGES 145–151

in publishing the ad because it had articles in its own files that would have demonstrated the falsity of some of the ad's allegations. Finally, the Alabama Supreme Court declared that no privilege of free speech or of the press could be attached to the ad because "the First Amendment . . . does not protect libelous publications," and the "Fourteenth Amendment is directed at state action, not private action."

68. 376 U.S. at 279–80.

69. *Id.* at 270.

70. *See, e.g.,* Harry Kalven, *The New York Times Case: A Note on "'The Central Meaning of the First Amendment,'"* 1964 SUP. CT. REV. 191, 221 (1964).

71. 376 U.S. at 271–72.

72. The Court later made that conclusion explicit in Philadelphia Newspapers v. Hepps, 475 U.S. 767 (1986).

73. The language describing those categories of "public figures" comes from Foretich v. Capital Cities/ABC Inc., 37 F. 3d 1541, 1551–52 (4th Cir. 1994).

74. 388 U.S. 130 (1967).

75. *Id.* at 163–64.

76. *Id.* at 163.

77. 418 U.S. 323 (1974).

78. *Id.* at 339–41. Emphasis supplied.

79. 376 U.S. at 272–73.

80. 497 U.S. 1 (1990).

81. *Id.* at 4–5.

82. *Id.* at 18–20, 24.

83. Dun & Bradstreet v. Greenmoss Builders, 472 U.S. 749 (1985). Six members of the Court also concluded in *Dun & Bradstreet* that there was no distinction between media and nonmedia defendants with respect to the constitutional privileges accorded in defamation cases. *Id.* at 783–84. That issue had been open since *Gertz,* where Justice Powell's opinion referred to the constitutional requirement of establishing at least negligence in cases where a private citizen was defamed on a matter of public concern, as applying where "publishers or broadcasters" were defendants. *Gertz,* 418 U.S. at 418.

84. RESTATEMENT (SECOND) OF TORTS, § 652 (1977).

85. Cox Broadcasting Corp. v. Cohn, 420 U.S. 469 (1975).

86. Bartnicki v. Vopper, 532 U.S. 514 (2001).

87. *Cox Broadcasting;* The Florida Star v. B. J. F., 491 U.S. 524 (1989).

88. Shulman v. Group W. Prods., Inc., 955 P. 2d 469 (Cal. 1998).

89. *See* William L. Prosser, *Privacy,* 48 CALIF. L. REV. 383, 398 (1960). The *Restatement* contains a second requirement that the defendant knows of the false light or recklessly disregarded it. RESTATEMENT (SECOND) OF TORTS

§ 652E (1977). But that appears simply to be incorporating the constitutional requirement, rather than stating the prior common law rule.

90. Time Inc. v. Hill, 385 U.S. 374 (1967).

91. In Cantrell v. Forest City Pub. Co., 419 U.S. 245 (1974), the Court majority noted that the jury had been instructed that liability could be imposed for false statements made about the plaintiff only if they concluded that the statements were deliberately and recklessly false (*New York Times*'s "malice") and that "consequently [the] case presents no occasion to consider whether a State may constitutionally apply a more relaxed standard of liability" when a private individual claimed injury under a false-light theory of liability. The Court then cited *Gertz*, suggesting that that case may have had implications for false-light privacy as well. 419 U.S. at 250–51.

92. Zacchini v. Scripps-Howard Broadcasting Co., 433 U.S. 562 (1977).

93. Winter v. DC Comics, 30 Cal. 4th 881 (2003).

94. *Zacchini* at 575.

95. Winter v. DC Comics, 69 P. 3d 473 (Cal. 2003).

96. Hustler Mag., Inc. v. Falwell, 485 U.S. 46 (1988).

97. Snyder v. Phelps, 562 U.S. 443 (2011).

98. 559 U.S. 460 (2010).

99. 564 U.S. 286 (2011)

100. "Violent video games" were defined as those in which "options for players included depictions of killing, maiming, dismembering, or sexually assaulting" images of human beings, which were presented in a fashion that a "reasonable person . . . would find patently offensive to prevailing standards in the community as to what is suitable for minors." California Assembly Bill 1179 (2005), Cal. Civ. Code Ann. Sect. 1746 (d) (1) (A) (West, 2009).

101. 567 U.S. 709 (2012).

102. *Id.* at 717–18.

103. *Brown* at 791, quoting *U.S. v. Stevens* at 468; *U.S. v. Alvarez* at 716.

104. *U.S. v. Stevens* at 470–72.

105. *U.S. v. Alvarez* at 722.

106. See *Gertz* at 339. We think that it would be a mistake to interpret this statement even more broadly, to mean that under the First Amendment, there can be no tort liability for the expression of an idea. There is no decision of the Supreme Court that goes this far. A moment's reflection reveals why: speech resulting in such liability is not always protected. For example, if there can be criminal liability for expressing ideas that incite immediate violence, as there can be, then imposing tort liability for such expression must also be permissible. For more detail, *see* KENT GREENAWALT, SPEECH, CRIME, AND THE USES OF LANGUAGE 87–134 (1989).

107. *See* Milkovich, *supra* note 80, at 21–22.
108. One can see this feature of disparagement law in the allowance of "puff-ing" about products as a complete defense to disparagement claims, in-cluding "puffed" statements making implicit comparisons between a manufacturer's product and those of competitors. If a statement "puffing" a product is deemed to be not capable of being proven true or false, it cannot be treated as grounds for a disparagement suit. *See* WILLIAM L. PROSSER AND W. PAGE KEETON, THE LAW OF TORTS 964 (1984 ed.), where the authors stated that "the puffing rule amounts to a seller's privilege to lie his head off, so long as he says nothing specific, on the theory that no one would believe him or . . . would be influenced by such talk."
109. *See, e.g.,* Della Penna v. Toyota Motor Sales, U.S.A., Inc., 902 P. 2d 740 (Cal. 1995) (indicating in a suit for interference with prospective eco-nomic advantage that the defendant warned its dealers not to do business with certain third parties).
110. *See Snyder* at 451–52.
111. *See, e.g.,* Haynes v. Alfred A. Knopf, Inc., 8 F. 3d 1222 (7th Cir. 1993). The Su-preme Court has not expressly adopted a requirement that for true infor-mation to be disclosed with impunity it must be "newsworthy," principally because in all of the Court's true disclosure privacy cases the information disclosed was either available in public records, legally obtained, or plainly newsworthy. *See, e.g.,* Cox Broadcasting v. Cohn, 420 U.S. 469 (1975) (iden-tity of a rape victim obtained when a television reporter was permitted to inspect the indictment, disclosed on television broadcast); The Florida Star v. B.J.F., 491 U.S. 524 (1989) (name of a victim of sexual assault identified on a police report to which a newspaper reporter had access); Bartnicki v. Vopper, 532 U.S. 514 (2001) (a telephone conversation about a school labor dispute illegally intercepted but then lawfully obtained by a radio com-mentator who broadcast it; the Court emphasized that the subject of the conversation was a matter of public importance).

In Shulman v. Group W. Prod., Inc., 19 Cal. 4th 200 (1998), a victim of a motor vehicle accident was filmed in a weakened condition at the site of the accident and being transported to a hospital in a helicopter. The film was subsequently broadcast on a local television station. The victim sued for intrusion and true disclosure privacy, and the station asserted First Amendment privileges in both actions. The California Supreme Court concluded that there was no First Amendment "newsgathering" privilege in intrusion actions where the intrusion was "offensive to a rea-sonable person." But it also assumed that any true disclosure suit would not succeed because the disclosure of the plaintiff's condition was obvi-ously newsworthy.

112. *See Virginia State Board of Pharmacy* at 765.
113. *See* RESTATEMENT (SECOND) OF TORTS § 623A (1977).
114. 620 F. 2d 1301 (8th Cir. 1980).
115. 458 U.S. 886 (1982).
116. The Boycott, Divestment, and Sanctions (BDS) movement is a global campaign promoting various forms of boycott against Israel until that nation meets what the campaign's organizers believe are its "obligations under international law." CHARLES TRIPP, THE POWER AND THE PEOPLE: PATHS OF RESISTANCE IN THE MIDDLE EAST 125–26 (2013). Numerous states have passed legislation or executive orders either deploring the activities of BDS or proposing that states divest themselves from companies engaging in BDS activities. One illustration is a June 5, 2016, executive order of New York governor Andrew Cuomo calling for the divestment of state assets in any company listed as participating in the BDS movement. *See* Lara Friedman, *The Pitfalls of the New York Executive Order on BDS,* PEACE NOW, June 7, 2016, https://peacenow.org/entry.php?id=18551#.XIkbbBlJYaig. That order has raised constitutional objections on the grounds that economic boycotts are protected forms of speech under *NAACP v. Claiborne Hardware,* and that states placing companies participating in BDS on lists and ceasing to do business them chills that speech. Friedman, *supra.* We are inclined to agree that *NAACP v. Claiborne Hardware* governs governmental efforts to regulate BDS's objectives because the boycotts constitute speech about a matter of public concern.

5. TORTS WITHOUT NAMES, NEW TORTS, AND THE FUTURE OF LIABILITY FOR INTANGIBLE HARM

1. KENNETH S. ABRAHAM, THE FORMS AND FUNCTIONS OF TORT LAW 61 (5th ed. 2017).
2. *See, e.g.,* Dillon v. Legg, 441 P. 2d 912 (Cal. 1968) (adopting liability for negligent infliction of emotional distress by relaxing no-duty restriction on liability); Kline v. 1500 Massachusetts Ave. Apartment Corp., 439 F. 2d 477 (D.C. Cir. 1970) (adopting negligence liability for a landlord's failure to maintain adequate security by relaxing no-duty restriction on liability).
3. In the past, tort law has tended to protect against physical harm—bodily injury and property damage (and their consequences)—and to compensate victims who suffer those physical harms more rigorously than other forms of harm, such as "pure" (freestanding) emotional suffering and economic loss. *See* ABRAHAM, *supra* note 1, at 2–3. In this chapter we use the term "tangible" to refer to overtly physical forces and overtly physical

harms, and the term "intangible" to refer to forces (cyber invasions for example) and harms (emotional and economic loss, for example) that are not overtly physical. Obviously, we recognize that cyber invasions have a physical component, even when that component is not overt and observable. In addition, by describing emotional and economic harm as "intangible," we do not mean that these harms are any less real or important than physical harms. Rather, our reference to "tangible" and "intangible" forces and harms is a shorthand designed to capture the general distinction between two subject matters that the law of torts, as it now stands, usually treats differently.

4. Oliver Wendell Holmes, Jr., *Privilege, Malice, and Intent,* 8 HARV. L. REV. 1, 3 (1894).

5. *Id.*

6. *See* David H. Burton, *The Intellectual Kinship of Oliver Wendell Holmes, Jr., Frederick Pollock, and Harold J. Laski,* 119 PROCEEDINGS OF THE AMERICAN PHILOSOPHICAL SOCIETY 133 (1975).

7. OLIVER WENDELL HOLMES, JR., THE COMMON LAW (1881).

8. For more detail on Pollock's early scholarship, *see* NEIL DUXBURY, FREDERICK POLLOCK AND THE ENGLISH JURISTIC TRADITION 20–27 (2004).

9. HOLMES, *supra* note 7, at 65, 110.

10. *Id.* at 190–92.

11. FREDERICK POLLOCK, THE LAW OF TORTS 21–23 (4th ed. 1886).

12. Holmes, *supra* note 4, at 3. First, he acknowledged that a finding of "malice" might in itself subject a party to tort liability even if his conduct was not otherwise unlawful. "Malice" was no longer subsumed in the category of "intent"; it was an independent basis of liability. *Id.* Second, whereas in THE COMMON LAW Holmes had treated "malice" as part of a continuum "of foreseeability that also included 'intent' and 'negligence'" (see OLIVER WENDELL HOLMES, THE COMMON LAW 126–27 [2009 ed.]), which might serve to clarify whether a defendant's conduct had violated a standard of liability, his analysis of "malice" in *Privilege, Malice, and Intent* was now centered on justification and excuse. Intentional injury resulting in "temporal" damage was now presumed to be actionable unless a defendant could show that his or her actions were not "malicious" because they were justified. *See* Holmes, *supra* note 4, at 3.

For a discussion of the evolution of Holmes's thinking and an account of the rise of prima facie tort, *see* Kenneth J. Vandevelde, *A History of Prima Facie Tort: The Origins of a General Theory of Intentional Tort,* 19 HOFSTRA L. REV. 447 (1990).

13. 167 Mass. 92 (1896).

14. Vegelahn v. Guntner, 44 N.E. 1077 (Mass. 1896).

15. *Id.* at 105–6.

16. He believed that since his opinion apparently took the side of labor against capital in an industrial dispute, it would end up being something he "may have to pay for, practically, before I die." Holmes to Clare Castletown, November 21, 1896, *Oliver Wendell Holmes Papers*, Microfilm Edition (1985), quoted in G. EDWARD WHITE, JUSTICE OLIVER WENDELL HOLMES: LAW AND THE INNER SELF 289 (1993).

17. In Plant v. Woods, 176 Mass. 492 (1900), a majority of Holmes's Massachusetts judicial colleagues ended up agreeing with him that justifiability was the critical inquiry in such cases, and that justifiability was a matter of social policy. But once again, in a labor dispute, the majority found that efforts by workers to disparage their opponents were not justifiable and thus actionable if they could be shown to produce damage. "The necessity that the plaintiffs should join this association is not so great," the majority declared, "such as to bring the acts of the defendant under the shelter of trade competition." The plaintiffs had "a right . . . to be free from molestation." *Id.* at 494–95.

    Similarly, in Moran v. Dunphy, 177 Mass. 485 (1901), the defendant made comments about the plaintiff to the plaintiff's employer that eventually caused the employer to fire the plaintiff. The plaintiff sued for intentional interference with contractual relations, a recognized tort. Holmes, overruling a demurrer to the action granted by a trial court, held that "to induce a third person to end his employment with another," when done "maliciously and without justifiable cause," was "an actionable tort." *Id.* at 485–87. Technically, the decision only allowed the case to go forward: Holmes and his colleagues did not pass on the justifiability of the defendant's actions, or even note what the defendant's purported justification was. Moreover, Holmes treated the case as involving intentional interference with contract rather than a prima facie tort. But his analysis suggested that he was inclined to extend his emphasis on justification to other torts in which persons intentionally interfered with the business relationships of others The cognizability of the tort of intentional interference with contract, at a time when the concept of an all-purpose tort of intentional, unjustifiable infliction of temporal damage was still largely unrecognized, can be put down to the value afforded "rights" of property and contract, and the importance attributed to preserving the stability of contracts, in late nineteenth-century America. *See* Stephen A. Siegel, *Understanding the Nineteenth Century Contracts Clause*, 60 S. CAL. L. REV. 1, 8–9 (1986); Henry N. Butler & Larry E. Ribstein, *The Contract Clause and the Corporation*, 55 BROOKLYN L. REV. 767, 778 (1989).

18. 195 U.S. 194 (1904).

19. *Id.* at 201–2.
20. *Id.* at 204. Emphasis in original.
21. *Id.* at 205.
22. *Id.* at 206.
23. *Id.*
24. 1 Q.B. 715 (Eng.).
25. 119 N.W. 946 (Minn. 1909).
26. *Id.* at 947.
27. *See, e.g.,* Dunshee v. Standard Oil Co., 132 N.W. 371 (Iowa 1911) (holding that an action would lie when agents of the defendant conveyed false information about the plaintiff and harassed its employees); Hutton v. Waters, 179 S.W. 134 (Tenn. 1915) (upholding a cause of action against the defendant who out of ill will attempted to drive a boardinghouse out of business).
28. WILLIAM L. PROSSER, HANDBOOK OF THE LAW OF TORTS 1015–17 (1941).
29. RESTATEMENT (SECOND) OF TORTS § 766B (1977).
30. RESTATEMENT (THIRD) OF TORTS: LIABILITY FOR ECONOMIC HARM § 17, Reporter's Note at 51 (2019).
31. *Id.* at § 17 (b).
32. Della Penna v. Toyota Motor Sales, U.S.A., Inc. 902 P. 2d 740 (Cal. 1995).
33. 140 N.E. 203 (N.Y. 1923).
34. *Id.*
35. *Id.* at 205.
36. *Id.*
37. For example, Minnesota, where *Tuttle* was decided, now characterizes the case as establishing a cause of action for wrongful interference with non-contractual business relationships. Witte Transp. Co. v. Murphy Motor Freight Lines, Inc., 193 N.W. 2d 148, 151 (Minn. 1971).
38. Mangum Electric Co. v. Border, 222 P. 1002 (1923).
39. *Id.* at 1004.
40. *Id.* at 1008.
41. 191 N.E. 713 (N.Y.1934).
42. *Id.* at 714.
43. *Id.*
44. 70 N.E. 2d 401 (N.Y. 1946).
45. *Id.* at 402.
46. *Id.* at 403. Emphasis in original.
47. *See* Reinforce, Inc. v. Birney, 308 N.Y. 164 (1954); Ruza v. Ruza, 146 N.Y. S. 2d 808, 811 (1955); Brant v. Winchell, 127 N.Y. S. 2d 865, 867 (1954).
48. As the (as yet unnamed) prima facie tort seemed to be establishing itself in New York, the first Torts *Restatement* adopted § 870, somewhat buried

under the category of "Miscellaneous Rules," which provided that "a person who does any tortious act for the purpose of causing harm to another or to his things or to the pecuniary interests of another is liable to the other or harm if it results, except where the harm results from an outside force the risk of which is not increased by the defendant's act." RESTATEMENT OF TORTS § 870 (1934). That formulation was curious. The term "tortious" seemed to suggest that all the section was doing was allowing recovery for purposeful acts that were torts. The limitation appeared to be only directed toward causation. No mention was made of justifiability. Although a Comment suggested that it might provide a basis for recovery in cases where specific torts were unavailable because of technical limitations on them, *id.* at cmt. c, on its face the term "tortious" in the section seemed to presuppose that the elements of particular torts had been satisfied. Read that way, the section only codified intentional torts that resulted in harm to persons, property, or pecuniary interests, all of which were already in existence.

49. RESTATEMENT (SECOND) OF TORTS § 870 (1979).
50. *Id.* at cmt. e. Whether the Reporters for the Second *Restatement* (first Prosser and then John Wade) intended § 870 to function as a residual category, or instead to serve as a placeholder for new, named intentional torts, is not completely clear. Comments to the last draft before adoption stated, "This Section is intended to supply a generalization for tortious conduct involving harm intentionally inflicted. . . . It has traditionally been assumed that intentional torts developed separately and independently, and not in accordance with a unifying principle. This Section purports to supply that unifying principle, and to explain the basis for the development of the more recently created intentional torts." RESTATEMENT OF THE LAW, SECOND, TORTS, Council Draft No. 39, § 870 cmt. a (November 19, 1975). The first portion of this passage suggests that the section reflected a residual category, but the second suggests a somewhat different ("unifying") function.
51. Examples include RESTATEMENT (SECOND) OF CONTRACTS § 90 (1979) (adopting promissory estoppel) and RESTATEMENT (SECOND) OF TORTS § 402A (1965) (adopting strict products liability).
52. *See* Porter v. Crawford & Co., 611 S.W. 2d 265 (Mo. Ct. App, 1980).
53. *See* Schmitz v. Smentowski, 785 P. 2d 726, 734 (N.M. 1990).
54. Bagpaygee v. Rolthermich, 372 N.E. 2d 817, 821 (Ohio Ct. App. 1977).
55. "Missouri courts, while recognizing prima facie torts at least nominally, do not look upon them with favor and have consistently limited the application of the prima facie tort." Hertz Corp. v. RAKS Hosp., Inc., 196 S.W. 3d 536, 549 (Mo. Ct. App. 2006).

56. Vandevelde, *supra* note 12. *See* Newell Co. v. William E. Wright Co., 500 A. 2d 974, 981 n. 4 (Del. Ch. 1985); Frontier Mgt. Co. v. Balboa Ins. Co., 658 F. Supp 987, 994 (D. Mass. 1986).

57. *See* Mark P. Gergen, *Tortious Interference: How It Is Engulfing Commercial Law, Why This Is Not Entirely Bad, and a Prudential Response*, 38 ARIZ. L. REV. 1175, 1217 (1996) ("But the theory of prima facie tort disappeared as a legal principle, other than in New York [and perhaps a few other states], which adopted the theory in the crystallized form of the doctrine of prima facie tort. The crystallized doctrine has proved inert") (footnotes omitted).

58. RESTATEMENT (THIRD) OF TORTS: INTENTIONAL TORTS TO PERSONS § 104, Reporters Notes to cmt. a, at 117–18 (Tentative Draft Number 1, April 8, 2015).

59. Porter v. Crawford & Co., *supra* note 52, at 272.

60. Schmitz v. Smentowski, 785 P. 2d 726, 734 (N.M. 1990).

61. Beavers v. Johnson Controls World Services, Inc., 901 P. 2d 761 (N.M. Ct. of App. 1995).

62. RESTATEMENT (THIRD) OF TORTS: LIABILITY FOR ECONOMIC HARM (2019).

63. RESTATEMENT (THIRD) OF TORTS: INTENTIONAL TORTS TO PERSONS (Tentative Draft No. 1, 2015).

64. On this score, theories of torts often have little to say. For example, the most prominent civil recourse theorists have written extensively on what characterizes torts, and have sought to explain why torts are legal wrongs even when they are not moral wrongs, but say much less about why some acts or omissions that might count as legal wrongs do not. *See, e.g.,* John C. P. Goldberg & Benjamin C. Zipursky, *Torts as Wrongs*, 88 TEX. L. REV. 917, 937 (2010) ("In part out of a sense of the limitations as to what sorts of interferences and injuries are justiciable, and in part for policy considerations that have changed over time, with changes in social norms and economic and political circumstances, courts and legislatures have never sought to render interferences with [significant aspects of a person's well-being] actionable"). In later work the same authors elaborated only a bit more. JOHN C. P. GOLDBERG & BENJAMIN C. ZIPURSKY, RECOGNIZING WRONGS 4, 234 (2020). Similarly, corrective justice theorists explain the structure of tort liability but not why certain injustices are not subject to tort liability. The closest statement addressing this issue we have found in the work of one of the leading corrective justice theorists, for example, is that "plaintiff's injury must be to something, such as personal integrity or proprietary entitlement, that ranks as the embodiment of a right." ERNEST J. WEINRIB, THE IDEA OF PRIVATE LAW 134 (1995). Nor have we found anything expressly addressing the issue in one of the leading

instrumental works, WILLIAM M. LANDES & RICHARD A. POSNER, THE ECONOMIC STRUCTURE OF TORT LAW (1987).

65. As we noted at the outset, we use the term "intangible" to denote loss falling outside the classic contours of damages for bodily injury and property damage. We include pure economic loss in that category when it is caused by an intangible force such as digital hacking.

66. *See, e.g.,* STEPHEN J. SCHULHOFER, UNWANTED SEX: THE CULTURE OF INTIMIDATION AND THE FAILURE OF LAW (1998); John V. Decker & Peter G. Barioni, *"No Still Means 'Yes,'"* 101 J. CRIM. L. & CRIMINOLOGY 1081 (2011).

67. CATHERINE A. MACKINNON, SEXUAL HARASSMENT OF WORKING WOMEN 164–74 (1979).

68. For recent examples of major data breaches, *see* Vindu Goel & Rachel Abrams, *Hackers Stole Data from Millions of Cards at Sacks,* N.Y. TIMES, April 2, 2018, at B2; Tara Siegel Bernard *et al., Equifax Attack Exposes Data of 143 Million,* N.Y. TIMES, September 8, 2017, at A1. One 2017 survey of credit card statistics stated that 46 percent of Americans had been victims of credit card fraud in the past five years. Rebecca Lake, *23 Frightening Credit Card Statistics,* Credit Donkey, February 1, 2017, https//www.creditdonkey.com/credit-card-fraud-statistics.html.

On the general lack of exposure of consumers to liability for unauthorized transactions on their credit cards, *see* John S. Kiernan, *Credit Card and Debit Card Fraud Statistics,* Wallet Hub, February 1, 2017, https://wallethub.com/edu/credit-debit-card-fraud-statistics/25725/.

69. *See* Nicole Perlroth, *Hospital Company Attacked, Affecting 4.5 Million Patients,* N.Y. TIMES, August 19, 2014, at B4; Henry F. Lee, *Hackers Tap Thousands of Students' Key Records,* S.F. CHRONICLE, May 9, 2009, at B1; Nate Lord, *10 Top Biggest Healthcare Data Breaches of All Time,* Digital Guardian, June 25, 2018, https://digitalguardian.com/blog/top-10-biggest-healthcare-data-breaches-all-time.

70. *See, e.g.,* Gerry Stith, *Facebook Admits Year-Long Data Breach Exposed 6 Million Users,* Reuters, June 21, 2013, https://www.reuters.com/article/net-us-facebook-security/facebook-admits-year-long-data-breach-exposed-6-million-users-idUSBRE95K18Y20130621. Facebook also releases vast amounts of private information by design. Gabriel J. X. Dance *et al., Device Companies Have Vast Access to Facebook Data,* N.Y. TIMES, June 4, 2018, at A1.

71. Danielle Keats Citron, *Sexual Privacy,* 128 YALE L. J. 1870, 1908–21 (2019).

72. *See, e.g.,* Charles Arthur, *Google Raises Privacy Fears as Personal Details Are Released to App Developers,* GUARDIAN, February 25, 2013, https://www.theguardian.com/technology/2013/feb/25/google-privacy-fears-app-developers.

73. Vicki Schultz, *Reconceptualizing Sexual Misconduct, Again,* Yale L. J. Forum 22, 27 (June 18, 2018).

74. Anita Bernstein, *How to Make a Tort: Three Paradoxes,* 75 Tex. L. Rev. 1539, 1545 (1997).

75. *See* Schultz, *supra* note 73.

76. *See* W. Page Keeton et al., Prosser and Keeton on the Law of Torts 59 (noting that "liability of course cannot be extended to every indignity") (5th ed. 1984).

77. 42 U.S.C. § 2000e *et seq.*

78. Robson v. Eva's Super Mkt., Inc., 538 F. Supp. 857 (N.D. Ohio 1982).

79. Coley v. Consol. Rail Corp., 561 F. Supp. 645 (E.D. Mich. 1982).

80. Henson v. Dundee, 682 F. 2d 897 (11th Cir. 1982).

81. E.E.O.C. v. Int. Profit Assoc., Inc., 647 F. Supp. 2d 951 (N.D. Ill. 2009).

82. For discussion, *see* Kevin Gomez et al., *State Regulation of Sexual Harassment,* 18 Geo. J. Gender & L., 815 (2017); Kristen N. Colletta, *Sexual Harassment on Social Media: Why Traditional Company Sexual Harassment Policies Are Not Enough and How to Fix It,* 48 Seton Hall L. Rev. 449 (2018); Ramit Mizrahi, *Sexual Harassment after #MeToo: Looking to California as a Model,* 128 Yale L. J. Forum 121 (2018); Jessica Fink, *Gender Sidelining and the Problem of Unactionable Discrimination,* 29 Stan. L. & Pol'y Rev. 57 (2018).

83. See Vicki Schultz, *The Sanitized Workplace,* 112 Yale L. J. 2063 (2003) (arguing against legal standards that attempt to banish sexuality from the workplace).

84. *See* Kenneth S. Abraham & Daniel Schwarcz, Insurance Law and Regulation 102 (7th ed. 2020) (indicating that most courts hold that insurance against liability for intentional wrongdoing violates public policy).

85. Most liability insurance policies cover both indemnity and the costs of defense but included the latter only when incurred to defend a suit that would be covered by the policy if it were successful. *See id.* at 577.

86. For discussion of the distinction between safety levels and activity levels, *see* Steven Shavell, *Strict Liability versus Negligence,* 9 J. Legal Stud. 1 (1980).

87. *See, e.g.,* Galella v. Onassis, 487 F. 2d 986 (2d Cir. 1973) (applying an anti-harassment statute to a suit by Jacqueline Kennedy Onassis against a photographer who stalked her and her children).

88. *See* 15 U.S.C. § 1643 (2012) (limiting liability of cardholders); 12 C.F.R. § 12 (2018) (same). These consumers may nonetheless have indirect or consequential losses, resulting from the inconvenience of setting up new accounts and the possible short-term lack of access to credit while new accounts are established.

89. *See* Catherine M. Sharkey, *Can Data Breach Claims Survive the Economic Loss Rule,* 66 DEPAUL L. REV. 339, 346 (2017) ("Privity . . . exists between the issuer bank and the payment card network, as well as between the acquirer bank and the payment card network").

90. *See id.*

91. For example, *see generally Symposium, Privacy, Data Theft and Corporate Responsibility, Twenty-Second Annual Clifford Symposium on Tort Law and Social Policy,* 66 DEPAUL L. REV. 311 (2017).

92. The banks are not in direct privity with the merchants but are in indirect privity by virtue of the membership in the Visa or MasterCard networks that contract with the merchants. For discussion, *see* Sharkey, *supra* note 89, at 361–62. With respect to contracts between banks and consumers, Mark A. Geistfeld suggests that whether the economic loss rule applies in data breach cases will typically turn on whether a consumer has sufficient information to protect his or her confidential information by contracting with a business over reasonable security for that data. Mark A. Geistfeld, *Protecting Confidential Information Entrusted to Others in Business Transactions: Data Breaches, Identity Theft, and Tort Liability,* 66 DEPAUL L. REV. 385, 394 (2017).

93. Sharkey, *supra* note 89, at 346, suggests that privity of contract does not "always exist between consumer credit card holders and merchants."

94. *See, e.g.,* Julie Creswell & Nicole Perlroth, *Ex-Employees Say Home Depot Left Data Vulnerable,* N.Y. TIMES, September 20, 2014, at A1.

95. *See* Sharkey, *supra* note 89.

96. *See, e.g.,* Metro-North Commuter R.R. Co. v. Buckley, 521 U.S. 424 (1997) (disallowing a claim alleging fear of cancer resulting from exposure to asbestos).

97. *See* RESTATEMENT (THIRD) OF TORTS: LIABILITY FOR PHYSICAL AND EMOTIONAL HARM § 47 cmt. k.

98. *See* ABRAHAM, *supra* note 1, at 278.

99. There is an analogy here to the requirement some jurisdictions apply in suits involving negligent infliction of emotional distress resulting from witnessing the death of another person, that the plaintiff has suffered distress beyond that which would have been experienced by a disinterested party. *See, e.g.,* Thing v. LaChusa, 771 P. 2d 814, 815 (Cal. 1989).

100. *See* In re Anthem Inc. Data Breach Litig., 162 F. Supp. 3d 953 (N.D. Cal. 2016); Reed Albeson & Matthew Goldstein, *Hackers Breached Data of Millions, Insurer Says,* N.Y. TIMES, February 5, 2015, at B1.,

101. *See* Dino Grandoni, *Ashley Madison, a Website for Straying Spouses, Is Hit By an Online Attack,* N.Y. TIMES, July 21, 2015, at B3.

102. *See Anthem Inc.* at 1016.

103. *See generally* Robert L. Rabin, *Enabling Torts,* 49 DePaul L. Rev. 435 (1999).

104. *See, e.g.,* Koeppel v. Speirs, 808 N.W. 2d 177 (Iowa 2011) (holding that installation of a nonfunctional camera to view female employees was actionable).

105. Most of the prominent seclusion cases involve only a single victim or a small number of victims. *See, e.g.,* Nader v. General Motors Corp., 25 N.Y. 2d 560 (1970); Dietemann v. Time Inc., 449 F. 2d 245 (9th Cir. 1971); *Galella;* Shulman v. Group W. Prod., 18 Cal. 4th 200 (1998). *See generally* 5 David Bender, Computer Law, sec. 41 (6 vols. 2018) (summarizing additional cases).

106. For a contrary argument, *see* Daniel J. Solove & Danielle Keats Citron, *Risk and Anxiety: A Theory of Data Breach Harms,* 96 Tex. L. Rev. 737 (2018).

107. We have been unable to find an authoritative statement to this effect, but we also have not been able to identify any cases in which liability was imposed for negligent disclosure. We are therefore confident that the assertion we make in the text represents the law on this issue.

108. There are at least a dozen federal statutes addressing data security, but they obviously have not deterred the many data breaches that have occurred in the past few years. Some are probably obsolete, given technological advances. *See, e.g.,* Family Educational Rights and Privacy Act of 1974, 20 U.S.C. § 1232g (regulating the privacy of educational records); Computer Fraud and Abuse Act of 1986, 18 U.S.C. § 552a (regulating computer tampering); Video Privacy Protection Act of 1988, 18 U.S.C. § 2710 (regulating the privacy audio and visual rental and purchase records); Health Insurance Portability and Accountability Act of 1996, 42 U.S.C. §§ 1320d–1320d-9 (regulating the security of health information); Financial Services Modernization Act of 1999, 15 U.S.C. §§ 6801–2 (2012) (regulating the development of financial institutions' data security plans).

109. *See* the discussion in Ward Farnsworth, *The Economic Loss Rule,* 50 Val. U. L. Rev. 545, 554–55 (2016).

110. *See* Abraham, *supra* note 1, at 320, citing Ultramares Corp. v. Touche, 174 N.E. 441, 444 (N.Y. 1931 Cardozo, C.J.) (describing the courts' traditional concern about threatening liability "in an indeterminate amount for an indeterminate time to an indeterminate class").

111. Judy Greenwald, *Cyber Insurance Policies Vary Widely and Require Close Scrutiny,* Business Insurance (May 10, 2015), http://www.businessinsurance .com/article/00010101/NEWS06/305109992/Cyber-insurance-policies -vary-widely-and-require-close-scrutiny.

Conclusion

1. *See generally* CHANGE AND CONTINUITY IN TWENTIETH-CENTURY AMERICA (John Braeman *et al.* eds., 1964).
2. RESTATEMENT (SECOND) OF TORTS § 46 (1965).
3. *See id.,* § 652B (1977).
4. *See, e.g.,* Pritchett v. Bd. of Comm'rs, 85 N.E. 32 (In. 1908) (observing the plaintiff from outside her property); McDaniel v. Atlanta Coca-Cola Bottling Co., 2 S.E. 2d 810 (Ga. 1939) (recording conversations).
5. On the other hand, much that now falls within the privacy torts of false light and appropriation of name or likeness could well have fit within expanded versions of defamation and conversion. Something like that might well have occurred had Prosser not contended early on that a single tort of invasion of privacy was emerging, as we described in chapter 4.
6. Code Civil, arts. 1382–83. *See* CEES VAN DAM, EUROPEAN TORT LAW 56 (2d ed. 2013).
7. Burgerliches Gesetzbuch (BGB) §§ 823, I, 823 II, and 826; VAN DAM, *supra* note 6, at 79.
8. The other two "privacy" torts posed little challenge in this regard. False light was a close relative of defamation, and appropriation in many instances involved the wrongful use of a commercial asset.
9. *See* RESTATEMENT (SECOND) OF TORTS § 46 cmt. h (1965).
10. The exception was commercial appropriation when the plaintiff sought to recover commercial losses.
11. For example, the "impact rule" that was in force for the first several decades of the twentieth century required that the plaintiff have suffered a physical contact of some sort, even if not an injurious contact, in order to recover damages for emotional distress resulting from fear of injury. *See* KENNETH S. ABRAHAM, THE FORMS AND FUNCTIONS OF TORT LAW 272–73 (5th ed. 2017). Part of the reason for this reluctance was that the courts lacked confidence in the verifiability of such loss. But another reason was the difficulty of valuing the losses even when there was no doubt that they had occurred.

    Similarly, until well into the twentieth century, awards for the emotional losses suffered by survivors resulting from the wrongful death of a loved one were either expressly precluded (though the fact that juries awarded such damages anyway was an open secret) or subject to a definite, and low, monetary ceiling. *See id.* at 255. The major form of intangible loss that was recoverable at that point was of course the pain and suffering associated with bodily injury. But awards for pain and suffering were comparatively low until the middle of the twentieth century, and awards were anchored in practice to the seriousness of a tangible physical injury. For example, as late as 1961 a decision from the California Supreme Court affirming a negligence judgment for $187,000, including $53,000 for pecuniary losses, for injuries involving serious, painful, and permanent injury to the plaintiff's foot elicited a dissent from Justice Roger Traynor, arguing that the award of $134,000 for pain and suffering was excessive. Seffert v. Los Angeles Transit Lines, 364 P. 2d 337, 344 (Cal. 1961) (Traynor, J., dissenting).

12. *See* Rory Lancman, *Protecting Speech from Private Abridgement: Introducing the Tort of Suppression,* 25 Sw. L. Rev. 223, 260 (1996).

13. Edwards v. Louisville Ladder Co., 796 F. Supp. 966 (W.D. La. 1992); Federated Mut. Ins. Co. v. Litchfield Precision Components, Inc., 456 N.W. 2d 434 (Minn. 1990).

14. *See* Terry R. Spencer, *Do Not Fold, Spindle, or Mutilate: The Trend toward Recognition of Spoliation as a Separate Tort,* 30 Idaho L. Rev. 37, 53 (1993).

15. *See, e.g.,* Schaefer v. Universal Scaffolding & Equipment, LLC, 839 F. 3d 599, 611 (7th Cir. 2016) (requiring only that the plaintiff prove that there would have been a reasonable probability of success if the missing evidence were available); Danna v. Ritz-Carlton Hotel Co., 213 So. 3d 26, 37 (La. Ct. App. 2016) (adopting a presumption that spoiled evidence would have been unfavorable to the party who failed to preserve it).

16. Oliver Wendell Holmes, Jr., The Common Law 88 (G. Edward White ed., 2009).

INDEX

"actual malice" in defamation cases involving public figures, 144–48

Addison, Charles, 65, 236n17

Advance Music Co. v. American Tobacco Co. (1946), 176

African Americans. *See* racial minorities and women

Aikens v. Wisconsin (1904), 170–71, 176, 177

Alabama, defamation law in, 257–58nn66–67

Alcorn v. Mitchell (1872), 251n138

ALI. *See* American Law Institute

Allen, Anita, 108–9

"all things considered" determinations in negligence cases, 38

Al Raschid v. News Syndicate Co. (1934), 175–76

alternative liability exception to proof of causation requirement, 11

American Historical Review, 15

American Law Institute (ALI), 74–75, 243n105

American Law Register, 36

American Law Review, 168

Ames, James Barr, 70–71, 73, 92, 240n77

Anthem (health insurer), data breaches at, 191, 195

appellate cases: on invasion of privacy, 113; opinions in premodern cases, 42–46; prima facie tort in, 174, 175–76; witness disqualification rule, effects of repeal of, 38

appropriation of name or likeness, 110–11, 121, 123–25, 127, 152, 250n131, 271n5, 271n8

Ashley Madison (marital dating site), data breaches at, 191

assault/battery: conceptualization of tort law and, 60, 63, 65, 66, 68, 76, 78, 80–82, 84–85, 92, 242n97, 244n119; discreteness as necessary element of, 207; IIED and, 101–2; intentional infliction of temporal damage and, 177; offensive battery, as dignitary tort, 97, 99–100, 122–27, 130; sexualized misconduct not coming within definitions of, 183, 184, 187

Associated Press v. Walker (1967), 147–48

atomistic approach to conceptualization of tort law, 85, 90–91

attorney compensation, 209–10

autonomy/liberty, dignitary torts protecting, 123–24, 127

Bacon v. Charlton (1851), 234n77

bank losses due to cyber-related harm, 189, 269n92

Bartnicki v. Vopper (2001), 260n111

battery. *See* assault/battery; offensive battery

Beardsley v. Kilmer (1923), 174–75, 176, 178

Bentham, Jeremy, 35, 52

Bernstein, Anita, 184

Bethel's Case (1681), 29

Bigelow, Melville, 68–69, 71, 73, 240n77

Black, Hugo, 256n35, 256n40

Black community. *See* racial minorities and women

black-letter rules, 90, 105, 112, 114, 143, 240n81

Black Lives Matter, 164

Blackmun, Harry, 141, 256n40

Blackstone, William, 66, 92, 231n60, 238n41